Jinx Dogs Burns Now Flu

Alex Gordon

Ringwood Publishing

Glasgow

First published in Great Britain in 2015 by

Ringwood Publishing

7 Kirklee Quadrant, Glasgow G12 0TS

www.ringwoodpublishing.com

e-mail   mail@ringwoodpublishing.com

ISBN 978-1-901514-28-5

British Library Cataloguing-in Publication Data

A catalogue record for this book is available from the British Library

Typeset in Times New Roman 10

Printed and bound in the UK

by Lonsdale Direct Solutions

About the Author

Acclaimed author Alex Gordon has spent almost half a century at the sharp end of publications after joining the Daily Record national newspaper at the age of fifteen in 1967. Glasgow-born, he celebrated his sixteenth birthday on the Sports Desk and was appointed Chief Sports Sub-Editor at the age of twenty-three. He became Sunday Mail's Sports Editor at thirty-five in 1987, before taking over as Managing Director of 7 Day Press, one of the UK's biggest freelance sports agencies, in 1994. Alex was also the Scottish correspondent for the prestigious French publications L'Equipe and France Football, while penning a monthly column for World Soccer for over a decade. He has had eleven football books published and his debut novel, *Who Shot Wild Bill?*, hit the book shelves in August 2013. He finished one follow-up novel, *What Spooked Crazy Horse?* and is currently working on the third of the series, entitled *Who Stole Sitting Bull?*.

PREVIOUS BOOKS BY ALEX GORDON

SPORT

CELTIC: The First 100 Years (Purnell, 1988)
LISBON LIONS: The 40th Anniversary (Black and White, 2007)
A BHOY CALLED BERTIE: The Bertie Auld Story (Black and White, 2008)
THE QUIET ASSASSIN: The Davie Hay Story (Black and White, 2009)
SEEING RED: The Chic Charnley Story (Black and White, 2009)
CELTIC: The Awakening (Mainstream, 2013)
KING AND COUNTRY: The Denis Law Scotland Story (Birlinn/Arena, 2013)
ALL THE BEST: The Tommy Gemmell Story (CQN Publishing, 2014)
YOGI BARE: The John Hughes Story (Self-Published, 2014)
CAESAR AND THE ASSASSIN: The Billy McNeill and Davie Hay Story (CQN Publishing, 2014)
THE WINDS OF CHANGE: Celtic Managers from Brady to O'Neill (CQN Publishing, 2015)

NOVEL

WHO SHOT WILD BILL? (Crime Lab, 2013)

Acknowledgements

There are so many folk who have helped make my journey through journalism so memorable. Here are a few:

Editors (in succession): Derek Webster, Bernie Vickers, Endell Laird and Noel Young.

Bill Aitken, Ronnie Anderson

Rodger Baillie, Nicola Barry, Matt Bendoris, Sandy Beveridge, Dixon Blackstock, Gordon Blair, Jim Blair, John Blair, Bobby Bogan, Eddie Bonner, Carole Brash, Ian Broadley, Danny Brown, Norman Brown, John Burrowes

Randolph Caughie, Ginny Clark, Johnny Clyde, Jack Coll, Copy Cat crew (Anne, Anna, Billy), Davie Coupar, Liz Cowan, Eric Craig, Jim Cullen, Dick Currie

Marge Davidson, Mike Davidson, Larry Diamond, Alan Dick

Fraser Elder

Billy Fagan, Hugh Farmer, Ricky Fearon, Len Findlay

Ken Gallacher, Lorne Gardner, Joe Gillan, Ian Gibson, Martin Gilfeather, Phil Gordon

Bill Harley, Jim Hendry, Gerry Hogan, Ian Howie, George Hunter, Frank Hurley

David Kelso

Ken Laird, David Leggat

James McBeth, Gerry McCabe, John McCall, Alex McCallum, Malky McCormick, Alex McDonald, Bill Macfarlane, Charles McGhee, John McGurk, Henry McInnes, Kevin McKenna, Wallace McLeod, Alan McMillan, Alex McLeod, Rod McLeod, Archie Macpherson, Dougie McRobb, John Maddock, Donna Marshall, Robert Melvin, Wallace Moore, Brian Morgan, Don Morrison, Alastair Murray, Jim Murray, Jack Myles

Alister Nicol

Bob Patience, Norman Pollock

Jim Rankin, Isabell Reid, Dougie Ritchie, David Robertson, Scott Robertson

Steve Sampson, Jim Savage, Scott Savage, Stan Shivas, Charlie Smith, Phil Smith, Gordon Stephen, Mark Sweeney

Hugh Taylor

George Wilkie, Vic Wood, Lorraine Woods, Martin Wright, Bill Wylie

A special round of applause must go to Anna Smith, author of the wonderful Rosie Gilmour books, for her exceptionally kind words.

Sandy Jamieson and Laure Deprez at Ringwood Publishing for their excellent support and encouragement.

Allan Rennie, Editor-in-Chief of the Daily Record and Sunday Mail, deserves a special mention, too, for his generous assistance and kind permission to replicate some of the pictures within the following pages.

The invaluable and unstinting help from the extremely accommodating Daily Record folk Jackie Hyndman, Julie Bryceland, Maureen Collins and Campbell Thomson who also contributed to putting the pictorial jigsaw together.

Bob Smith, who listened to some of the tales and prompted the book in the first place. He gave me a nudge when I most needed it.

Last – and certainly not least – I have to thank my wife Gerda for all her assistance in putting these memoirs together. Her expertise was greatly appreciated. The steady stream of coffee and bacon butties helped, too.

If I have overlooked anyone, please forgive me. So many people played a role and, trust me, they will never be forgotten in a location where it matters most.

Dedication

This book is dedicated to the memories of Alex Cameron and Jack Adams, two stalwarts of the newspaper industry.

Two fine men and, I'm delighted to say, two great friends.

There would be no such tome as *Jinx Dogs Burns Now Flu* if it hadn't been for these two gents. The assistance they afforded a raw teenager stepping into the crazy world of journalism back in the late sixties is inestimable. Cherished and appreciated for all time.

We had some outrageously fabulous times over the years, in and out of the office. Hopefully, some of the tales told within will make you smile and, maybe, give you some sort of insight into life on the two best-selling newspapers in Scotland at the time, the Daily Record and Sunday Mail.

I had my opportunity to say farewell to Chiefy, as Alex was known, before he passed away peacefully at his home in Strathblane on July 23 2003. He was seventy-four years old. His beloved wife Jan was by his side.

Time, alas, did not afford me that opportunity with Jack. I had arranged a family holiday in Cyprus at the same time as Jack was heading for his beloved Greek island of Kos. We agreed to meet up for lunch when we returned; food, as usual, would no doubt be required as blotting paper for what would have most assuredly followed.

That meeting never took place. Jack died in Kos on May 22 2004 at the age of sixty-six. That man's great passions were his family, football and what was commonly known as 'a snifter'. He passed away, while on a break with wife Beth, watching the Scottish Cup Final between Celtic and Dunfermline on TV in his apartment. A cold gin and tonic was nearby.

With the most awful of ironies, I found myself writing both obituaries of these wonderful newspapermen. And even better human beings.

Alex Cameron and Jack Adams, on separate occasions, both took a young journalist aside early in his career and informed him, 'It won't always be easy.'

As ever, they were both correct.

But when Alex and Jack were around, it was a lot of fun, too. Unforgettably so.

An indebted Alex Gordon

Part One

Setting the scene

Chapter 1

What's in a title?

JINX

DOGS

BURNS

NOW

FLU

Yes, I know it looks like a random selection of words plucked from the dictionary and haphazardly thrown together. Well, if something called *Drop the Dead Donkey* can win two Emmys, one BAFTA, twelve other glittering top television awards, run for eight years and attract millions of viewers to Channel 4, then you have got to wonder what's in a title.

Well, quite a lot, really.

The excellent writers of *Donkey*, Andy Hamilton and Guy Jenkin, were actually going to call their outrageous and devastatingly accurate sitcom, set in a fictional TV newsroom called GlobeLink News, *Dead Belgians Don't Count*. But, after spending some time observing journalists in the BBC London newsroom, they decided that *Drop the Dead Donkey* sounded more interesting and could be something someone might shout out minutes before production. 'Drop the such-and-such a story and replace it with such-and-such.'

I also realised that Frank McGhee, the Daily Mirror's Chief Sportswriter in England for many years, had originally thought of the title *Forgive us our Press Passes* for the autobiography he never got round to writing. Very clever. So clever, in fact, it was used in an anthology of sports reporting by Fleet Street's finest in a 1983 publication.

Then I thought of *Chiefy, Grizzly and a Guy Called Ali*. Made sense to me, but, possibly, not to the most important person - the potential book buyer who is persuaded to shell out some hard-earned cash to actually purchase the publication.

Chiefy? That was the nickname of Alex Cameron, the Daily Record Chief Sports Editor. *Grizzly?* That was the moniker given to Jack Adams, the Sports Editor of the same publication, when he was foolhardy enough to embark on some wild hirsute adventure. Even after Jack decided it was a reasonable idea to forget his attempt to resemble a bear hunter and take a flame thrower to the foliage, he was still answering to 'Grizzly' many years later. *And a Guy Called Ali?* No explanation required, I hope.

So Bob Smith, the individual largely to blame for this stumble down the cobwebbed memory lane of newspapers, and I were discussing the possibility of the tome in a Glasgow city centre hostelry one evening. Some ideas for a title were bounced around, but, funnily enough, the one that struck the right chord came after the seventh or eighth pint. Strange, that.

Jinx Dogs Burns Now Flu is one of the finest headlines that never made it into print. It was put forward as a suggestion by a sub-editor for a sports story in the Daily Record in the sixties, but was bombed out by Jack 'Grizzly' Adams. He asked the sub to think again; the headline made no sense. Now, back in those dark days when you were forced to get out of your seat to switch TV channels, LSD meant pounds, shillings, and pence, men were men, and women were grateful, archaic newspaper technology had remained anchored well and truly in the past. Newspapers were produced by nineteenth-century hot metal typesetting.

A headline writer would be given a point size and how many decks of words over a certain amount of columns. Say, for instance, a sub-editor was handed a headline style for 84pt caps (or lower case) across three columns. The point size of a headline dictated the impact and importance of the story. Something in the region of 84pt would be a lot more eye-catching than something, say, in 24pt.

The sub would then count out the characters to fit the allocated space on the page plan. The word 'ONE' would be a count of three, one for each letter. 'TWO' would be three-and-a-half because the 'W' counted as one-and-a-half. 'T' and 'O' would be one apiece. 'FIVE' would be three-and-a-half because 'I' would be a half a character while the others are one each. Simple, eh?

The problem with hot metal was that it was rigidly inflexible. These days, headlines can be extended, squeezed, tightened, elongated with a couple of key strokes. Back in the sixties, there was no such luxury. So, when a sub-editor was working on a headline, there was absolutely no margin for error. The character count had to be fairly spot on or else there were huge chunks of space where there shouldn't be huge chunks of space. 'Tasteful white', it would probably be called today.

The journalist who was given the type size for the story for *Jinx* would have had a heading size that would have been a maximum count of five characters running across three columns and five decks down the page. For instance, 'HOODOO' couldn't have been used instead of 'JINX' because it had a count of six and would have 'burst' by one. Six into five just wouldn't go in hot metal. So, the headline was worked out thus:

JINX (a count of three-and-a-half).
DOGS (four).
BURNS (five).
NOW (three-and-a-half).
FLU (three).

The sub would have been fairly satisfied with his effort; it wasn't a bad fit, at all. Not a lot of wastage in evidence. Unfortunately, the Sports Editor just couldn't fathom the meaning.

'*Jinx Dogs Burns Now Flu*? Sorry, try again, please.'

There wasn't the time to explain the headline. A footballer by the name of Burns had just returned after a lengthy period out due to injury. As bad luck would have it, the unfortunate guy then caught a bug and was sidelined again. Hence, *Jinx Dogs Burns Now Flu*. Explains everything, doesn't it? The sub who had that headline knocked back kept the apparently reckless assortment of words in his memory bank.

I knew they would come in handy some day.

Chapter 2

Welcome to the crazy world of newspapers

My dear old mum was from the polite school of always knocking before entering my bedroom. On Saturday, May 20 1967, she almost bulldozed the door from its hinges.

It was around eight o'clock in the morning and my mum, Mary, was clearly in a state of high excitement. She was holding a letter. 'It's for you,' she cried out eagerly. 'It's from the Daily Record.'

Suddenly, I was wide awake. I was handed the white envelope which was franked 'Daily Record' and was adorned with that famous little red lion crest. Inside the covering lay my destiny, although, to be honest, that was not how I viewed it at the time. I had celebrated my fifteenth birthday just under four months beforehand and there was a lot I still had to discover about the world and its workings. Still the same today, as a matter of fact.

Back then, though, in my small bedroom in our two-up three-apartment council house in Castlemilk on the south side of Glasgow, I was simply intrigued to discover the contents of the letter. I ripped open the envelope, swiftly read the tight two paragraphs and leapt out of bed. Thankfully, for my mum, I was wearing pyjama bottoms, although I don't suppose she would have seen anything she hadn't seen before.

'I'm in,' I screamed at the top of my voice. I had forgotten Mr McLay, in the bedroom directly above, worked constant nightshift. I don't suppose he appreciated the impromptu early alarm call.

The previous morning, at precisely ten o'clock, I had been summoned to 67 Hope Street in Glasgow's city centre. That was the address of the Daily Record newspaper and I'll admit I was shaking like a leaf caught in a storm. I had an appointment with a Mr Ian Merry, who was the Assistant Chief Accountant of the newspaper. I was accompanied by my dad, John.

He was bowled over by the fact a commissionaire, wearing all sorts of gold braid, opened one of the massive heavy wooden-framed, glass-fronted doors to allow us to enter the rather opulent foyer of the grand old building.

Wait a minute, though. How did this remarkable situation come about in the first place? Only a week or so beforehand, I was saying my farewells and walking out of my secondary school, St.Margaret Mary's, without a qualification and without a clue of what lay ahead. My deputy headmaster was a character called Mr Carroll (I've no idea what his Christian name was; we were never close on a social level). He was a mean-looking, beady-eyed, hawk-faced, hook-nosed individual. (I never made my observations known to him, by the way.) He also doubled as my English teacher.

I thought he was a decent enough bloke, but he certainly had an over-fondness for using the strap to mete out instant justice. He kept the leather belt straddling his left shoulder under his suit jacket. He had perfected the art of whipping the vile instrument of pain from its lair with his right hand and whipping it down across a miscreant's exposed palms for spontaneous reprisal against heinous crimes such as breathing out of turn or possessing too many freckles. He was so skilful it became sheer poetry in wicked motion, an abominable fusion of power and precision. It's not what I thought at the time as my palms turned crimson after another assault with that three-tongued leather contraption.

He will never have known this - our paths never crossed again after I walked through those school gates for the last time - but I owe him a great debt of gratitude. If it hadn't been for his intervention, I would never have been in a position to go for my interview with Mr Ian Merry on May 19 1967. In all probability, I would never have been given another chance to enter the world of newspapers.

I was offered the opportunity to stay on at school and go for my O-levels in fourth year and my Highers the following year. I suppose I did reasonably well at school without ever getting close to egghead level. I had always been in the A class, the top tier in a system that was graded very simply from A to F. If someone was so unfortunate not to be deemed clever enough even to claim a place in the F class, they were packed off to the school's annex somewhere in the back of beyond. I had a cousin, a year younger than me, who was stuck in that annex for three years. I asked him one day, 'What do you do in that place?' He answered, 'Oh, we're making a boat.'

Presumably, The Queen Mary was assembled more speedily than anything that ever came out of the annex (although I sincerely doubt if anything seaworthy was ever produced in that wee hideaway). Looking back, the annex was like the room in the old haunted castle no-one was allowed to enter. It was kept hidden away from prying eyes or inquisitive minds. God only knows what REALLY went on it that place. Once they allow my cousin, who has long since shed his Christian name of John in favour of Igor, out into the daylight he may be in a position to give us a clue.

This is the bit where I am beginning to feel like Ronnie Corbett sitting in The Big Chair while rambling all over the place attempting to tell a joke. After about five minutes, you've lost the thread of the tale and, possibly, the will to live. Annoying, isn't it? But, please, bear with me. Anyway, I had made up my mind I was quitting school as early as possible and fifteen was the permitted leaving age at the time. My top subjects at school were English - yes, I thought that might surprise you - Art and Sports. I got the hang of arithmetic and my French, Latin and History were reasonable. However, I'm afraid algebra and geometry were complete gobbledygook and remain so to this day. I could never see how A over Z equalling 3 would ever be helpful to me later in life. Pythagoras' Theorem could have been an emerging pop band challenging Pinkerton's Assorted Colours for a place on Top of the Pops for all I knew or cared.

Also, I had a very nervous Science teacher by the name of Mr Rodgers who looked even more anxious when he saw me going anywhere near a Bunsen burner. He was probably breathing a little more easily when he was informed I was leaving school at the age of fifteen; his precious lab enjoying a stay of execution.

I enjoyed Art and my teacher was an excitable Italian/Scot by the name of Signor/Mr Franchetti. He must have been good because he kept popping up on an STV news programme called *Here and Now* giving his 'expert' opinion on all sorts of weird and wonderful creations. Franchetti, in fact, was a bit of an Einstein lookalike - even more so when he stuck out his tongue. He liked me and continually nominated me to represent the school at the Kelvingrove Art Gallery and Museum where I vied with budding Leonardos from other schools for an assortment of awards. My style, if that grand title could be bestowed upon it, owed more to Spike Milligan than Michelangelo. I never won anything; I never even hit the bar. I think I might just have been there to make up the numbers.

As I prepared to launch myself upon the universe, I was told of an opening at a sign writers' studio in the East End of Glasgow. I went for an interview, was handed a pencil and a piece of paper and was asked to copy the lettering of the Greek alphabet. I must have done well enough, because I was offered the job there and then. 'When could I start?' Small problem with that, I told them. I actually hadn't completed my school term - I think I still had about two months to go - and, to my utter horror, Mr Carroll refused to allow me to leave ahead of schedule. I begged, pleaded, offered my pocket money, even my twenty-one year old sister Betty, but he was resolute and was having none of it. The sign writers informed me they couldn't keep the post open and it went to someone else. Thank God! Thank Mr Carroll! (I doubt if the two ever met, though.)

Around that time I sent letters, in my best handwriting, to four newspapers; the Daily Record, the Daily Express, the Evening Times and the Evening Citizen. Basically, I asked them the same question, 'How do I go about attempting to get into newspapers?' I received one reply: from the Daily Record. It wasn't a form letter, either. I still have that priceless (to me) piece of paper to this day. Here it is, dated April 5 1967, reproduced word for word.

Dear Alex,

Thank you for writing to me about a job in the Daily Record.

There are two main ways to enter a career in newspapers. The first, is to get a position as a 'Junior' - either as a clerk or a messenger - and then to graduate into more senior work. The second, is to get higher educational qualifications first, and then enter a small newspaper - preferably a weekly newspaper - as a journalist and then graduate to a larger newspaper on the editorial side.

Most editorial jobs require a high standard of education and boys who have not got this background often find they don't get a chance of becoming reporters, but are left doing more routine jobs.

If you are interested in joining the Daily Record as a 'Junior' you should apply to the Chief Accountant.

Wishing you luck in your career.

Yours sincerely,

Derek A Webster

Editor

It was sent to:

Master Alex Gordon

54 Dougrie Road,

Castlemilk,

Glasgow S5

The door had edged open an inch and that was all I needed. A letter winged its way to the Chief Accountant of the Daily Record the following day. Now it was just a question of waiting, hoping and praying while checking the post every morning. A month crawled by at a pace worthy of a snail with arthritis. On May 15, something remarkable occurred in my young life. A letter dropped through the door and I think I caught it before it hit the floor. Again, it was easily identified with the Daily Record stamp. It was from a Mr G Hogan, Chief Accountant, and I was being told to make myself available for a meeting with his assistant, Mr I Merry, at the Daily Record building at 10am on Friday, May 19. If I could not make the appointment, I was asked to respond.

Snipers posted on every rooftop in Glasgow's city centre couldn't have prevented me getting to the front door at 67 Hope Street that day.

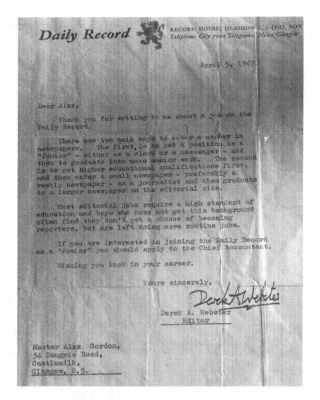

The letter that changed my life

I took along a couple of scrapbooks I had put together. I had faithfully cut out football photographs and written my own match reports at games I had attended. I trained with Queen's Park at the time and took in a few games at Hampden, which was about ten minutes on the No.37 bus that linked Castlemilk with Springburn. The route also took in Cathkin Park, the home of the now-defunct Third Lanark. Unaccompanied, I observed the action involving the wonderfully nicknamed 'Hi-Hi'. Most of my friends, Catholics and Protestants alike, were a cross section of Celtic and Rangers supporters. I saw a lot of Jim Baxter, John Greig and Willie Henderson at Ibrox while still getting the opportunity of watching the likes of Jimmy Johnstone, Tommy Gemmell and Billy McNeill across the Clyde at Celtic Park.

I catalogued everything fairly neatly and, I thought, artistically. Mr

Merry looked through a couple of my offerings and complimented me on my English. He asked me a few questions and, after about thirty minutes, which seemed like the clichéd eternity, he thanked me for coming in, shook my hand and told me he would be in touch. I went home in a daze. My dad, John, kept asking me how it had gone. I couldn't tell him for one very good reason; I hadn't a clue myself. I didn't even know if Mr Merry was one bit interested in football. (I later discovered he was a Rangers season ticket holder.) He must have been reasonably impressed because his was the name at the bottom of the letter that arrived the following morning, the message that had sent my dear old mum into orbit. I wasn't far behind, mind you. I was told to report to a Miss E Thomson, of Finances, on the first floor at 9am sharp. My starting wage was £4 per week; £3.10s (£3.50) after tax and national insurance.

Do you know, I can remember exactly what I wore my first day at the Daily Record, when I turned up early in my best bib and tucker on May 22 1967. I sported a dark tan suede jacket, light fawn trousers (razor sharp crease), brown suede Hush Puppies shoes, white plain shirt and a dark green tie. I must have worn black socks because I have never worn any other colour. Charity shops have been the beneficiary of many unwanted gaudy Christmas gifts around the second week of January every year.

My mum had a card for a shop called Goldbergs in Glasgow that allowed her to purchase goods on tick. (Hire Purchase to the good people of Newton Mearns.) She hopped on a bus that Saturday afternoon, got to the shop and bought me an Omega sports wristwatch with a black plastic strap. Believe it or not, I had never owned a wristwatch in my life. God bless her.

I'll talk about some of the larger-than-life characters I met during my early days in newspapers if, of course, you haven't already found a use for this book to balance that shoogly leg on the dining room table, returned it early to the library or hit the relevant button on your Kindle to obliterate it from your files. Quickly moving on, while I've still got your interest, I found that being a 'junior' in a vast newspaper office was just below the level of dogsbody. I was at the beck and call of everyone, and I do mean *everyone*. The cleaning ladies often sent me to make their tea. If someone needed their shoelaces tying on the seventh floor, I was their man; just give me ten seconds to race up the stairs while the two elevators were occupied.

One marvellous aspect of this job was that I very quickly got on first-name terms with all the bosses in the building while I delivered their morning newspapers. One such gaffer was, in fact, Mr G Hogan, Chief Accountant. He told me to call him Gerry. I found out he was a Celtic fan and we would have a brief natter most mornings about football. He was a prepossessing individual with a daunting physical presence, about 6ft 4in tall and well built, and always immaculately dressed. He was also one of the most approachable blokes you could ever hope to meet. And, thank goodness, that worked hugely in my favour one day.

I didn't have to spend too long racing around as a 'junior/dogsbody' when, about six weeks later, I was 'promoted' to Advertising Accounts. I hated the job. I spent most of my time licking envelopes and stuffing them with bills or receipts. I hadn't signed up for this. I would turn up in the morning and half expect Rod Serling to show me to my desk. (For younger readers, those of you who have stuck to the task of reading this merely for curiosity purposes, Rod Serling was the presenter on an American TV show called 'The Twilight Zone' which was dedicated to supernatural bunkum. It ran from 1959 to 1964. I can barely remember it, but I just know it will be on UK Gold any time soon.) My boss was an anonymous fellow by the name of Jack Bartholomew. He had a skin pigmentation that left him looking as though he had spent all day under a sunlamp. Of course, he was known as 'Black Bart'.

There was another guy called Colin who arrived every day on a moped. (Not at the desk, he parked it downstairs.) I recognised his daredevil spirit from day one; clearly, he was Advertising Accounts' answer to Evel Knievel. Hail, rain or shine, Colin always sported layer after layer of protective clothing. Not for him, though, the lightning flashes or the skull and crossbones on his sensible black helmet. He would remove the head gear carefully and then the balaclava under that. Next up, it was the goggles, followed by the spare set of goggles for the emergency pair of goggles. He then stored away the huge latex gloves followed by the ordinary pair of cloth hand coverings. Bright yellow bri-nylon jacket to match the bright yellow bri-nylon trousers was next to be shed. Special clip-ons for the trouser bottoms gave way as did the protective rubber overshoes. By the time he had struggled clear of his outer clothing, it was time to put it all back on again and go home.

I felt as comfortable in that department as Danny DeVito would on a basketball court. I had to escape. After about a month, I was cheeky enough to knock on the door of Mr G Hogan and ask for a meeting. Now he could have told me to get lost, he was working on the annual budget for the entire organisation or he was just about to begin a big crossword. Luckily, he nodded, offered me a seat and said, 'What can I do for you, Alex?' I was amazed he remembered my first name, but, as I got to know later, that was typical of this gentle giant.

'I can't work in Advertising Accounts,' I said.

'What's the problem?' he asked.

'Do you know what I do there?' I returned.

'I know what EVERYONE does on the commercial floor,' he smiled.

'Then, in that case, you'll know why I want to leave.' If I had spent time working on that line, rehearsing those words or polishing that delivery, it could never have come out better.

'You're clearly unhappy. What can I do for you?'

'I want to work in the editorial.'

'Do you, indeed?' He leant forward and looked me straight in the eye. 'Do YOU know what they do in that department?'

'I've got a good idea,' I ventured.

'I doubt it,' grinned the Chief Accountant. 'Even I don't know what on earth goes on in the editorial. I would like to keep it that way.'

Undeterred, I said, 'I would like to give it a go. That's why I joined newspapers in the first place.'

What happened next took me hugely by surprise. Gerry Hogan said, 'Be back here in an hour. I'll see what I can arrange.'

That sixty minutes took an age before I knocked on his door again. I was told to enter and there was a guy I didn't recognise sitting on the edge of the Chief Accountant's desk. He looked an affable enough bloke with an enormous grin like a cartoon cat. I was introduced to him; he was Bill Harley, Editor of the Noon Record. The newspaper was an offshoot of the Daily Record, but was purely a sports paper, mainly horse and dog racing with football dotted around its thirty-two or so pages. It was named the Noon because it only went onto the presses when the Daily Record's run was complete. It was on sale long before midday, of course.

'So, you want to join the crazy people on the third floor?' asked Bill Harley warmly.

I suppose he could have framed it more attractively. 'Yes,' I said without hesitation. For reasons that will become obvious, I thought I had the necessary qualifications to fit snugly into that environment.

'It will mean constant back shift,' warned the Noon's Editor. 'Anti-social hours. No more going out with your chums every night. You'll be working on a Sunday, too. No more weekends free. You won't be able to go to the football on Wednesdays.'

He wasn't doing too good a job of selling the job to me. I didn't care. My mind was made up and I was ready to make the sacrifices. The Holy Grail was within touching distance.

'Do you want time to think it over, Alex?' asked Gerry Hogan. 'It's a big step.'

Funnily enough, although the next answer would change my entire life, professional and personal, upside down, I never wavered for a moment. 'That's what I want to do.'

The Chief Accountant and the Noon Record Editor looked at each other, had a quick confab and Bill Harley said, 'Do you want to start on Sunday? Three in the afternoon until ten?'

'Sure thing,' I heard myself say. My heart was pounding. I've never taken drugs in my life, but I don't think you could have filled me with any amount of hallucinogenic substance that would have made me feel higher than I was at that moment. I was exhilarated. It was a Wednesday afternoon. I floated the thirty yards or so from the Chief Accountant's

14

office to the Advertising Accounts and told Black Bart I was leaving on Friday. If he was disappointed, he hid emotions spectacularly well. 'Okay,' he said while continuing to peer at an account.

Colin probably didn't notice my absence for about another year or so. If at all.

The Daily Record Editorial at Anderston Quay. It's so quiet this snap must have been taken on a Sunday morning.

Chapter 3

Chiefy and the Munich Massacre

The crackle on the telephone line was not a faulty connection; it was machine gun fire. I later discovered the pop-pop-pop sounds were those of AK-47 pistols. On the other end of the line was Alex Cameron, Chief Sports Writer of the Daily Record. It was the early hours of September 5 1972, during the second week of the Munich Olympics and the horrific massacre of the Israeli athletes was taking place.

The Palestinian Black September group had infiltrated the Olympic Village where security was remarkably, and intentionally, lax. The West German Olympic Organising Committee had actively encouraged a friendly and open atmosphere in the Village. The idea behind the thinking was to eradicate memories of the strict militaristic image of wartime Germany. The organisers had secretly tagged it the 'Carefree Games' and it was accepted that athletes were coming and going without presenting proper identification, while many bypassed the security checkpoints altogether, stepping over small chain-linked fences before strolling off to do a bit of sight-seeing.

Alas, the lack of security was to be brutally exposed at the cost of lives of the innocent: six Israeli coaches, five athletes and a West German police officer. Five members of Black September were also shot dead. It was an atrocity that shocked the world, and Chiefy, as he was known to his Daily Record colleagues, was determined to be one of the first on the scene to report on the story as it was unfolding.

Prior to that fateful morning, Chiefy had been waxing lyrical about the Games and the wonderful feelgood factor and unsurpassable facilities. The press area was 'unbelievable', he assured me. 'Spacious with everything at your fingertips.' So, the Games were going according to plan. As you might expect, covering the event for Scotland's National Newspaper, our man put a focus on home talent such as David Wilkie (swimming),

Ian Stewart and Ian McCafferty (5,000 metres), Lachie Stewart (10,000 metres), and David Jenkins (400 metres), while hoovering up the thoughts of the other hopefuls. However, his remit was to cover EVERYTHING, all the main events, the gold medal finales, giving progress reports on the likes of Mary Peters (women's pentathlon), David Jenkins, David Hemery, Alan Pascoe and Martin Reynolds (men's 4x400 metres relay), and Alan Minter (boxing). It was a daunting, demanding task Chiefy relished.

The botched hostage-taking of Israeli athletes and the ensuing disastrous shoot-out between terrorists and security were unpredictable and abominable occurrences not on Alex Cameron's agenda. Try stopping him, though, from attempting to get into pole position to file a report.

Chiefy realised something untoward was taking place with the sudden activity around 4.30am local time outside the area designated for the world's press. He was aware of strange noises coming from the Village. Later, he described them to me as intermittent dull thumps, nothing at all like a car backfire. Now, he could have pulled the sheets over his head and continued to slumber. Just some hyped-up athletes making a nuisance of themselves. But his journalistic instincts had been alerted, the antennae was buzzing. There was nothing else for it; he would have to investigate. I rarely ever saw our reporter without a suit, shirt and tie. I've always had this image of him playing golf booted and suited, straight from Savile Row to the first tee. The press corps had been presented with a range of sportswear by the Olympic authorities, but I still can't get my head round the thought of Chiefy in a tracksuit and trainers. He slipped into the latest in the Adidas range and, for reasons known only to himself, hauled his favourite tan camel-haired coat from a wardrobe. Then he went to explore.

After the welcome freedom of the previous days, he was surprised to be stopped in his tracks by an anxious machine gun-toting policeman as he headed towards the athletes' premises. Chiefy's grasp of the native tongue could very well have been restricted to 'Wodka, Tonika, kein Eis' - vodka, tonic, no ice - but he quickly got the notion that the armed personnel waving a deadly weapon under his nose was not inviting him round for drinks with his colleagues at the 'Polizeistation'. Thinking on his feet was never a problem for my old mate. He straightened his back, pulled his coat tightly over his tracksuit and took a chance that the policeman was not a keen linguist. 'I am Russian official,' said Chiefy, in some sort of weird dialect. 'I must be allowed passage.'

Remarkably, the officer put away the machine gun and actually waved Chiefy through. 'Just like that,' I was told by my chum. 'I walked through and didn't look back.' At that stage, our intrepid reporter couldn't have had an inkling what was happening, but he followed 'the strange noises.' His progress was halted again by two more policemen, but once again Chiefy did his best to mimic Leonid Brezhnev and, incredibly, he was allowed to carry on.

'Why a Russian official?' I had to ask.

'There were some Russian weightlifters arriving back late at the time and that must have triggered off my thought process,' answered Chiefy. 'Anyway, I didn't think I would get away with Mexican.'

Chiefy edged ever forward. 'Obviously, I knew it was serious,' he said. 'The penny was beginning to drop. The press had been lectured about the possibility of terrorist attacks. Unfortunately, these sporting global events attract audiences of vast millions and if anyone is determined to get their message across to the rest of the world it is an ideal platform. Sad, but true.'

The Record's top man espied a public telephone booth, partially hidden by bushes and not too far away from the commotion which was taking place at a small building in an isolated part of the Village next to a swing gate which was not manned. Chiefy quickly discovered the building housed the Israeli Olympic squad. A horrible jigsaw was coming together. He telephoned the Sports Desk in Glasgow. At that time, only one or two staff might have been expected to be in attendance with the vast majority of editions already heading for most parts of the country.

As it happened, there were a few of us at the desk that morning, including Sports Editor Jack Adams. We were having a beer while a few of our colleagues played cards. No-one found it unusual that we would still be kicking around the office at that time. Unless, of course, they were on 'a promise'. Some of the hacks would leave with the usual, 'If I'm not in bed by two, I'm going home.' Apart from the Press Club in West Regent Street, there were very few places to go after the midnight hour those days. With the Olympic Games taking place, we would more than likely have worked up to 1am and beyond. I've often been asked about journalists' strange nocturnal habits. I have always answered, 'If you finish work at 6pm, do you want to be tucked up and sleeping an hour or so later?' Adrenalin could often still be pumping after a particularly exhilarating evening and a sporting event such as the Olympics would certainly evoke excessive stimulation in the system.

Jack Adams answered the ringing telephone. It could have been a drunk wondering what had won the sixth at Shawfield. His expression changed immediately. I heard him say, 'Christ Almighty! Hold on, Alex, I'll alert the copy takers.' There might have been one such operator on at that time of the morning and Jack handed me the telephone as he prepared to race along the editorial floor to the copy room. 'Talk to Alex; keep the line open.'

Back then, you had to continue chatting on a call coming in from a foreign country. Overseas telephone switchboard operators would often listen in to the calls and if they heard silence they would assume the call was over and immediately disconnect you. I may have only been twenty years old at the time while working on the Sports Desk for the best part of five years, but I had already had experience of a line going dead and then being forced to go through the annoying rigmarole of attempting to revive it. Obviously, I can't recall exactly what I said to Chiefy that morning, but I can reveal we did end up speaking about the weather just to continue talking in case an operator listened in, detected nothing but silence and hit the switch that cut off all communication.

I could detect a muffled, sudden report every now and again in the background. 'What the hell's that racket?' I asked. I will always remember Chiefy's reply: 'I hope to God it's fireworks.' Then he added swiftly, 'Don't think so.' Looking back after all these years, I realise what a surreal situation was developing in Munich that morning. Chiefy, in the guise of an anonymous Russian official, had somehow managed to annex a public telephone in the Village as armed police swarmed around.

'They began cordoning off everything,' Chiefy told me later. 'I got some strange looks, standing in a glass-fronted phone booth, but they hardly took any notice of me. Obviously, they didn't believe I posed a threat. Mind you, what on earth I would have been doing there at that time in the morning with all hell breaking loose and quietly minding my own business while making a phone call is anyone's guess. I did discover later that the police were more concerned about people trying to get OUT of the Village rather than someone apparently quite content to hang around and make a phone call.'

This, of course, all sounds far fetched, but if you had ever met Alex Cameron, you would have accepted it, without the merest hesitation, as being utterly true. Our daring reporter could get caught up in the most extraordinary situations and live to write the tale. Think of a hurricane whirling its destruction as it lays waste an entire city, cars being sucked out of their parking areas, lampposts and trees being uprooted and being propelled crazily through the skies, parts of bricks, mortar, glass and manhole covers zipping around hither and yon. And then conjure up an immaculately-tailored figure, not a hair out of place, stepping out of the carnage and debris, notepad in hand and a pen in the other, and you have Alex Cameron. Trust me, nothing fazed this guy.

Jack Adams eventually located a copytaker whiling away the hours in the downstairs library. He was swiftly pressed into action. Once he was seated, with the cans on his head, five pieces of paper, carbon in between each sheet, in the typewriter, we switched Chiefy over to him.

Of course, Alex's knowledge of events at that time was all a bit sketchy, but the wire services had by now kicked into action. Reuters, I remember, were quick off the mark. It would normally be a one-line message stating 'Disturbance in Olympic Village'. That snap would be updated every five minutes or so until it emerged 'Shots heard in Olympic Village. Police on the scene'. And so on for the next hour or so.

The News Desk and the backbench had been alerted to the dramatic developing story. On TV, it would be done as one of those live broadcasts, 'I am standing here at the scene of the crime' pieces. Chiefy, skilfully and swiftly, put together his eye witness account. He was the only journalist from the world's press covering the story at the actual scene at that time. It was sheer, taut, good old-fashioned journalism. Sports, News and Picture Desks combined at breakneck pace in an attempt to get the sensational story into the final editions of the newspaper. Possibly, we only managed to get a few thousand out at the end of a run because it was not easy to replate so many pages in the machine room back then.

What mattered most to me, though, was how Chiefy reacted to a breaking story with such awesome awareness and vigilance. His response was extraordinary and, to me, if any tale was typical of Chiefy's sheer professionalism it was that one.

One evening, in January 2003, thirty years and four months after Munich, Chiefy telephoned me at home. I had left the Sunday Mail in 1994 after taking over as Sports Editor in 1987. Naturally, Alex and I had

21

kept in touch and there was such a (dis)organisation as the Wednesday Club where Chiefy, Don Morrison, Dixon Blackstock and David Leggat, three of my former colleagues at the Sunday Mail, Phil McEntee, formerly of the Sunday Express and Daily Mail, and a few 'special guests' would meet for a beer, a blether and a bite. Chiefy, of course, bodyswerved the beer for his time-honoured 'vodka, tonic, no ice.' Our chosen rendezvous was The Montrose Bar on Carrick Street on Glasgow's Broomielaw.

After we had put the world to rights - again - and Chiefy had devoured another plate of mince and tatties, his absolute favourite meal, he pulled me aside. 'Are you at home tonight?' he asked. 'Yes, I've nothing planned,' I replied. 'I'll call about nine,' he said, putting the forefinger of his right hand to his lips. All very mysterious and clandestine, I thought, but I knew when not to ask questions.

Later that evening, the phone duly shrilled and I answered; it was Chiefy. There was no preamble, which was most unlike him. 'I am phoning a handful of friends I know I can trust. Have you noticed anything different about me recently?' he enquired.

'Yes,' I said. I was not going to lie to one of my dearest friends. 'I've noticed a few things.' The previous January, Alex and I, with our respective wives, Jan and Gerda, were booked for an eight-day break in Playa Blanca in Lanzarote to celebrate my fiftieth birthday. A few days before we were due to fly out, Alex got in touch to say he had a bad cold and wouldn't be able to make the trip. That didn't sound like him, but, of course, I accepted the situation. Alarm bells weren't immediately ringing. Things, though, were nagging away at me throughout 2002. Alex was becoming a little forgetful, not quite as sharp in his actions. I accepted, at that stage, he was seventy-three years old, but, remember, I had only ever known this individual to possess such a keen, active and inquisitive mind. I saw him changing before my very eyes, but, thinking positively, I always believed he would return to the Chiefy of old.

'I've got Parkinson's,' he said and added, as though he were discussing an ingrowing toenail, 'Bloody thing.'

I didn't know how to react. Parkinson's? What exactly was that?

Chiefy answered the unasked question. 'It's a degenerative disorder of the central nervous system.'

I won't dwell on the remainder of the conversation. Alex, though, did promise, 'I'll fight this, you can be sure of that.'

Now I could fully understand the change in my old mate. An exceptionally proud and dignified human being, he attempted to disguise the disease. In the end, he realised he would have to acknowledge it. I later discovered he telephoned another five people that night. I hadn't realised I was in such exalted company.

On July 23 2003, I received another call at home. On this occasion it was Don Morrison. 'Chiefy's passed away,' he told me.

It wasn't totally unexpected, but the news still struck me like a jackhammer. Both my parents died within eleven weeks of each other in 1982 and I had got through it. Inevitably, I knew I would overcome the death of such an incredible man, who had gone out of his way to look after me during my career. It was Alex who promoted me to Chief Sports Sub-Editor on Scotland's biggest-selling daily newspaper when I was only twenty-three and by far the youngest guy on the Sports Desk. My best mate on the desk at the time was a bloke called Ian Gibson and I think he was eight years older than me, the nearest to my age group. I had left school at the age of fifteen without a single qualification, but that mattered not a jot to Chiefy when he gave me that job. The bond between us was unbreakable, I believed, but I accept there is little you can do when the light goes out for the last time.

You know, Alex left me with one major regret: he never wrote his autobiography. I pleaded with him and I prompted him, but all I ever got back was, 'Och, who's interested in me? Who wants to read my story?' Alex had worked for more than fifty years in journalism, kicking off with his local paper, the Stirling Journal, before moving onto the Daily Mail in 1952. He was there for sixteen years before joining the Daily Record in 1968. I was there to welcome him that day at the front door of the building in Hope Street. He arrived as Sports News Editor, became Chief Sports Writer and was then put in overall charge as Chief Sports Editor. He continued until he retired at the age of seventy in 2000. ('I think I've done my stint,' he told me.) His Candid Cameron column became the widest read in the country. He was a frequent face on television for thirty years and he was a regular voice on radio. He was an instantly recognisable figure everywhere he went.

And, just to refresh your memory, Alex is the only journalist in history who covered the following:

Eight Olympic Games

Seven World Cups

Seven Commonwealth Games

Four World Athletic Championships

Two World Boxing Title fights.

In 2001, he received a lifetime achievement from the Scottish Press Awards.

Aye, who would be interested in Alex Cameron's story? I hope Chiefy forgives me, but I, for one, was more than fascinated and there are a few more stories within these pages that have more than passing references to this doyen of the written word.

Broadway gave us Damon Runyan; Balfron gave us Alex Cameron.

If only he had written that damn book ...

Chapter 4

Ali boxing clever with Willie Henderson

Muhammad Ali was the hottest ticket in sport when he accepted an invite to visit Scotland in August 1965. Everyone wanted a piece of the brash youngster who had won the world heavyweight championship from Sonny Liston in June the previous year and successfully defended the crown with a first round knock-out against the man he christened 'The Big Ugly Bear' eleven months later.

It was the father of Tommy Gilmour, the legendary fight promoter, who somehow persuaded the self-proclaimed 'Greatest' to come to these shores. Tommy Snr, also in the boxing business, was friendly with Ali's manager Angelo Dundee and his brother Chris. Ali, at that time twenty-three years old, was resting before his next fight against former champion Floyd Paterson on November 22 in Las Vegas. Angelo and Chris assured their boxer he would thrive on the 'bracing airs' of Scotland.

I doubt if Ali came within sniffing distance of Loch Lomond, but he was whisked off to Celtic Park and Ibrox Stadium to meet the players of Celtic and Rangers. It was a PR man's dream. The world's most talked-about sportsman even agreed to pose in a kilt when he arrived in the East End of Glasgow. He hammed it up for the photographers and then met some of the Celtic stars, Tommy Gemmell among them.

'He was an awesome presence,' said Gemmell, who would become a European champion within two years. 'You saw him on the telly, but you never really appreciated the size of the guy or his fabulous physique. The dimensions of his hands were like sides of ham. You could only imagine what the width and depth would be when they were encased in boxing gloves. If he struck you square on the face, he would have hit everything from the top of your forehead to the tip of your chin. And, of course, he was such an immaculately-honed sportsman with incredible good looks. Apart from that, he was just an ordinary fella. I was talking to him and asked where he was off to next. He told me he was travelling across Glasgow to meet with the players of Rangers.

A born showman ... Muhammad McAli

'They a good team, these Rangers folk?' he asked me.

'Not as good as us,' I replied.

'I hope they better-looking. You guys all look as though you train by letting the punch bag hit you.'

'I wasn't going to argue, but I did tell him to look out for a particular Rangers player who was a friend of mine, Willie Henderson. Wee Willie's knowledge of the pugilistic sport was breathtaking. Honestly, you could mention a boxer at any weight and Willie could rattle off his history, wins, draws, losses, etc. He could tell you his opponents and his best fights. Willie actually looked a bit like a boxer with his squashed nose.'

Ali and his entourage duly arrived at the home of Celtic's fiercest rivals and the planet's finest exponent of fisticuffs went through the same routine with the Rangers players. Nothing was too much trouble for a genuinely charismatic human being. Willie Henderson, as expected, took the opportunity to introduce himself. They shook hands and Ali looked at the player's nose.

'You a footballer?' he asked.

'Aye,' answered Willie.

Ali took another glance at the Rangers player's mangled hooter.

'Man, I'm sure glad I'm a boxer,' he said.

Part Two

Managers : clubs and papers

Chapter 5

Big Jock the PR man

George Taylor sounded an awful lot like Jock Stein. I discovered very quickly there was a very good reason for that: George Taylor was, in fact, Jock Stein.

If Jock Stein hadn't attained legendary status as manager of Celtic, I have absolutely no doubt he would have been a roaring success in PR. Big Jock was light years ahead of anyone else in football after he returned to take over as team boss of an ailing Parkhead side in March 1965. His successes as a football manager are well-documented. However, I was always taught to write a story for the man who had just dropped in from the moon and required background on a story he was reading for the first time, so here's his silverware collection: ten league championships, nine Scottish Cups (one with Dunfermline), six League Cups and, of course, one European Cup.

Back in 1967, after I had just joined the Daily Record Sports Desk, I was often left holding the fort between 9pm and 10pm while the sub-editors went for their break, almost exclusively in the general direction of the Garrick Bar. The laws of the land prevented me from working beyond 10pm. It would be another three years, when I reached eighteen, that my shift would change from 3pm to 10pm, to 5pm to 1am. I found that sixty minutes on my own at the desk of Scotland's national newspaper to be very illuminating; especially when George Taylor called.

One of the first of our 'chats' came at the start of February 1968. I answered the phone and on came the gruff tones of 'George'.

'Any writers there, son?' he always asked.

I gave him the stock reply, 'Just me and I'm nobody.'

'Aye, we're all somebody,' he said. 'Can you take this down, please? Celtic are going to play a Friendly with Newcastle United at St. James's

Park on Saturday, February 17. Three o'clock kick-off. A full team will turn out. Do you want me to repeat that?'

I went over it again and he agreed I had got it word for word.

'Make sure you get that in the paper tomorrow. Okay?' he said.

I had to ask. 'Excuse me, Mr Taylor, but how do you know this? I can't put anything in the paper until I'm certain of the facts.'

My query was met with laughter. I had long suspected George Taylor to be Jock Stein and the guy appeared to know an awful lot of what was going on within the walls of a certain team in the East End of Glasgow.

'Are you Jock Stein?' I blurted.

'Naw, naw, son, I'm no' Jock Stein. I'm George Taylor, Hughie Taylor's brother. Did you no' know that? Just make sure you get that story in the paper, okay?'

As far as I was aware, Hughie Taylor, our top sportswriter, didn't have a sibling. I knew, though, that there was every chance that Hughie would still be in the Garrick at that very moment. I raced round to the Waterloo Street pub to give Hughie the news. 'Who told you this?' he asked. 'Your brother,' I answered. Hughie smiled, obviously in on the joke. 'I don't have a brother, but I know George. The story will be good; you better get it in the paper.'

I sprinted back to the desk and wrote out the information in long hand - I was quicker at writing than typing at that stage - and sent the truncated story to the Caseroom department to be included in the 'Stop Press' gap in the back page. It was normally printed in red ink. If you don't know what 'Stop Press' was in a newspaper in the sixties and seventies, I can only say I envy you your youth. It was for little unexpected snippets that would bypass a pre-planned slot in the newspaper. Afterwards, the story would be taken out of the 'Stop Press' spot and rewritten and given more prominence in a later edition of the newspaper.

I can look back now and shudder if that had been one of those hoax callers who derive so much pleasure in dropping unsuspecting innocents in the brown stuff. Thousands of Celtic fans travelled to Tyneside on that particular Saturday - a crowd of 38,790 was recorded - to watch their team, with the likes of Lisbon heroes Ronnie Simpson, Billy McNeill, Tommy Gemmell and Jimmy Johnstone in the line-up, lose 1-0. I found it difficult to comprehend that I was one of the first persons on the planet to have knowledge of the arrangement of this game.

Now, I realise this may be a small point, but I believe it shows how clued up and tuned in Jock Stein was to the need for Celtic to claim column inches in Scotland's national newspapers. Actually, he was revolutionary in that role. Nowadays, there are press conferences called to notify the press of press conferences. Back then, though, there was no such thing.

Rangers, for instance, still sent letters to a journalist of their choice at a newspaper to 'cordially invite' them to a meeting with their manager. Normally, they gave two days' notice. Jock Stein brought an immediacy to the role. Whereas other football clubs plodded along the archaic path of sending communications through the post, he would pick up the phone and go straight through to a Sports Desk, have a chat, plant the story and move on to another newspaper. He did this without the aid of a PR department. In truth, Rangers and others were not so much sucked into a publicity vacuum as blown away by an unstoppable hurricane.

Anyone brought up on a staple diet of Sky TV will no doubt find it hilarious that there was no set routine for the press to talk to managers or players after a game. A hack might get lucky and catch a player leaving the ground, but it was as rare as hen's teeth for anything to be pre-arranged. Rangers manager Scot Symon, for instance, so rarely talked to newspapermen or other media outlets that hardly anyone knew what he actually sounded like. That's a fairly absurd situation when you consider he was team boss at Ibrox for THIRTEEN years and had been registered as a player for another nine. No-one can remember him doing a TV or radio broadcast.

Bertie Auld would often insist, 'The foxes took to the hills when Big Jock was in town.' It's intended as a compliment. Jock Stein saw an opening for him to exploit on behalf of Celtic. He would often make time for the Sunday newspaper reporters in the immediate aftermath of a game on a Saturday while inviting the daily hacks to Celtic Park around 11am on a Sunday where, after some vital hours to digest what had happened in the previous match, he would always give them something newsworthy.

The reporters were being spoonfed stories and they weren't going to complain. When the pages were being drawn up for the Monday editions of the papers, a massive space was always left for Celtic because Sports Editors were well aware that something of note would be coming from Jock Stein that day. It took Rangers years to get wise to this 'tactic' by their rival across the Clyde. Rangers could have a particularly good result on a Saturday, Celtic might scrape through, draw or even lose and they would more often than not be the greater presence on the back pages on Monday. Simple and effective.

Here's another little gem that marked Jock Stein as being more than just slightly streetwise. He would often plan ahead to make certain Rangers did not have a free run at the back pages. The Ibrox side could be about to play a big game with Celtic having a free day and, naturally enough, that would mean the men from Govan commandeering precious space in the nationals. Big Jock would go into overdrive in his bid to hijack the back page and sabotage the attempts of his club's oldest foes.

Rangers were due to play Dundee in a Scottish Cup-tie at Ibrox on February 17 1974. Sunday football was unusual in the seventies - satellite TV was still almost two decades away - and this encounter had caught the public's imagination. (A crowd of 64,672 turned out that afternoon.) Big Jock knew he would have to derail the Rangers publicity juggernaut. He had been pondering over a move for an Anglo-Scot to boost his first team squad. Big Jock had the deal in the bag days before he unveiled the signing, coincidentally on the same Sunday Rangers were playing host to Dundee. Jimmy Bone cost £25,000 from Sheffield United and was paraded that very afternoon meaning Rangers no longer had exclusive rights to the back pages of the press. On this occasion, though, the Celtic manager might have wondered if it had been worth his bother; the Ibrox side were thumped 3-0 on their own pitch by the Tayside outfit.

He didn't often get it wrong as he pushed Celtic to the forefront on the pitch and in the press. Certainly, he wasn't shy of appearing in front of a camera or a microphone. Unlike Scot Symon at Rangers, everyone was well-aware of the thick tones of Jock Stein.

Jock Stein – or is it George Taylor?

Me? I thought he sounded uncannily like a guy called George Taylor.

Chapter 6

Waddell and the charm offence

'Who the bloody hell are you?' There was no disguising the hostility in the guttural growl.

I had been warned that the individual on the other end of the telephone could be rude or carnaptious or obnoxious. I felt privileged. He had put himself out to merge all three distasteful characteristics just for me.

Alex Cameron used to do a fair impersonation of Willie Waddell, then the Rangers manager. He would nudge his specs down to the tip of his nose, peer over them in a mock menacing manner and say in intimidating tones, 'What the bloody hell do you want?'

Until that moment, I hadn't realised what an uncanny take-off that was of the Ibrox boss who didn't appear to have to work too hard on his belligerence.

It was the early seventies when SHOOT! Editor David Gregory telephoned me to say he was going to kick off a Scottish column in the magazine, calling it *Tartan Talk*. He required regular columnists from Celtic and Rangers and asked me to name names. Immediately, I put forward John Greig for the Rangers angle. It would be fairly accurate to say David Gregory wasn't quite up to scratch with Scottish football. I got the impression that anything north of Watford was a mystery. But even he had heard of the Rangers captain.

He revealed the financial package, asked me to get in touch with the player and see if he was interested. I did this and John Greig couldn't have been more accommodating. There was absolutely no hassle, but he asked could I please get in touch with the manager, Willie Waddell, to give him his place and get his permission. 'There won't be a problem, Alex,' I was reassured. Oh, yeah?

I put a call into Waddell at the manager's office at Ibrox. I talked to a secretary, who, extremely diligently, asked me for all my details and to what the enquiry pertained. I mapped it out and she asked me to call back in about an hour. I duly did this. 'Mr Waddell has the details and asks could you call him again in an hour,' I was informed. Fair enough. Sixty minutes later, I was actually talking to the Rangers manager. Or, more accurately, he was grunting at me.

An exclusive snap of Willie Waddell almost smiling

'Who the bloody hell are you?' he snarled. I identified myself and why I was calling. 'Who the bloody hell are you again?' he interrupted. 'I'm the writer who has been asked to ghost the John Greig column in the SHOOT! football magazine,' I explained for a second time. 'You're the writer?' Again, the unmistakeable rumble of someone who sounded as though he had just awakened from a deep and troubled slumber.

Before I could even answer, he added, 'I'm not talking to you. I don't talk to monkeys. Get me the bloody Editor.' With that, the phone line went dead. Immediately, I realised the Rangers manager and I wouldn't be mingling socially any time soon.

I phoned John Greig and told him about the one-way 'conversation'.

He didn't seem unduly surprised about the uncalled-for rancour from his manager. I got the drift that I hadn't caught Waddell on a rare off-day. 'So, what do we do now?' asked the Rangers skipper. I told him I would get in touch with the Editor and let him attempt to make progress on what should have been a simple, straightforward matter. I was to learn there was no such thing when Waddell was around. To me, he came across as being an unreasonable, unhelpful character who was always content to place as many obstacles as possible in your way for absolutely no good reason.

David Gregory was more than little astonished at the reaction of the Rangers manager. At that time he had George Best, Kevin Keegan, Bobby Moore and Billy Bremner as columnists in his magazine. 'I've never had an ounce of bother from Matt Busby, Bill Shankly, Ron Greenwood or Don Revie,' he said. 'This is a first.' I passed on Waddell's number and the SHOOT! Editor said, 'Leave it with me. I'll sort it out.' He also asked me to get cracking on the first John Greig column. They wanted to introduce in the magazine with a bit of a fanfare, bells and whistles and all that. I kept the Rangers player up to speed and we agreed to go ahead with the first interview. John Greig, unlike his manager, couldn't have been more co-operative. I typed up the first-person piece and posted it to the magazine offices in Farringdon Street, London, later that day. It duly appeared a couple of weeks later and everyone was happy.

After a few months, I asked David Gregory about his telephone call to Willie Waddell. 'Oh, him,' said David. 'I just ignored that bloke. I don't talk to guys like that.' The column ran for about seven years and no-one heard a murmur from Waddell. Ignorance is bliss? Yup, that would be the phrase.

I wasn't one bit surprised when I learned that Jock Stein and Willie Waddell did not like each other. Of course, the public face was quite different as it had to be in the volatile market place of the Old Firm. Any misplaced word or expression would be seized upon. In a powder keg city such as Glasgow, that could have sparked chaos.

The managers of Celtic and Rangers were often photographed at functions, shaking hands warmly and smiling brightly for the snappers. Away from the cameras, it was a different story. There was a genuine discord between two strong personalities.

Stein had never forgotten an article that had been penned by Waddell in his guise as a sportswriter with the Daily Express. In a strongly-opinionated piece, Waddell blamed Stein, acting as caretaker manager of the international side, for Scotland's 2-1 World Cup qualifying defeat by Poland at Hampden in 1965. The Scots were leading 1-0 with six minutes remaining when the Poles struck twice to leave 107,580 fans - me included - struck dumb. Waddell went to work and, basically, slaughtered his former Old Firm adversary. Stein never forgot nor forgave what he perceived to be a very personal attack on his abilities.

Waddell would often goad Stein in private by asking him how many times he had played for Scotland. The answer, of course, was none, while Waddell had represented his nation on eighteen occasions. Stein would reply in kind by asking how many medals he had won as a manager. For the record, the Celtic boss won twenty-six (one Scottish Cup with Dunfermline) and the Rangers gaffer picked up three (one league title with Kilmarnock). And so it went on. To the innocent onlooker, it may have come across as some jolly banter between two heavyweights of the game. Below the surface, there was a fierce antipathy between the individuals who would never choose to spend time in each other's company. On occasion, it appeared they found it close to intolerable to share the same city.

In truth, both could be gruff and certainly neither suffered fools gladly or otherwise. Stein was already the boss of the Parkhead side when I took my first tentative steps into the world of sports journalism in 1967 and Waddell would arrive at Ibrox in 1969.

Remarkably, Waddell had quit as manager of Kilmarnock only months after leading them to the old Scottish First Division championship in 1965. He re-entered the newspaper world as a sportswriter with the Daily Express (he had an earlier stint as a youngster with the Glasgow Evening Citizen) and, that being the case, you may have thought he may have been sympathetic to those in that industry when he returned to football. You would be wrong. Waddell was a nightmare to deal with and I had a few run-ins with the guy. Never speak ill of the dead, they say, but I have no intention of being a hypocrite, either. I didn't like him and I'm fairly certain that emotion was mirrored perfectly by Waddell.

By the way, I was also told Waddell used to grill trainee journalists who applied for jobs in Rangers' publications. How many sought a new career path after a meeting with this chap, I wonder?

Chapter 7

Why so glum, Jum?

Surely I am not alone in believing Jim McLean, the former Dundee United manager, is a trifle odd?

I recall enjoying a journal's spoof on a 'Day in the life of Jim McLean'. I think it may have been penned by the excellent Phil Differ, of *Only An Excuse?*, *Rab C Nesbitt* fame. It started off with McLean waking up in the morning and 'having a maddy'. Getting out of bed and 'having a maddy'. Getting dressed and 'having a maddy'. Going for breakfast and 'having a maddy'. And so on throughout the day. For the uninitiated, 'having a maddy' is a West of Scotland phrase for going doolally.

Fighting mad ... Jim McLean

I spent a few years sparring with the Tayside 'legend' and, as a consequence, the Sunday Mail was often barred from reporting on games at Tannadice. Needless to say, these bans do not work; they are a complete waste of everyone's time.

Wee Jum, as he was known, once took umbrage at a match report in the Sunday Mail on March 28 1993. He didn't believe his team had been given enough credit for their efforts, the summary was slanted and, basically, the overall account favoured the other side. I re-read the report. The scoreline was: DUNDEE UNITED 2, CELTIC 3. The match was covered by David Leggat, who, I can reveal, possesses a nose that is of a distinctly blue hue. It must have broken poor old Leggo's heart to scribble out so many words of acclaim for the men from the east end of Glasgow after their excellent triumph. Leggo, to be fair, was nothing more than straight-down-the-middle in his match chronicles. If not, he wouldn't have been anywhere near Tannadice that March afternoon.

I tried to reason with Wee Jum - no easy task, I hasten to say. He wasn't having any of it and I was informed the Sunday Mail would no longer be given access to his club's press box. We were persona non grata in his wee part of the universe. Oor tea was oot on Tayside. The biggest-selling newspaper in the country, regularly edging towards the one million mark in sales, had got the elbow. Now I didn't believe for a moment that we would be given the sine die treatment and I also realised it would blow over in time. It was the immediate that concerned me. So, what was I going to do when United were due to play their next home game in a fortnight's time? That was easy - I was going to send Leggo back to Tannadice with a photographer in tow.

Our esteemed hack had a penchant for fedoras back then; or maybe he was merely paying homage to the flamboyant Malcolm Allison, the former Manchester City mannequin manager. I thought it best if he left the fancy headgear at home on this occasion. As expected, our reporter was denied access to the press area and was turned away by a steward. The snapper clicked to capture the moment. Leggo then paid in and took his seat in the stand, as close to the press box as possible. More photographs with our intrepid reporter posing with what was known as the office's 'talking brick'. There were no such things as mobile phones at the time, but we had this telecommunications monstrosity that looked like the sort of walkie-talkie you would see John Wayne screaming into in the old war movies when he ordered his company to get over the top and wipe out hundreds of 'commie scum'.

We carried the match report under the bold strapline, 'THE PAPER THEY CANNOT GAG', accompanied with the snaps inside and outside the ground of a hatless Leggo. Mission accomplished; Wee Jum no pleased. It was an action replay two weeks later. Eventually, Wee Jum reluctantly relented and the ban was lifted. Would you believe he stepped down as United manager in July that year after a reign of twenty-one years and seven months? If only he had chucked it a decade or so earlier I wouldn't be grey-haired today!

On another occasion, we were crossing swords over something else that had irked the Dundee United manager. It was so inconsequential, I can't even remember what it was. Anyway, Wee Jum did make a reasonable point. 'I always read your newspaper on a Sunday and I see a lot of things I don't agree with,' he said. 'But I know you guys don't work on a Sunday, so I can't get in touch with you. And you're off on a Monday, too. By the time you go back to work on Tuesday, I've normally calmed down.'

'Okay,' I said, 'if you're upset on a Sunday why don't you phone me? Here's my home phone number.'

I duly divulged my unlisted number. 'Phone any time and we'll discuss it. Okay?'

I wondered if I had let myself in for a barrage of phone calls every Sunday morning, even before I have had my welcome first cup of tea. That said, I thought it was at least some sort of compromise and if it prevented the Sunday Mail from being given the bum's rush every second week, then it was a small price to pay. Do you know how many times the Dundee United manager phoned me on a Sunday? Not once.

I travelled up to see Wee Jum one day with the newspaper's Chief Sports Writer Don Morrison after yet another fall-out. Frankly, I was getting a bit tired of all the hassle and thought a face-to-face might help clear the air. We sat in the manager's office where we were served with tea and Abernethy biscuits. Wee Jum declined my offer of a lunch in the city as he was going to watch an Under-11 boys' game elsewhere that afternoon. As we sat and talked, each having his say, I noticed a piece of paper on McLean's desk. On it was etched numbers about three inches deep. I was attempting to read it when Wee Jum said, 'Aye, it's your phone number; I've still got it.'

After about an hour or so, Don and I got ready to leave. There is a little kitchen just off the manager's office and McLean shouted through, 'Just leave the dishes, Anne. I'll get them later.' The little lady who had made the tea emerged, said thank you and left sharpish. The picture of the United manager in a pinny and scrubbing cups and saucers wasn't an easy one to facilitate. Anyway, we shook hands and he thanked me and Don for taking the trouble to travel up from Glasgow. Apparently, it was 'much appreciated'. He may have been a complex, complicated human being, but Jim McLean was a marvellous coach and he deserved every bit of credit and success that came his way. Having said that, I was just thankful that my journalistic beat wasn't on Tayside.

There was another afternoon when Wee Jum ordered a Sunday Mail reporter - David Leggat again! - out of a press conference after the Scottish Cup Final between his United side and that of wee brother Tommy's Motherwell in 1991. It had been billed as 'The Family Final' and it was an encounter worthy of its blue riband status at the national stadium with the Fir Park side just edging it 4-3. Wee Jum was in a foul mood as he attended the aftermatch conference. It had nothing to do with the result. It was something else altogether and, on this occasion, I didn't blame him one little bit.

He was grim-faced as he entered the press room and, before even taking his seat, he snarled, 'Who's here from the Sunday Mail?' Leggo identified himself. 'Out!' barked McLean unceremoniously. 'There will be no press conference while you're here. Get out!'

Our puzzled reporter didn't even get the opportunity to ask what on earth he had done to bring about this rebuke from the United manager. Having no intention of creating an unnecessary fuss, he left quietly and immediately phoned me at the Sports Desk. He relayed what had just happened. We were both in the dark. I made a couple of enquiries and a few minutes later I had the answer. I could hardly believe it. My own newspaper, without my knowledge, had sent a news reporter to the home of McLean's mother while the game was going on. Sadly, the McLean brothers had lost their father a couple of days before the match. The brothers wore black ties and dark suits as they led out their teams at Hampden. It said a lot for their fortitude that they could carry on in such exceptionally painful circumstances.

I thought the actions of someone on the News Desk that day were reprehensible. I've never been tempted to change my mind. There are times and places and that was neither. Surely, the widow should have been given the opportunity to grieve in peace after the sudden loss of a loved one? But, behind my back, the News Desk had sent a journalist to knock on Mrs McLean's door safe in the knowledge both sons were elsewhere. No-one ever stepped forward to take responsibility, but I have my own thoughts on that. I was more than a little dismayed at the antics of my fellow-hacks and I didn't trust a couple of them inside the Sunday Mail editorial offices ever again. To my mind, they had earned that disrespect and contempt. Neither works at the newspaper today.

I found it rather amusing, if not incongruous, that Jim McLean actually ended up having a column ghosted in the Daily Record which ran for over two years. Possibly its strapline owed something to the day Wee Jum banjoed unsuspecting BBC reporter John Barnes; it was entitled 'The Column That Packs A Punch'. There was a wee photograph of McLean, doing his best to look mean and menacing, holding up his fist. Maybe the Beeb hack required smelling salts every time he turned to that particular page once a week. I'm told Wee Jum, serial blackballer of journalists and newspapers up and down the country, was paid a jaw-dropping £900 a pop for his 'hard-hitting' column.

There was a time the notion of Jim McLean working in the press would have been as likely as the Duke of Edinburgh being asked to become Honorary President of the Diplomatic Corps.

Chapter 8

Clive's swansong

Clive Sandground was Editor of the Sunday Mail from 1973 until 1981 and, unfortunately, I never got the opportunity to work with this colourful character who had a penchant for heavy tweed checked three-piece suits and garish bow-ties. He sported a wiry beard that would have been the envy of Ian Anderson, the bug-eyed, flute-playing, wild lead singer of Jethro Tull (the rock band, not the 18th Century English agriculturist). In fact, Clive, who had an artificial leg, looked as though he had just limped out of the pages of Jeeves and Wooster.

Clive Sandground ... or frontman for Jethro Tull?

There is little doubt the man possessed a sense of the ridiculous - and not just in his dress sense. He was Editor of the Scottish Daily

Express when it went into a circulation nosedive and couldn't prevent being overtaken and left in the slipstream of the rampant Daily Record in the late sixties and early seventies. The Express had reigned supreme for decades, but collapsed at the first sight of blood. The Glasgow office was hurriedly closed and the 'Scottish' edition was put together in Manchester. Sandground might not have been physically capable of dancing a celebratory jig when he got his pay-off. What he did, though, was buy a rather splendid boat, moor it beside his Wigtown hideaway and name it 'The Golden Handshake.' The man had class.

It wasn't long before Sandground fetched up at the Sunday Mail. One female reporter, clearly concerned, asked what had happened to his leg.

'They cut it off,' he replied matter-of-factly, smiling under the explosion of hair he called a beard. With that, he hobbled off.

It must be said that the work force at the Sunday Mail loved the guy. He treated them exceptionally well. The Daily Record editorial, where I worked at the time, was situated on the second floor at Anderston Quay while the Mail was a floor below. We would often hear gales of laughter travelling up the stairs and corridors from their editorial and only wonder at what the madcap Editor was up to today. He thought nothing about hiring boats and taking his staff 'doon the watter' on a Tuesday if he was particularly pleased with the previous weekend's edition.

He was also fond of what became known as 'hero-grams'. If he believed one of his operatives had done exceptionally well, a bottle of the best champagne would often wing its way to their front door on a Sunday morning. Chocolates and roses were other favourite rewards for females for a job well done. He would often insist on four-hour liquid lunches for his grateful staff. Alas, I missed him by six years at the Sunday Mail. Damn!

Sandground's reign at the newspaper came to an abrupt end on April 15 1981. The party line from the newspaper's bosses informed us he had resigned following 'policy differences which could not be resolved.' Poppycock and balderdash, as Clive might have said.

The Brixton Riots had taken place four days earlier when there was a bloody clash between the Metropolitan Police and protesters in

Lambeth, South London. There were almost 300 injuries to police and 45 to members of the public. Over 100 cars were burned, including 56 police vans. Almost 150 buildings were damaged and thirty were burned to the ground. There were 82 arrests and it was reported almost 5,000 people were involved.

All of this, rather remarkably, hardly got a mention even in the later editions of the Sunday Mail the following day. Instead, the main story was about thugs throwing heavy objects at swans in Rouken Glen Park. A huge colour picture dominated the front page of two of our feathered friends sedately paddling around and obviously totally at peace with the world. It was a splash that signalled the end for the eccentric Editor. It became known as 'Sandground's Swan Song'.

He picked up his P45, said farewell to crestfallen, near-suicidal members of staff and then admitted that the terms under which he was leaving were 'generous'.

Someone observed, 'Well, at least, Clive's landed on his foot again.'

Chapter 9

Graeme Souness: Welease Wodewick

There is a saying among footballers that some players are 'hard men without portfolio'. Basically, they are calling these guys fakes and phonies. These individuals play to the stands and hope they are deceiving the support. Just about every team has one. They go crunching in when they know it's safe and it looks fairly spectacular. The fans are supposed to believe they are wholehearted characters who would give their all for the team. Their fellow professionals are never duped.

It would be fair and accurate to report that I have never heard Graeme Souness being labelled a 'hard man without portfolio'. Souness was the bone-shuddering, snarling, growling real deal. No-one messed with the lad from the prefab in the working class area of Saughton Mains in Edinburgh. (As a Glaswegian, I was surprised to discover there were such things as council estates in our capital city. They kept that quiet.)

Graeme 'Smiler' Souness

If anyone who turned up at La Parmagiana Italian restaurant on Great Western Road one April afternoon in 1989 expecting to witness the then Rangers manager in full ranting, muscle-flexing, teeth-gnashing mode, they would have been very much disappointed. There is another side to the individual and that particular day something had touched his funny bone. As a matter of fact, Souness had watched the film of Monty Python's *Life of Brian* the previous evening and he kept getting flashbacks all the way through lunch.

He clearly enjoyed the bit when Pontius Pilate (Michael Palin), with the slight speech impediment, addressed the crowd. 'People of Jewusalem, Wome is youw fwiend. To pwove ouw fweindship it is customawy at this time to welease a wongdoer fwom ouw pwisons.' Then we go through the entire 'Welease Woger' and 'Welease Wodewick' before settling on 'Welease Bwian'. There was little chance of getting a hard-hitting interview with this genuine tough guy that afternoon. I made a mental note not to arrange an interview with Graeme Souness again when the Pythons were due on television.

I mention this meeting with the former Scotland captain because I get the drift many believe he is a mirthless individual. Nothing could be further from the truth. Yes, when he adopted his single-minded attitude towards success, he was a determined, mean professional. Grannies stayed out of his way. However, he clearly lived and died by the adage, 'Show me a good loser and I'll show you a loser.' The guy was a winner; pure and simple. Second was nowhere for Graeme Souness and that shone through when he was out in the football field or in the dug-outs at Rangers, Liverpool, Southampton, Blackburn Rovers or Newcastle. I'll take the word of others that it was the same story at Galatasaray, Benfica and Torino.

Souness in full flight must have been a fairly fearsome sight and I'm glad to tell you I never witnessed it. However, a Sunday Mail reporter was on the receiving end when a semi-naked Souness booted him out of Ibrox one Friday afternoon in September 1989. Our guy, a Rangers fan, as it happens, turned up for the routine Friday conference and was milling around with the other hacks in the marble hallway at the front door. Souness must have come straight from the shower, covering his modesty only with a towel, and still soaking wet, padding around in flip-flops, to tell our reporter to 'Get out!' Our guy, unsurprisingly, beat a hasty retreat from this Spartacus from Saughton Mains and fled onto Edimiston Drive and disappeared over the horizon.

I had just returned from a fabulous fortnight doing nothing (which I do very well, by the way) in St. Ives, that beautiful little corner of Cornwall. The feelgood factor disintegrated the moment I was informed the Sunday Mail was banned from Ibrox. I telephoned the reporter. 'What's the problem?' I asked. He told me he didn't know. If he thought he had offended the Rangers manager and expected some sort of reprisal, he might have thought about arming himself with an elephant gun, he reasoned.

By the time I got this knowledge, it was Friday evening and I was due back in the office the following morning. The previous Saturday, September 16, the reporter in question had been at Ibrox where Rangers, after being two goals ahead, drew 2-2 with Dundee. I re-read the summary of the game. Yes, he had set about his favourite team with the tackety boots, probably as disappointed as Graeme Souness and any Rangers player with the dropped points. Obviously, he had let personal feelings come into play and I would have a word with him about that. Neutral has to be the watchword on matchday and, to be fair, the reporter normally followed that rule of thumb. I knew Souness refused to take phone calls on a Saturday as he prepared his team for a game; quite right, too. He took his team to Dunfermline that afternoon, so I made a point of either phoning him or going to Ibrox to see him early the following week to nip this in the bud.

I spoke to him on the Wednesday with Rangers due to host Hearts three days later. Were we in? Or were we out? Thankfully, Souness agreed with me there was nothing to be gained by a ban, so we would be allowed access. 'Tell your man to be careful what he says in the future,' said Souness, rather cryptically. 'Tell him to tone it down, too.' And that was that. However, even for my own personal delectation, I had to know what he was referring to. I asked my guy and he thought hard before saying, 'Christ! I was in a restaurant on Saturday night with a mate after the game and I was still fizzing. I said a few things I probably shouldn't. I was sitting in a booth. Do you think someone was listening?'

Unfortunately for our reporter, I discovered shortly afterwards there was a Rangers player sitting directly behind him in a Cantonese restaurant in Glasgow's city centre. Rather helpfully, the Ibrox star with the big ears and the bigger mouth couldn't wait to tell his manager everything that had been said at the table beside him. When the penny dropped, the Sunday Mail hack was more than a little embarrassed.

Wed-faced, in fact, as Pontius Pilate would have said.

Chapter 10

Pressing times with Billy McNeill

First class ... Billy McNeill

Billy McNeill was clearly startled. 'Are you joking?' he asked me. 'Are you serious?'

It was July 1991 and Billy had been sacked as Celtic manager two months earlier following the completion of a traumatic and trophyless season. The Parkhead side simply could not compete with big-spending Rangers, so the board did the natural thing and handed their team boss his P45.

Celtic, back then, were nicknamed 'The Titanic' by the press because the club had so many leaks. As Sports Editor of the Sunday Mail, I could hardly complain about having knowledge of what was happening at the very heart of the inner sanctum of the club. I saw that as part of my job to keep readers of the newspaper informed of what was happening out there on the mean streets; or, more accurately, inside the Celtic boardroom.

The jungle drums (no pun intended) had been beating long and loud about Billy's future at the club. In truth, he was treated appallingly. I knew the board was deliberately not keeping him informed about their closed-door meetings and that, inevitably, will bring about a breakdown in communication and trust between the manager and his chairman. It's a recipe for disaster. And so it proved.

On the Saturday evening of December 15 1990, I received a telephone call at the Sports Desk. It was from a prominent member of the board. Celtic had just lost 2-1 to Dunfermline in Glasgow and I was told, 'It's not looking good for Billy.' The individual didn't have to elaborate. I got the drift that a change of manager at Celtic was imminent. The club had appointed Terry Cassidy as their first-ever Chief Executive in December 1990 and he was an abrasive, outspoken character who, quite clearly on the occasions I had met him, had no fondness for Billy McNeill. He told me so on several occasions. I relayed his thoughts to the manager. He wasn't surprised. The charmless Cassidy was sacked in October 1992 after a disastrous spell at the club. If Liam Brady ever allows me to write his autobiography about his life and times as Celtic manager, I can tell you Cassidy will require a chapter to himself. Maybe two.

Okay, so I'm sitting at the Sports Desk on a bleak December evening, traces of snow beginning to form on the pavements of Glasgow, and the first edition of the newspaper is heading for airts and pairts of the country. It's a breaking story from an impeccable source and I know it is back page splash material. I have never hidden my respect for Billy McNeill and what he achieved for Celtic as a player and as a manager. I also liked the guy as a damn fine human being. It was never a chore to spend some time in the company of this witty, clever bloke.

I telephoned him at his home in Pollokshields. I wouldn't name my source - I never did and I also realised Billy would never push me to reveal an identity - but I had to tell the Celtic manager his job was on the line. As I expected, he took the news with his usual poise although I realised he must have been hurting like hell at that moment. I didn't want him picking up his Sunday Mail from the doormat the following morning (I was aware he bought our newspaper) and being slammed with the news he was about to be sacked. There has got to be better ways of discovering you are about to lose the job you love. I did a new lay-out for the back page of the Sunday Mail and wrote the headline, 'BILLY ON THE BRINK'.

There are occasions when you dislike your chosen profession and, undoubtedly, this was one of them. It was a genuine, exclusive story and, without attempting to sound like one of those irritating 'I'm-so-important' blowhards, I knew full well I had a responsibility to the person who shelled over hard-earned cash for their favourite Sunday newspaper. The machine room replated and we ran the story from the first edition onwards. It would be reasonable to estimate almost 2.5 million Scots would have read that news with their tea and toast the following morning.

After that, it was only a matter of time. On Wednesday, May 22 1991 - only eleven days after Celtic's 3-2 win over St. Johnstone to bring the curtain down on an underwhelming campaign - an emergency board meeting had been called at 10am at Celtic Park. Billy was informed of the high level pow-wow by Cassidy as he was leaving the ground the previous day.

'Of course, I knew what was coming,' said Billy. 'I telephoned my lawyer and he advised me to get in touch with my accountant, Frank Walker. He reckoned it would be more beneficial to have a money man sitting beside me when the axe fell. As it happened, the meeting was very brief. Chairman Jack McGinn expressed "deep regret" about the "painful" decision and that was that. Jack also talked about a financial settlement over the course of the next few days. You would have thought the board would have had plenty of time to put that package together over the months of speculation. I wasn't having any of it. I told them, "I'm not leaving until we settle it here and now." It was my turn to take them by surprise. I meant it, though. I was not going through that door until I was satisfied with the pay-off.'

The board had already issued a press statement saying Billy McNeill had left the club. The board detested the word 'sacked'; people always parted company with Celtic by 'mutual consent'. It seemed a very genteel way of saying some poor unfortunate has just seen his world collapse around his ears. Four years before Billy, Davie Hay was in the same situation. The club wanted him to sign a declaration that he had resigned. Davie, politely, of course, told them to get lost. He told me, 'I was never going to have anyone believe I would ever dream of quitting Celtic. If they wanted to fire me, they were going to have to come out and say so. Eventually, they saw I would never change my mind and, technically, the history books will show I was the first manager to be sacked by the club; apparently, everyone else had quit.'

On that gloriously sunny afternoon in May, months away from the heavily-swollen skies of December when I first took the call from my Celtic mole that Billy was heading for the firing squad, the board had backed itself into a corner. The press had been alerted and reporters, camera crews and radio stations were setting up in the car park outside the front door of Celtic Park. Billy forced their hand. Swiftly, they put together a settlement, Billy and his accountant poured over it and only when they were satisfied did the newly-fired Celtic manager agree that his time at the club, where he walked in as a teenager in 1957 and won a landslide of trophies, medals and personal honours, was at an end.

Billy, straight-backed as ever, chest thrust forward, went to meet the journalists and supporters at the front door. The man obviously knew his gallows humour. He expressed surprise, 'What? No guillotine?' That was for the cameras. He told me he broke down in tears when he got home.

So, a couple of months later, I have Billy McNeill on the other end of the telephone line. 'Are you joking?' he repeated.

'Deadly serious,' I said. 'I would like you to join the Sunday Mail.'

Billy, I knew, was interested in the media. He had an inquisitive mind and would continually ask newspapermen about their job. He would sit down with them on away European trips and enquire about their calling. One of his particular favourites was our mutual friend Alex Cameron. Chiefy had co-authored Billy's excellent autobiography *Back to Paradise* in 1988. Jim Black followed up with the equally-superb *Hail Cesar* in

2004. Billy was always comfortable around hacks and I thought he might be able to contribute something to the Sunday Mail.

I had allowed the dust to settle. Billy had told me he was uncertain of his next move. Did he want to go straight back to mainstream management? I can tell you he could have stepped into Dundee's dug-out only a week or so after vacating the premises at Celtic. The Dens Park secretary, Ian Gellatly, got in touch with Billy and asked him to think about it. Billy admitted to me he spent a fairly sleepless night before telephoning the Dundee official the following day to say, 'Thanks, but no thanks.'

So, armed with that knowledge and the fact I was aware Billy, at the age of fifty-one, was not one to spend all his time pruning the roses, I invited him out for a relaxed lunch at the Pavarotti Trattoria restaurant in Cambridge Street just opposite Glasgow's Thistle Hotel. Again, the sun was splitting the sky as I walked up from the Sunday Mail offices at Anderston Quay (I was thirty-nine and must have been fit back then). I realised Billy was interested, but could we afford him? We both arrived at the Italian eaterie at the same time and I was delighted to see the smile had returned to his face. We took a table in the corner and had a wee natter before we got down to discussing business matters. There had been a story in that day's papers about some Rangers fans complaining about a pole restricting their view at Ibrox. Billy seized upon it. 'Glad to see the buggers got something wrong.'

We chatted, ate a sumptuous meal and had a few Peroni lagers. I outlined my thoughts to the legendary sportsman. I wanted him to sit side-saddle with one of our reporters, Don Morrison, Dixon Blackstock or David Leggat, and give his verdict on the big match of the day. There was also scope for a column on his views on something that was topical during the week. He looked happy enough with that. We shook on it and I underlined one thing. As soon as he wanted to end the arrangement and go back into football there would be no problem. This was no binding contract, no Philadelphia lawyers were required. I was happy, Billy was satisfied and there only remained the little matter of ordering up some celebratory bottle, or two, of Pavarotti's finest white wine.

I was walking back to the office that beautiful afternoon when something struck me. Billy and I had spent the best part of three hours blethering away, but I hadn't got round to financial matters. He never even asked what we were prepared to pay for his expert views every week. We had shaken hands, Billy had agreed to come down to the office later in the week and I would set up an advert for Radio Clyde to announce 'the Sunday Mail's big-name signing for the new season.' No talk, though, of financial recompense. The bean-counters at the newspaper had given me a ball-park figure to play around with. I didn't even get the opportunity to put it on the table. I went back to the office and asked for £100 more or the deal was off. 'Billy's a tough negotiator,' I told them. Billy got the extra cash, I'm happy to say.

Immediately, I was struck by the professionalism of the guy. We had organised the Radio Clyde advert and Billy came into our office, made the call to the commercial radio station, was given the green light and said, 'Hello, this is Billy McNeill. Read my exclusive, hard-hitting big match verdicts only in the Sunday Mail every week. It's the column no sports fan will want to miss.' There was a bit more to those words, but Billy did it in one take. As bright as ever, he asked me about his first assignment: which match had been selected for him to sit in with a reporter and give his forthright analysis?

'Can't you guess?' I asked.

'I'm going to Ibrox, ain't I?' he smiled.

'Got it in one,' I replied.

Rangers were due to launch the new season with a home game against St. Johnstone on August 10 1991. As champions, the unfurling of the flag was due before the kick-off and there would be usual songs of delight and joy from the Rangers support. Ironically, the last time Billy had seen the Perth side in action had been his final game in the Celtic dug-out almost three months earlier. The following day, I used a huge picture of Billy and Don Morrison on the back page of the Sunday Mail and our 'big-name signing' was even game enough to hold up the Rangers programme as though he was reading it. A superb bit of improvisation. He may have wanted to be anywhere else on the planet that afternoon, but now he was there he was going to play the part. Impeccably, as usual.

Billy was with us for a full season and did a splendid job. I had no doubt he could have made a career in the inky trade if he hadn't been such an accomplished footballer. It was a pleasure and a privilege to work alongside him.

Football's gain was journalism's loss.

Chapter 11

Big Eck's a smart Alex

Alex McLeish is a dangerous guy to know. Please don't take that the wrong way. I think the world of the big fella and I've known him for years, but there are occasions when his sense of humour can be a little suspect.

I'll give you a quick example. It was the aftermath of yet another excellent Scottish Football Writers' Player and Manager of the Year awards ceremony in Glasgow. As you might expect, there were a few of us, managers, footballers, journalists, all sorts of imbibers, who still had the notion that more booze was a reasonable idea and, therefore, we had repaired to the late-night (early-morning?) bar.

Big Eck ambled over and enquired innocently enough, 'Alex, have you heard the Gestapo joke?'

'No,' I said.

'LIAR!' shouted Big Eck and slapped me smack across the kisser.

I can tell you, that big lad doesn't know his own strength. I wasn't quite forced to take my dinner through a straw for the next few days, but you get the drift.

I've spent some quality time with Alex over the years and I have to say he is wonderful company. He's a bright, entertaining lad, but as you may have guessed, he is one to watch when his funny bone is twitching.

I've seen the other side of him, too. How ironic is this? It was a freezing Hogmanay afternoon as 1994 prepared to bid us all a fond farewell and I was sitting with Alex in the cramped confines of his manager's office at Fir Park. It was one of those bitingly cold days when even the penguins refused to venture out. So, of course, I didn't hesitate when I was offered a cold can of lager. Alex had just seen his Motherwell side lose 3-1 to

Rangers and he was cursing his team's luck. He had a fair point. At 0-0, Motherwell had a superb chance to score, but a shot hit the woodwork and spun back straight into the grateful arms of young goalkeeper Colin Scott. A few minutes later, Rangers went up the park, had a shot at goal, it thumped against the post and rebounded against the back of keeper Steve Woods and bounced into the net. Goalscorer? A guy called Stuart McCall. Aye, fine margins between failure and success in this game. Miss Marple qualities were not required to detect Alex had been hurt by the result. That was his private face and the public saw another one entirely.

Of course, he was all smiles in December 2001 when he waved a Rangers scarf above his head outside the main gates at Ibrox Stadium after being named as successor to Dick Advocaat. It took a big man to take on that job at the time with Martin O'Neill ruling the roost. I can tell you Alex, then the manager of Hibs, did not hesitate for a split-second before taking that post. I think he received the rewards his courage deserved in his five years as Rangers gaffer.

And he did a fine job as Scotland manager, too, when he answered another SOS in January 2007, taking over from blundering Berti Vogts. Who could forget the night in Paris when Scotland beat France 1-0 at Parc des Princes on September 12 later that year with James McFadden's sixty-fourth minute wonder strike? Well, I'm ashamed to admit this, but I could. I was on holiday in Plakias, in Crete, at the time and, try as I might, I could not find a taverna that was showing the Scotland game live. A friend, Pavlos, owned a bar called Kyma and he had a giant screen which showed games from all over the world. Unfortunately, England were playing Russia at Wembley in a European qualifier that evening and, as I was probably outnumbered twenty to one, I was told their game was being shown live, but Pavlos offered to tape the France v. Scotland encounter and I could watch that in its entirety afterwards.

Great idea, but one major snag. Crete was two hours ahead of Paris and London. The England encounter was due to kick off at 10pm Cretan time with Scotland coming on at midnight. I'm as patriotic a Scot as the next bloke, please believe me, but I reckoned, with the best will in the world, I might just have managed to catch the start of the game in France, but there would be no guarantees I would still be awake to hear that final toot of the referee's whistle around 2am. I decided it would be best to sleep on it and attempt to catch up with the action the following day.

Before the kick-off in Paris, I sent a text message to Alex which simply read, 'Bonne chance, Grande Eck.'

The following morning I awoke to a text from the Scotland manager. 'Mon Plaisir, Grande Alexandre!'

That big guy's class - dodgy sense of humour, though.

Chapter 12

The grapes of wrath

Bernie Vickers was the colourful Editor of the Daily Record during the seventies and eighties. I lost count of the amount of times he fired me. I loved working for that man.

Bernie hailed from Manchester and preferred to talk about himself in the third person. In his distinct Mancunian accent, he would say, 'T'Editor's not fookin' happy with you, lad.' And then he would sack me. Bernie liked a drop of vino collapso the way most people enjoy oxygen. It appeared obligatory, even mandatory, for our maverick boss to go one over the eighty on a daily basis. Trust me, though, Bernie Vickers, stone cold sober, was as good as any Editor with whom I worked. Even blotto, he could certainly have edited one of that number into embarrassment.

Top class ... Bernie Vickers

I recall being 'invited' into his office one evening. I had received a call from his secretary Kaye that it was 'very urgent'. I hadn't a clue what to expect. He asked me to sit down and pull up a chair. He handed me a piece of copy paper. A freelance reporter had phoned in a tip-off that informed Bernie that a very famous Scottish international footballer's marriage was breaking up. It wasn't amicable, either, according to the source. The Editor let me digest the words placed in front of me and I realised what was coming next.

'You know this footballer quite well, don't you?' he asked. There was an edge to his tone and I knew immediately he was wearing his Editor's hat.

'Yes,' I answered. 'He's a mate of mine.'

'Then it would be reasonable to assume you know all about this situation, then?'

'That's right,' I said. I saw no point in even attempting to lie.

'I want you to go out and sit in with a News reporter and tell him everything you know. Okay?' Bernie was being forceful.

Now, I accept that when a footballer's marriage hits the rocks there is every chance he is the guy wearing the black hat. On this rarest of occasions, though, I knew exactly what had happened and the player was not the guilty party. He telephoned me around 3am a week or so earlier and was sobbing down the phone. He revealed he had caught his missus in the act with another sportsman (not a footballer). Either my pal missed his vocation as a Hollywood actor or he was telling the God's honest truth. I believed him. Genuinely, he was broken-hearted and it couldn't have been easy for him to tell me such a tale. He admitted his parents didn't even know the full facts of a messy situation.

'Is there a chance of getting back together?' I asked.

'No fuckin' chance,' was the vehement response.

So, there I am sitting in the Editor's office at the Daily Record and he has put me right on the spot. 'Okay?' he repeated.

'Nope,' I said, shaking my head. 'As far as I'm concerned, it was a private conversation and that's the way it will stay. Sorry.'

'Sorry?' said Bernie. 'You'll be sorry when you're out of a job this time tomorrow. Do you want time to think about it?'

'Not really,' I answered. 'I am not going to fill in the blanks. That's personal and not for public consumption.'

Bernie gave me his best T'Editor's glower. 'I'll let you have half an hour,' he said. 'I'll get Kaye to phone you and you can come back and we'll discuss the situation. Okay?'

I nodded and left the office. I knew I would not change my mind. Bernie could have given me thirty minutes or thirty years, I still wouldn't have exposed the truth of the matter. That's the reason I will not name the player in question today. I don't think I'm giving away any clues when I tell you he is now happily remarried and still a very close friend. I have never even told him this story. Why would I? Nothing could ever be gained by it.

Sure enough, the telephone came to life on my desk exactly half an hour after I had left the Editor's office. It was Kaye again. 'Bernie wants to see you,' she said. 'I'll be right there,' I replied.

The walk from the Sports Desk to the Editor's office is the longest possible trek on the editorial floor. I had to walk past the Features Desk, then the backbench, the News Sub-Editors, the News reporters and, finally, the Pictures, along a small corridor and then knock on the door to be told 'Enter.'

'Have you changed your mind, young man?' asked Bernie. I wasn't even worthy of my Christian name.

'Sorry, Bernie, but I'm afraid it's still no.'

'Your job could be on the line here, you know.'

I nodded.

'No chance of changing your mind?' Bernie was handing me one last opportunity to give up the details that would have embarrassed my mate and followed him around for the rest of his life, never mind his career.

'Sorry, Bernie, but it's still no.' I then awaited my fate. It's funny what goes through your mind in such a situation. Would I have to tell my wife I had lost my job? Or would I 'merely' be demoted from Chief Sports Sub-Editor? Would I be out the door completely? I knew the NUJ would fight my corner, but had I acted unprofessionally? The story would have been a front page splash and I was denying my own newspaper that opportunity.

Bernie stared at me. I looked straight back at him. A few seconds passed. Then, amazingly, he burst out laughing. 'T'Editor's not fookin' happy,' he said. 'T'Editor's not fookin' happy one little bit.' Pause. 'You're a useless newspaper man, Alex,' - I was delighted to get my first name back - 'but you're not a bad human being.' And with that, he ordered Kaye to fish two bottles of white wine from the fridge. 'Two glasses, as well, Mr Vickers?' asked the secretary. I wondered if the Editor was in the habit of scoffing two bottles on his own. I decided the likelihood was not beyond the bounds of imagination. 'Two glasses, Kaye, please. One for me and one for Alex. A bottle each, please.' He smiled a roguish smile. I had seen it before, normally just before he told me I was fired. On this occasion, though, there was no follow-up.

Kaye didn't need to ask the Editor about his preferred measure as she poured the wine right up to the brim. She picked up my bottle and I said, 'I'll have the same as the Editor, please.' She left us on our own and we clinked glasses; to any onlooker the best of mates. Only thirty minutes beforehand my career was hanging by a thread.

After a couple of glasses, Bernie whispered almost conspiratorially, 'Okay, Alex, what is the real story? Completely off the record, of course.'

'Maybe some other day,' I said. Possibly he thought a couple of glasses of very nice Chardonnay might loosen my tongue. We drained our glasses and I got up to leave. 'Kaye!' shouted Bernie. 'Another two bottles, please, for Alex and I.' He never mentioned that story again and I never volunteered the information even after the divorce was complete. The 'inside' story was never told.

I rated Bernie very highly. I saw him close-up dealing with breaking stories and he was an excellent operator. His handling of the Iranian Embassy Siege, which lasted from April 30 to May 5 in 1980, was simply outstanding. The Daily Record wiped the floor with every rival on that story and that was down to the leadership shown by Bernie Vickers. When the work needed done, he was first in line. But he did have this irritating penchant for wanting to hand people their P45.

On another occasion, he rolled up to the Sports Desk. I recall it was a very busy European night when we would have had both Old Firm teams, Celtic and Rangers, plus Aberdeen and Dundee United in action. The good old days. Bernie was more than tipsy. He wouldn't have realised it, but he was interfering in the midst of a hectic period. I told him, 'Go and bile yer heid, Bernie.' I wasn't sure if our resident Mancunian even understood the translation of that little nicety. Anyway, he toddled off back down the editorial floor.

The following day, he returned and stood at my desk. He looked at me, put his hand on my shoulder and said, 'So, you would like T'Editor to go and bile his heid, would you?' Frankly, I was astonished he could even remember what had happened the previous evening. His powers of recollection were never put to the test again.

On another occasion, he put Kermit The Frog in charge of the Sports Desk. The Muppets were all the rage in the mid-seventies and Bernie somehow had managed to get his hands on full-size puppets of Kermit and Fozzie Bear. (God knows what happened to Miss Piggy.) Grinning from ear to ear, he meandered up the editorial, stopping at the Features Desk to plant Fozzie Bear in the Features Editor's chair. Then he noticed our Sports Editor, Jack Adams, had gone for a well-earned break. Bernie sauntered forward, sat Kermit on Jack's chair and declared to everyone, 'T'Editor has just appointed Kermit The Frog as the new Sports Editor. Okay? I fookin' expect you all to do as Kermit fookin' tells you. Okay?'

Huge overhead fans had just been introduced to the editorial because we were not allowed to open windows. It had something to do with the continuing threats about the place being blown up by all sorts of angry organisations. I've still no idea how a locked window is going to save you from being blasted to Kingdom Come. Maybe some helpful person from Health and Safety might provide a clue. Anyway, the propellers on the fans attached to the roof had speeds of up to five - hit that number and it was like a helicopter trying to land on your head.

If Bernie had bothered to look over his shoulder as he strolled back towards the backbench, he would have witnessed Kermit The Frog swirling around by his tongue at about twenty revolutions per second. Kermit was clearly abusing his new position of power. Surely a sacking offence if ever there was one.

Bernie never did, in fact, actually fire me. When I was leaving to join the Sunday Mail in 1987, he asked me to come through to his office to see him. I was happy to observe two bottles of Chardonnay on his desk and two empty glasses primed and ready to go. 'Sit down, Alex,' he offered. 'We've had some good times, eh? We've had some laughs. You know I would never really have sacked you, don't you?'

'You were pretty convincing at times, Bernie,' I answered.

'Just T'Editor playing his little games.' Then he was serious for a moment. 'I'm not going to ask you to stay at the Record. You've obviously made up your mind. Please go to the Mail with my best wishes. I'll be watching you, be sure of that.' I smiled because I knew he meant every word of it. We tanned the two bottles of wine; those suckers didn't stand a chance. Now, although Bernie liked a small libation along with the best of us, he never stepped foot in the office pubs, Off The Record, The Montrose or the Copy Cat. Dick's Bar was too far away to even contemplate making his way there and back. So, I was more than a little surprised when he said, 'T'Editor would like to buy you a drink. Let's go down to that pub, Off The Record. What do you say? Do you want a drink with T'Editor?' I thought it was a fabulous gesture and an offer I accepted in a heartbeat. It was a wonderful way to say farewell to my time at the Daily Record; twenty, mainly fond, years working with some outrageous, eccentric, memorable, gifted individuals.

Bernie Vickers was very near the pinnacle of that exalted list.

Chapter 13

Welcome to Celtic, Mr Brady

Managers of the Old Firm often talk about the pressures of the job being akin to unbearable. Away from the glare of cameras and the eavesdropping of dictaphones, I've been in the company of Celtic and Rangers bosses when they have talked freely and candidly about the burden that is on their shoulders on a daily basis. 'Awesome,' was a word often used by Graeme Souness. 'Relentless,' was one of Billy McNeill's standards.

If I didn't know by then, I certainly did after a lunch with Liam Brady at Celtic Park shortly after he had taken over the job on June 19 1991. Although he had no experience of managing at any level, the Irishman was clearly a character of exquisite quality with an unmatchable football-playing pedigree.

He had come out on top of a four-man shortlist that included his former Arsenal and Republic of Ireland team-mate Frank Stapleton, Ivan Golac, the manager who would go on to to steer Dundee United to their 1994 Scottish Cup Final success, and Tommy Craig, who had been assistant manager to the dismissed Billy McNeill. Brady was pitchforked into the spotlight after becoming the first Celtic manager never to have played for the club.

The astute Irishman once confided in me, 'Glasgow is such a fiercely divided city. I thought I was ready for it, but I wasn't. Nothing prepares you for that sort of rivalry. Absolutely nothing. When things weren't going too well, I tried to ride out the storm, but, unfortunately, I discovered I couldn't.' Honest and frank words from a bright individual who spent just two-and-a-half trophyless seasons in the dreaded hot-seat in the East End of Glasgow.

Liam Brady ... welcome to Glasgow

I was with him one afternoon in the Brother Walfrid restaurant at Celtic Park - Brady rarely ventured too far from the team's base - when a frail-looking old lady came over to our table. She was very polite and apologised for breaking into our conversation. She shook Brady by the hand and whispered, 'Are you going to win the league this year, young man?'

The Celtic manager grinned and nodded, 'You can be sure we will be doing our very best, ma'am.'

The rather gaunt expression on the lady's face gave way to a small smile. 'That would be good,' she said in hushed tones. 'You see, I've been told I don't have long to live. I would love to see Celtic win the championship again before I pass on.'

Brady tried to disguise the look of trauma in his expression, but his eyes betrayed him. She apologised for the interruption and made her way back to her company at another table.

'Awesome' and 'relentless' don't really come close, do they?

Chapter 14

Solving the Brady mystery

The Scottish sportswriting corps in its entirety had been looking for Liam Brady for two full days without success. It would be fair to say I was more than delighted at their lack of powers of deduction.

The Irishman had quit as manager of Celtic Football Club after a 2-1 defeat against St. Johnstone in Perth on the evening of October 7 1993. He had been in the job since June 19 1991.

Brady actually made up his mind to leave the post while on the team coach carrying the Celtic party back to Glasgow an hour or so after the referee had blown for full-time, following another depressing display from the Parkhead team. His resignation filtered through to the Press the following morning. A statement, apparently from the exiting manager, stated, 'After recent results and performances, I have decided to resign. A tremendous pressure surrounds the club at the moment - the management staff, players, board and supporters alike. It is my responsibility as manager that this should not affect the players. I have not been able to do this. I have taken the decision to stand down.'

It was a formation of words straight from the PR Department.

Kevin Kelly, who had taken over from Jack McGinn as chairman, followed the party line. He was quoted, 'Liam always conducted himself with great dignity as Celtic manager. He did the honourable thing by resigning.' He added the board would consider as 'a matter of urgency' the question of a permanent replacement.

Brady had no intention of facing the media at a Press Conference. I was aware he didn't have a lot of time for my fellow-hacks. He came off everyone's radar as they frantically searched for his whereabouts. I had an inkling, but couldn't say or write a word.

As a Sunday newspaperman in these situations, you have got to hope your story remains exclusive until Saturday after the dailies had exhausted their sources in the pursuit of the awol Irishman. Even then, you have to make sure your Sunday rivals don't get a sniff. I had every confidence Brady would not speak to anyone else, even if there was big money on offer for a so-called scoop.

Twenty-four hours after Brady's announcement, Joe Jordan, who was expected to step up and take charge of the team, suddenly quit. It was obvious Jordan was extremely upset he wasn't immediately awarded the job as Brady's successor. My information at the time suggested the Celtic directors had already made an approach to Lou Macari, who was Stoke City's manager, with the offer of the post at his former team.

If that was the case, it would have been extremely difficult to believe the men who occupied the Celtic boardroom didn't realise Jordan and Macari were the best of pals, forging a friendship during their years together at Manchester United. Undoubtedly, Macari would have contacted his mate about the situation. For me, that would have sparked the reaction from Jordan on the Friday when he walked out of Celtic Park for the last time. He left saying, 'You've got to make these sort of calls.'

After determining his location, I contacted Liam Brady in Dublin on Friday afternoon. As ever, he was courteous and focused. There was no problem with a 'first-person' exclusive. I wasn't surprised there was no mention of a fee for his time. Under the banner headline 'PARADISE LOST', I ghosted the story everyone else wanted. With Liam Brady's name on the tale, it read thus:

'I was sitting on the team bus on a stretch of the M9 on Wednesday night when I made the decision to quit as manager of Celtic. I had just watched the team lose 2-1 to St. Johnstone and I was utterly dejected.

'I thought about that game - and the recent performances against Hearts and Kilmarnock - and I knew I couldn't shield the players from the pressures any longer. It was getting to me and it was getting through to them.

'I HAD TO GO.

'I approached the chairman Kevin Kelly and told him I had made up my mind to quit. He didn't even attempt to talk me into changing my mind.

'IT WOULD HAVE BEEN A WASTE OF TIME, ANYWAY!

'My mind was made up and, having come to such a momentous decision, I wasn't going to change it. It was the most difficult decision of my life. I leave Celtic with so many regrets. I would have loved to have given those wonderful fans a trophy. They deserved more than they got.

'But let's nail some of the rumours right now. I was NOT stabbed in the back by Joe Jordan or anyone else. I brought Joe to the club. He was my appointment, there can be no arguments on that.

'I HAD HOPED JOE WOULD GET THE JOB.

'I was amazed when I heard the news he had quit, too. Naturally, I can't go into that because I don't know the facts. I would like to say there were no running feuds with the board. I wasn't at their throats and they weren't at mine.

'Sure, money was tight. But I knew the situation at the club from day one. However, if anything, things got worse this year. Of course, the atmosphere could have been better. All the talk of the rebel takeover and so on kept on the pressure. It just never went away and it affected the club, the management and some individuals.

'And, yes, there was talk of the rebels putting in their own man as manager if they were successful. However, I stress I am NOT using that as an excuse. Things just didn't work out on the pitch. We didn't get results in my two years and that is what it is all about. No-one is more aware of Celtic's reputation than me. Okay, I didn't play for the club, but I was brought up in Dublin and the two teams everyone talked about were Celtic and Manchester United. Their flamboyance and style were well known. That was my aim. I wanted Celtic to continue to play with that flair.

'People have also been saying I was contemplating quitting after we lost to Rangers in the League Cup semi-final last month.

'BUT I CAN TELL YOU THERE IS NO TRUTH IN THAT.

'Yes, it was a huge blow losing that match at Ibrox ... but I believed we could pick things up again. That wasn't to be. Obviously, I am sad that some of the transfers I made didn't work out. The name Tony Cascarino continually crops up, but I would like to point out he is currently in the Chelsea first team. Why didn't he do the business at Parkhead? I believe the unique pressure of being involved with a Glasgow team got to him.

'To understand just how stressful life can be in Glasgow as a sportsman you really have to sample it. You have to be a certain animal to cope. It took me at least a year to understand it. Tony just could not settle and I believe he is finding life a lot easier in England.

'The same goes for Stuart Slater. I was greatly disappointed he didn't match up to expectations at Parkhead. The boy oozes talent and I'm sure we'll see him do the business at Ipswich. And who could have predicted that Tony Mowbray would have picked up such a series of injuries after joining us? I think he missed about four games in ten years at Middlesbrough, but that's the way things go. You have to be philosophical about it.

'What does the future hold for Liam Brady? I'll sit down and think about that when the dust settles. I'll talk over everything with my wife Sarah and I'll spend some time with the kids.

'I MAY EVEN STAY IN SCOTLAND.

'I have made some very good friends during my stay at Parkhead. Who knows what is around the corner in this game? Would I think about becoming a manager again? Anything is possible. Again, I won't be making any rash decisions.

'I hasten to add that I did not run away from things in Glasgow. That is not my style. I was already scheduled to be in Dublin at Jury's Hotel this weekend. It is a beautiful place to get away from the rigours of life. There is a dinner I have agreed to go to tonight. And I'll probably stick around for the Republic of Ireland's World Cup-tie against Spain on Wednesday.

'Meanwhile, I am still trying to come to terms with the fact I am no longer manager of Celtic.

'THAT FACT HURTS, BELIEVE ME.

Brady actually laughed. 'No, it wasn't quite like that, but I do have a file of memos from Cassidy. There are some classics in that collection. You never know, maybe some day I'll get them published as a book - it could be a best-seller! Yes, we had some stand-up rows, Cassidy and I. It did little for the morale of the place with things like that going on. I wanted to manage the side and do my level best to put out a team that deserved to wear the green and white hoops. Simple as that, but there was interference from every corner.

'When Cassidy eventually left, Celtic put in Michael Kelly to handle the club's Press Relations department and things didn't get any better. It all became a bit intense and it got to the stage that you had to continually look over your shoulder. So much for team harmony and pulling together. Yes, it was quite an experience managing Celtic Football Club!'

Any genuine newspaperman worth his salt will tell you they live for exclusive stories. I was overjoyed my Fourth Estate colleagues couldn't trace the former Celtic manager back in October 1993.

And I was fairly humbled that Liam Brady kept his word at a traumatic time in his life to speak to me about the situation. I can't think of too many who would have been so thoughtful in similar circumstances.

What is it they say? You can buy style, but you can't buy class? Liam Brady is a class act.

Chapter 15

The quiet assassin? I'll drink to that

QUESTION: How do you know a football manager is lying?

ANSWER: His lips are moving.

Old joke, I apologise, but, alas, all too true. I've known team bosses who will look you squarely in the eye and tell you a whopper. So many of them are more accomplished as liars than they are as team coaches. As we all know, in the good old days, a newspaper reporter's must-have requirements for interviews were a pen and a notebook. Latterly, mobile phones and dictaphones have come into play. Possibly a polygraph kit might also be useful in this new-fangled age. Somehow, though, you know the men in the dug-out would have the cunning to outfox a lie detector test.

So, when you find a rarity, a manager who is honest and truthful, you feel like having him stuffed and put in a museum as an exhibit for centuries to come. People in the future could queue up to witness 'THE MANAGER WHO DID NOT LIE'.

Davie Hay comes into that category. Okay, I admit here and now, he is a personal friend. Davie has been there, seen it, done it, got the t-shirt etc., but I have rarely come across a more down-to-earth and exceptional human being. Here's a wee instance. I was fortunate enough to co-author Davie's autobiography *The Quiet Assassin,* which was published in 2009. We arranged to meet at least once a week in the White Cart restaurant at the corner of East Kilbride Road and Busby Road. It was ideal, about equidistant from both our homes on the southside of the city. It was an perfect, secluded place in which to conduct interviews. I'm still trying to catch up with the twenty-first century and I still jot everything down on paper. No polygraph equipment was required on these occasions.

Between legends … Billy McNeill, yours truly and Davie Hay at the book launch of *Caesar and the Assassin*, my tribute to these wonderful individuals.

On one of the meetings, Davie apologised and said he would have to go after an hour or so as he had something urgent to attend to. No problem, we would charge ahead and see what we could get in the tank. Over the course of our chat, Davie told me why he had to leave so early; we had been known to relax over a beer or tidal wave during these interviews which could stretch to three and four hours. Remarkably, we still got the book out ahead of the scheduled publishing date.

Apparently, Davie had been shopping with his lovely wife Catherine in the Mearns Centre at Newton Mearns that morning. A complete stranger stopped him and asked him if he was Davie Hay. Davie nodded. This bloke then asked Davie if it was possible to get a signed Celtic shirt. Now, remember, Davie didn't know this guy from Adam, but immediately he said he would do his best. 'Great,' said the mystery individual, 'I'll see you here about five o'clock, then.' Let's face it, most people, never mind football managers, might have politely told the guy to go forth and multiply, in the nicest possible terms. Not Davie. He left me that afternoon, travelled to the superstore at Celtic Park, bought a top, signed it and was at the designated meeting place at the Mearns Centre at five o'clock. The fellow turned up, Davie handed over the autographed shirt and he never saw the character again. Davie told me, 'You know, I didn't even know his name.' That wee tale may actually embarrass my chum and I'll apologise for that, but I think it says all you need to know about him.

I've had some marvellous days out with Davie who is a genuine one hundred per cent man's man. I've never seen him turn his back on someone who has wanted to talk to him, get an autograph or a photograph. I speak from experience here. I'm the guy who often gets the mobile phone thrust at him and ordered to take the snaps. I've taken more photographs than David Bailey, although I have to say his subject matter may just be a trifle more attractive than anything I have ever had to deal with.

I recall one afternoon during a close season in the eighties when Davie was manager of Celtic. I was Sports Editor at the Sunday Mail at the time and I had arranged to see Davie at La Lanterna, a splendid Italian restaurant on Hope Street. Wisely, I had arranged to take a couple of days off. Three colleagues came along and we had a good old-fashioned natter over our steak piazzaiolas, risotas, pastas and whatever. Oh, did I mention the wine? Gallons of Frascati, Pinot Grigio and Soave appeared to wash up at our table. Now, I've got to say here that Davie Hay can drink. I don't even want to hint at an over-fondness of beer or grape, but Davie can hold his own. He has quite a substantial tolerance level as far as booze is concerned. Trust me, I know what I'm talking about.

On this particular gloriously sunny afternoon, as I recall, two of my Sunday Mail colleagues decided to call it a day after the Sambucas. Davie, myself and the other unnamed (for obvious reasons) reporter climbed the stairs out of La Lanterna into the inviting, if harsh, afternoon daylight of Glasgow's city centre. 'Fancy a quick one?' I said. 'One for the road?' Davie agreed. 'Good idea.'

No, it wasn't.

We tried a couple of nearby pubs, starting off, if I remember correctly, in The Alpen Lodge next door to the Italian eaterie. I think Denholms got a hit, too. Then up to The Toby Jug and then across to Archies (which was formerly The Garrick where I started my 'serious' drinking as an employee of the Daily Record Sports Desk). It was in that establishment that we realised my newspaper colleague's attention was beginning to wane. The clue was in the fact he was attempting to get to the Gents through the fruit machine which just happened to be to the left of the door leading to the loos.

Three down and two to go.

I've absolutely no idea what we had downed by the time six o'clock came around, but we were matching pint for pint and I was feeling quite proud of myself. One of us suggested going down to The Montrose at the Broomielaw. It was owned and run by a chap by the name of Jim Cullen and he just happened to be a pal of mine and Davie. So, off we toddled. After a few more bevvies, I could feel something tugging at my eyelids. Goodness only knows what had happened to my tongue, but it had ceased to function as an instrument of speech. I tried to focus on Davie.

The following morning I awoke in my bed, which in itself was a bit of a miracle. The long-suffering missus had obviously led me by the nose up to the room and dumped me. I was wearing my suit, shirt and tie. My shoes were still on. I felt as though I had taken a direct hit from a cannonball. I crawled down the stairs, even the dogs didn't want to come near me in that condition, to be met with a smug wife. 'Serves you right,' was the extent of the sympathy extended.

I wondered what had happened to the Celtic manager. I telephoned my host, Jim Cullen. 'Difficulty remembering getting home, Alex?' he practically giggled. 'Had to be poured into a taxi, my old son.' Nothing jogged my memory banks after the almighty assault from alcohol.

'How was Davie?' I managed to croak.

'Oh, I drove him up to Central Station,' replied Jim. 'He was getting the train through to Paisley to have a couple of drinks with some old mates.'

I crept back upstairs to my bed.

Chapter 16

Martin O'Neill and his promise to the press

Martin O'Neill fixed everyone in the room with a deadly stare and said, 'Just to be absolutely sure about this, I want you all to know that I bear a grudge. No, I'm not joking. Seriously, I do bear grudges. Honestly, I do.'

I had been invited to meet the new Celtic manager at the Crutherland Hotel, set back in beautiful gardens on the way to East Kilbride, on a gloriously sunny afternoon in June 2000. Me and about fifteen other sports journalists were being given the opportunity to greet the incoming team boss for the first time. So, O'Neill, fashionably about an hour late, was addressing a dining room packed with strangers. However, he wasn't hanging about as he laid it on the line during his 'maiden' speech at the end of a rather splendid lunch.

I sat opposite him for an hour or so that day and swiftly realised he wasn't a massive fan of mirth. He appeared to be solemn and withdrawn and made little effort to indulge in idle chit chat with anyone around about him, including me. However, I did get the distinct impression he was sizing up everyone in the room, making little mental notes and gathering strength. He was one serious hombre, I reckoned, with a mean glower to back it up.

When it came to coffee and liquors, the man given the task of breathing urgent life into the ailing giant that was Celtic Football Club moved to the top of the table to grab everyone's attention. He went through the usual preamble: 'Big club, big job, big test.' All that sort of stuff. Once he had got the formalities out of the way, the real Martin O'Neill took over and he had no intention of leaving anyone in that room in any shadow of doubt about what he expected in the coming years while he was manager of 'one of the greatest clubs in the world.' He wasn't just talking about his players, either. No member of the press left the Crutherland Hotel that day with any uncertainty about what was around the corner. The feeling was unanimous, 'Cross me and you're in trouble.' It was loud and clear.

Martin O'Neill: 'Don't mess with me.'

I sat back and I admit I had to admire the man. I'm fairly certain he didn't know too much about anyone in the room - with the possible exception of former Celtic player Davie Provan, who was representing SKY Sports - as he held court. Immediately, he came across as a single-minded, fiercely-committed individual who wouldn't lose a wink of sleep over slamming doors on people. I can still hear him going through his 'I bear grudges' speech. Anyone that day looking at the new Celtic boss and attempting to detect the hint of a smile while he uttered those words was wasting his time. He meant every syllable, no doubt about it. He was laying down the law, setting the ground rules and everyone was warned what to expect if they didn't toe the line. If he was looking for any favours from the media, I must have missed it. Nope, he was Martin O'Neill and it was his way or the highway.

It didn't take him long to wheedle out some information I just knew was part of his agenda that afternoon. He hated leaks from the dressing room, he said, and they would be dealt with. He wanted to know who had loose lips at Parkhead. Astonishingly, some helpful hack, no doubt trying to curry favour, practically put up his hand like he was sitting at a school desk. He outed goalkeeper Jonathan Gould as being a bloke who enjoyed a good relationship with the press.

'Really?' said O'Neill. 'That's interesting to know.' The rest of the media scrum groaned; another avenue of information turned into a dead end. It may be a coincidence, of course, but Gould disappeared off the first team radar after the opening thirteen games of the campaign. Robert Douglas was brought in from Dundee and it was curtains for the media-friendly Gould.

They say you only get one chance to make a first impression. I would say that most certainly is the philosophy of a fairly astute chap from Kilrea in Northern Ireland.

Chapter 17

Giving editors the willies

Malky McCormick was blessed with a wicked sense of humour. It came in handy in his profession as a cartoonist.

I first met Wee Malky in the late sixties when he contributed a full page cartoon strip in the Sunday Mail called *TellyToon*. It consisted of about twenty or so frames and told the story of the previous week's TV shows. It was innovative, witty and, above all, bloody brilliant. Malky's caricatures were spot on and his keen eye for detail was evident. If someone had a slight weight problem, that was their bad luck. Malky would lock into it and exaggerate it totally. Poor Bobby Murdoch, of Celtic. By the time Malky was finished with his image, Bobby often looked like a cross between Quasimodo and a blancmange. Unfortunately, for the legendary footballer, he was also instantly recognisable. Not too sure if my old mate always saw the funny side.

Malky McCormick ... deadly on the draw

Frankly, I thought the Wee Man was a genius. I was fortunate enough to work with Malky and Rod McLeod in my years at the Daily Record and Sunday Mail and, apart from being extremely nice guys, they were unsurpassable at their chosen profession. Both had acid in their ink and enjoyed different strengths. Rod's one-off pocket cartoons were unbeatable; just as Malky's strips were the best in the business.

In 1975, Malky teamed up with his friend and fellow banjo player Billy Connolly to give the Sunday Mail readers a full-page cartoon called The Big Yin. Malky devised and drew the graphic and, as you would expect, it was hugely successful. Malky maintained an excellent standard in this ground-breaking comic strip. However, there was one little problem - his apparent fixation for male genitalia. I commissioned a full front cover cartoon for a 1998 World Cup Special magazine and, sure enough, there was the offending dangly bit just peeping out from under the 'Tartan Barmy' fan's kilt. It had to be airbrushed into oblivion.

On the newspaper front, back in the seventies, it became a weekly battle of wits with Malky and the Sunday Mail Editors, first Clive Sandground and then Endell Laird. The cartoonist would attempt to disguise willies all over his creation. There was always a dog having a pee up against a lamppost, for instance. However, Malky's naughty side got the better of him when he tried to discreetly conceal a penis or two in his artwork. It drove the Editors potty.

Malky would appear with his handiwork and present it to them. For the next half-hour or so, it was scrutinised; where was the willy? Endell, in particular, went to great lengths (if you pardon the expression) to detect the camouflaged male genital organ. With a triumphant yell, the Editor would excitedly shout, 'I've found it!' Sherlock Holmes couldn't have been more satisfied with his powers of deduction and the family jewels were removed. Nothing was off limits to Malky in his quest to sketch in a mini-trouser snake; cigars, sausages, babies' arms, toes. You name it, Malky tried to mask it as he sought to get the better of the Editor.

Endell, though, was determined there would be no willies in his family newspaper and would meticulously examine every minute detail of Malky's weekly presentation. Then, and only then, was it allowed to be placed in the Sunday Mail. Endell would tell Malky, 'Aye, you almost sneaked that one through, didn't you? Better luck next week.' This went on for years until the Editor was convinced Malky had bowed to his superior detective work.

Endell Laird ... newspapers' answer to Sherlock Holmes.

If only Endell had paid more attention to Rod Stewart's nose ...

Chapter 18

On the bosses

Football managers. Don't you just love 'em? Or don't you just loathe 'em? Some were an absolute delight to work with and others, for no apparent reason, went out of their way to make your life a misery.

Some were witty; others were witless. Some were charming; others were charmless. Some smiled; others snarled. There is no identikit for the perfect manager. They come in all sorts of shapes and sizes and their intellects vary just as wildly. I've met many and, as they say, I've counted them in and I've counted them out.

My job dictated that I broke bread – yes, that euphemism again - with a variety of these guys on a weekly basis and, on occasion, it was sheer joy, a perk of the profession. Others, though, gave you the impression they were merely going through the motions and obeying orders from above to spend time with a newspaperman because the chairman required some publicity for his club. Those characters never worked too hard at disguising the fact they rated you just above something nasty they may have trod on. Common decency to some was a complete stranger.

Paul McCartney, of all people, has a great distrust of the press and, when you think about the column miles he has had in publications worldwide, you have to feel a little sad about the loss of several hundred Norwegian woods, sacrificed so that his every whim could be made public to a grateful planet's population over the decades. As The Beatles started their universal domination of pop, McCartney once observed, 'I looked at a writer from New Musical Express and I thought NME. Get it? NME? Enemy?' Very good, Paul, stick to being the 'most successful composer and recording artist of all time.' (Source: Guinness Book of World Records)

The team bosses you really had to be wary of were those who addressed themselves in the third person. 'The manager thinks this and the manager thinks that.' I guessed they might have been brought up on a staple diet of Noel Coward books and plays. Elsewhere, I've talked about Jock Stein and Willie Waddell. They were two cunning old foxes who sparred on the field and the dug-outs in colourful careers that lifted the expectation levels of a small country. Both were fairly rigid in their footballing beliefs and totally committed to the causes of their respective clubs.

Somehow I could never have quite envisaged either totally relaxing at home, slippered-feet cradled on a pouffe, cup of Horlicks in hand while guffawing merrily at the Morecambe and Wise Show of an evening.

Billy McNeill followed Jock Stein as Celtic manager in 1978 and, of course, it was a natural progression. He was also blessed with a sense of humour. Chic Charnley, that wayward nonconformist of a player who achieved legendary status at Partick Thistle, was often linked with his boyhood favourites. Possibly, the fact he had been sent off seventeen times in a somewhat turbulent career counted against his wish ever being granted. He came close in 1994 when Lou Macari was Celtic boss and the irrepressible Chic played in a Testimonial Match against Manchester United at Old Trafford and had the visiting fans chanting his name as the Glasgow side won 3-1. A permanent move never materialised, though.

A few years earlier, Chic decided to attempt to force the issue when Billy McNeill was in charge of Celtic second time around. Chic told me, 'I saw Big Billy at a sporting function and I took the bull by the horns. I went straight up to him and asked, "Why don't you sign me?" Billy looked back at me and replied, "Good reason for that, Chic, son. I like to sleep at night." I couldn't argue with that.'

John Lambie made certain the painters and decorators at Firhill were fully employed throughout the football season as he continually stripped the Dulux off the walls of the Firhill dressing room with his vociferous and liberal use of the f-word. He tells a good story about Chic, who is obviously a favourite son. 'You know, Chic doesn't sleep too well at night. Why? Well, he knows there are pubs open somewhere in Australia.' Very humorous, but I must jump to the defence of the player. I spent the best part of two months co-authoring his autobiography *Seeing Red* in 2009 and I have to dispel a few myths; Chic only drank Coca-Cola at every interview.

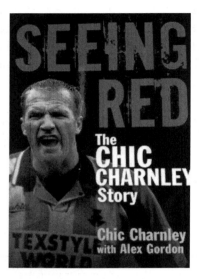

Partick Thistle's legendary Chic

Fraser Elder also tells a good story about John Lambie. The manager and the reporters were having a chat after a game at Firhill when one of the hacks asked the Thistle boss how his fixed odds coupon had done. 'Came very close,' he bellowed. 'Let down by fuckin' Sten-fuckin'-house-fuckin'-muir, for fuck's sake!' Cue a telephone call to the guy with the paint pot and brushes.

I recall a day back in 1968 when Alex Cameron asked me if I wanted to travel through to East End Park to watch a Scottish Cup replay between Dunfermline and Aberdeen. I couldn't turn down that invitation. George Farm, manager of the Fifers, and Eddie Turnbull, his counterpart with the Pittodrie side, were not the best of friends, I was told by Chiefy as he drove through to the game. I was informed they had 'a bit of history' dating back to the forties when both were team-mates at Hibs. Apparently, they had kept their personal feud going through the fifties when they played alongside each other in the same Scotland international team. 'Watch out for fireworks,' I was warned. Pyrotechnics? These guys were a level above anything I had encountered on Guy Fawkes' Night.

It was a real rough and tumble confrontation, as I remember, with both sets of players hurling into tackles. Every now and again, I let my attention drift to the dug-outs and, sure enough, there was a definite bit of needle between the two managerial protagonists. Dunfermline won 2-1 and Chiefy invited me down from the press box to the dressing rooms which was a completely new experience for me. Imagine my surprise when I witnessed Farm and Turnbull, booted and suited, going toe-to-toe in the privacy of the tunnel. Punches were flying around with great abandonment and it was clear these blokes would never kiss and make up.

Farm, who had a stint as a lighthouse keeper shortly after quitting football in 1974, died in 2004 at the age of 80. Turnbull passed away seven years later. He was 88. Now if these chaps had taken better care of themselves they might have been the recipients of a telegram from Her Majesty.

Ally MacLeod was a manager you couldn't fail to warm to. An entire nation agonised when the TV cameras panned onto a tortured soul on the touchline during the truly awful World Cup misadventure in Argentina in 1978. The photograph of the tormented manager with his head in his hands during the lamentable draw with Iran summed up a dreadful short stay in South America. It was an absolute disaster and the supporters turned on the manager. I was in Ally's company shortly before Scotland flew into their worst nightmare. He was ebullient, flamboyant and lived up to his nickname of 'Muhammad Ally'. The press had dubbed him the 'Fastest Gums in the West' and he was playing the role to perfection.

A month or so later, he was a broken man. Of course, blunders had been made during a haphazard build-up to soccer's biggest carnival. Ally admitted he hadn't bothered to spy on our first game opponents Peru in person and had relied on video tapes. He wrote them off as 'being too old and too slow'. They took Scotland apart and won 3-1 in Cordoba. That wasn't part of the script. The manager had also taken a player, Gordon McQueen, in his travelling squad when he was clearly unfit and would play no part in the finals. He left out Andy Gray, the Aston Villa striker who had won the Player AND Young Player of the Year awards after a remarkable campaign in England's top flight. Errors were made everywhere. The x-certificate stuff continued four days after the pummeling from the Peruvians at the same ground in Cordoba when the Iranians, who would have struggled to beat Millport Amateurs, ground out a 1-1 stalemate. An amazing 3-2 victory over Holland in Mendoza was too late to reverse the inevitable outcome. As Tommy Docherty observed, 'One thing is certain about Scotland and the World Cup Finals - the players will be home before their postcards.'

Eight days in Argentina completely changed the entire character of Ally MacLeod. I could hardly believe the transformation in the man when I met him at a game at Ibrox not so long afterwards. Rangers director Hugh Adam invited me along as his guest and Ally was also at our table. The one-liners had dried up, the charisma had evaporated, the magnetism had disintegrated. Sitting opposite me that evening was the hollowed-out shell of a human being I had seen, only months beforehand, eagerly looking forward to leading his nation onto the world's greatest stage. Ally was not quite prepared for the vitriol that spewed towards him when our hopes disappeared into a black hole of despair. He felt betrayed by his friends. Frankly, I don't think he recovered.

A decade later, in 1988, I was at Parkhead to witness Celtic defeating Ayr United 4-1 in a League Cup-tie. Ally MacLeod was in his third and final stint of the appropriately-nicknamed 'Honest Men'; Ally was that, without argument. I was in the press interview room under the main stand when Ally came in to discuss the game with reporters. He could barely look anyone in the eye. He fidgeted with the buttons on his blazer, his sparse hair looked as though it had been caught in a wind tunnel and he preferred to walk around the area, refusing to take a seat and face the press. Clearly, he was working off memory as he attempted to say something noteworthy.

Actually, and it saddens me to admit this, he had become something of a disturbing parody of his former self. Ten years earlier, newspapermen were hanging on his every word, pencils and pens scribbling furiously, tape recorders shoved under his nose. On this evening in the east end of Glasgow, the notepads had been put away. Billy McNeill had made his spiel and everyone was satisfied. 'Don't ask me about that referee,' said the Ayr United boss. In the good, old days that would have opened the door to a deluge of queries about the match official. On this occasion, no-one was tempted. He spent one more year at Somerset Park before having a season at Queen of the South. He retired from the game at the age of 61. Hardly anyone paid any heed. Game over for a decent man.

He died at the age of 72 in 2004 after a long battle with Alzheimer's Disease. The epitaph could have come from his own autobiography published in 1979. In it, he said, 'I am a very good manager who just happened to have a few disastrous days, once upon a time, in Argentina.' Amen to that.

At his zenith, Ally MacLeod was a newspaperman's dream. In that industry, he was known as 'good copy'. You couldn't say the same about Kenny Dalglish. The Scotland legend, who, to my mind, was one of the finest footballers our country has ever produced, must have concurred with Paul McCartney; the press were the enemy. Former England international striker Mike Channon was clearly unimpressed with the man away from the football pitch. He put it this way, 'Kenny Dalglish has about as much personality as a tennis racquet.' Well, he should know, I suppose.

I wrote a Kenny Dalglish feature for a magazine in the late nineties shortly after he had been sacked as manager of Newcastle United. I sympathised with the fact he had been only nineteen months in the job and, on Tyneside, Kevin Keegan would always be an extremely difficult act to follow. The Newcastle board allowed Dalglish to sign nine new players in the summer and fired him two games into the season. What on earth do they put in that Newky Brown Ale?

However, I did a sidebar piece on how Kenny Dalglish could make interviewers squirm on live television. Here is part of a transcript of the manager, going through his best dour Scot routine, talking to Garry Richardson, working on behalf of the BBC's *Football Focus* on January 27 1998.

RICHARDSON: 'What about your future? Because constantly the papers write these stories that, well, Kenny Dalglish won't be at Newcastle much longer. What do you say to them?'

DALGLISH: 'Justify it.'

RICHARDSON: 'There's absolutely no way you would leave

Newcastle United next week, next month, next year?'

DALGLISH: 'You never asked that. You asked a question earlier and I said in hindsight I'd take this job quicker than I did before - and I took it very quickly.'

RICHARDSON: 'Sure ...'

DALGLISH: 'And I don't regret for a second coming here. We've had disappointments in results. But you said you were going to do a balanced piece and you've not spoken about the Champions' League, you've not spoken about finishing second in the Championship last year, you've not spoken about us getting further in the Coca-Cola Cup this year. We're in the same round as the FA Cup as we were last year. But our league position isn't as good and that's the only thing that is disappointing. So, if you're going to do a balanced piece, I think you should start maybe discussing one or two of those things or certainly talking about them.'

RICHARDSON: 'Well, you've said some very, very positive things for Newcastle. You're optimistic, then, about the future?'

DALGLISH: 'Well, who knows what the future holds? But I'll tell you one thing, it won't be for the lack of trying.'

RICHARDSON: 'Are the pressures here like Liverpool? In your, sort of, final months at Liverpool, people said the pressures were great on you. Can you relate to the two situations, at all?'

DALGLISH: 'Your question doesn't even bear relation to both clubs.'

RICHARDSON: 'Why not?'

DALGLISH: ''Cause it's irrelevant.'

RICHARDSON: 'I think people would be interested to know, though, what you were sort of feeling about, er, the pressures of ... of working at a high-profile club ...'

DALGLISH: 'It's irrelevant. Your question's irrelevant. Your question's irrelevant.'

RICHARDSON: 'So, you don't feel under any pressure at all here?'

DALGLISH: 'I'm just saying your question is irrelevant. You're saying you're doing a balanced piece. But your questions have not been very balanced so far. They've all been negative.'

RICHARDSON: 'Well, what else would you like me to ask you?'

DALGLISH: 'You tell me. You explain to me the relevance of your questions in relationship to Liverpool and Newcastle. The Press man asked the same question and got the same answer. You tell me the relevance.'

RICHARDSON: 'What I'm really asking is, just to give us a little answer on the pressures you feel.'

DALGLISH: 'Well, that's different to the question you asked.'

The BBC man was later seen wandering around the streets of Newcastle town centre waving a massive placard emblazoned with the words, 'COME BACK KEVIN KEEGAN ... PLEASE!' (Allegedly.)

Tommy Burns had a good relationship with the press. The former Celtic manager, who died far too young at 51 in 2008, was brutally honest. If you asked him a question, you knew you would get a straight answer. I'm not sure if Tommy was a little forgetful, but I rarely heard him call anyone by name; everyone seemed to be christened 'Bud' in his world. Some very expensive Celtic players, Paolo di Canio, Jorge Cadete and Pierre van Hooijdonk among them, would certainly testify to the club legend possibly possessing a wonky memory bank.

One afternoon, he dragged the Celtic players back to Parkhead after a morning training session at Barrowfield. He was not satisfied with the way the defence was dealing with free-kicks or how the forwards were utilising them at the other end of the pitch. Taking a leaf from the great Jock Stein's book, he ordered some extra work. 'Go for a light lunch and be back here at 1pm prompt,' Burns ordered his players. 'And prepare for some hard work.'

The players, fearing a gruelling session, assembled back at the ground. They were stripped and ready to go at the appointed hour. They waited. And they waited. After an hour of milling around, one decided to see what was delaying the manager. He asked at the foyer and the receptionist looked a little surprised. 'Oh, Tommy left about two hours ago. Told me he was going straight home and he would see me tomorrow.'

Sean Fallon was Stein's trusted right hand man in the glory days, but the man from Sligo could get a little tongue-tied at times. He was in charge of the team while Stein recovered from the car crash that almost cost him his life in 1975. Sean rarely handled press interviews, but had to step into the breach during that particular season. I wasn't in attendance, but I am assured he did tell the press corps one day, 'McGroin's got a grain strain.'

Sean, who signed from Glenavon in 1950, lived in the South Side of Glasgow for over 60 years before his death at the age of 90 in 2013. He never lost his thick Irish brogue and, honestly, sometimes sounded as though he had just come off the boat from Sligo. I had to laugh, then, when I was talking to one Irish Celtic supporter who had attended a function thrown in Fallon's honour in his home town. 'Oh, we had a real problem with Sean,' he told me. 'How come?' I asked. 'Well, he's picked up a terrible Glasgow accent and we could hardly understand a word he said.'

Hal Stewart, the mercurial chairman of Morton in the sixties and seventies, was a slippery character. For a start, he didn't like his photograph being taken. The Daily Record had one fading, tatty image of the man, with a trilby hat covering part of the side of his face. He refused point blank to pose for a replacement. Let's put it this way, he liked his anonymity. However, it was the wheeling and dealing of this secretive character that kept the famous old Greenock club afloat in extremely trying financial times.

It was often alleged there was some sort of 'hidden' tie-up between Morton and Celtic while Hal was in charge and the story went around the newspapers that the Cappielow side owed the Glasgow club a reasonable amount of money. Jock Stein, we were informed, was given carte blanche to select any Morton player to wipe out the debt. Big Jock watched them a couple of times, but wasn't impressed. A few months later Joe Jordan joined Leeds United for a couple of quid. Oops. Even the greats can make an error in judgement.

Every penny was the proverbial prisoner when Hal was around. Davie Hayes was a great servant for the club throughout the seventies and early eighties. He was one of those old-fashioned doughty wee full-backs Scotland used to unearth in splendid abundance. I got to know Davie very well as I covered a pile of games at Cappielow in my early reporting days. It helped that he was a joiner by trade and I had just purchased an old piece of property in Burnside that required an awful lot of work. Davie and his dad set about it and transformed the place over the period of about a year. It was out on the football field, though, that I believed Davie did his best work (and I mean that as absolutely no disrespect to his carpentry skills).

Through my contact with 'Man-in-the-Know' Jim Rodger, I tried to get the right-back to England; with Hal's blessing, of course. I'm not saying this through friendship, but I never saw an outside-left give my chum the runaround. He would face the likes of wily Davie Cooper, at Rangers, or Arthur Duncan, a speed merchant at Hibs, and I don't recall him ever getting turned over. Jim Rodger persuaded Sunderland, on the look-out for a right-sided defender, to send a scout to watch Morton play in 1970, Davie's initial season.

My newspaper pal was informed the spy was impressed, but there was another Scot he was told to have a look at. He duly did and eventually signed the other player. There was no difference in the quality of their play or their overall ability, but Sunderland had signed the taller of the two. My mate was around the 5ft 9in mark while, unfortunately, his rival topped 6ft. Dick Malone was signed from Ayr United and went on to play over 200 times for the Wearside outfit while winning an FA Cup medal in 1973. Davie Hayes remained at Morton for fourteen years and turned out over 350 times in the first team. You can only imagine how his career would have materialised if he had been a few inches taller.

I was with him the night he was presented with the Morton Player of the Year award. Hal Stewart made the presentation and handed over an ornate carriage clock, which I thought was a rather generous gesture from the Morton supremo. Davie was bursting with pride when he showed me his well-deserved award. I noticed the inscription, 'Davie Hayes Morton Player of the Year 1972'. It appeared to be embossed on sticky-back tin foil. Davie picked at the edges until he could strip it away. Under it read, 'Borge Thorup Morton Player of the Year 1969'. The Danish full-back had apparently forgotten to pick up his award the year he left to join Crystal Palace.

Hal Stewart wasn't going to allow a perfectly good carriage clock, in full working order, go to waste, was he?

One manager who really irritated me - and I suspect millions of other Scots - was England's 1966 World Cup-winning boss Sir Alf Ramsey. When asked about what he thought was the best thing about Scotland, he answered, 'The road back to England.' I always thought he looked like a ventriloquist's dummy with his stiff upper lip and clipped tones. I was informed afterwards he had, in fact, taken elocution lessons when he was given the England manager's job. He was so good at delivering outstandingly dull monotone discourse he should have been sponsored by Mogadon.

I would have paid over the odds to have been in the Wembley dressing room when he was talking to Rodney Marsh before an international. Sir Alf wasn't a huge fan of flair players, but was under pressure from the Fleet Street scribes to give the Manchester City maestro his chance. Reluctantly, he bowed to their clamour for some flamboyance within the strict confines of his fairly boring team formation. He took Marsh aside before the kick-off and said, 'Now, remember, follow my instructions. You know what to expect if you don't.'

Emphatically, he added, 'I'll pull you off at half-time.'

'Gee, thanks, Alf,' answered Marsh. 'Normally, I only get a slice of lemon at City.'

Chapter 19

The night a light went out in Cardiff

I was in Cardiff the night Jock Stein died. If twelve or so yobs had got their way, I might have been standing right beside Big Jock in the queue at the Pearly Gates.

Let's set the scene. I knew if I wanted to attend the crucial World Cup qualifying tie against Wales at Ninian Park on September 10 1985, I would be forced to take holidays; there was no way I would get time off from the Daily Record simply to attend the game. I learned that lesson the hard way. Back in October 1977, I had made arrangements to travel to Anfield to watch Ally MacLeod's side face the Welsh on Scotland's triumphant march to Argentina '78.

Alex Cameron managed to get me tickets, two little pieces of cardboard stardust, and handed them to me. As I paid over the cash, he asked casually, 'Who are they for?' I responded matter-of-factly, 'Me.' 'Oh, you're not going to the game, Alex,' he said in an even tone. 'I'm leaving you in charge of the desk while I'm in Liverpool, sorry about that.' I was twenty-five at the time and I looked at Chiefy to make certain he wasn't smiling. He wasn't. I knew there was no scope for debate. I had just received two of the most sought-after briefs in football and, seconds later, any thoughts of cheering on my nation had been instantly extinguished.

I knew a mate of mine, a sub-editor on the Features Desk, was desperately seeking tickets for Scotland's biggest international game in years. I walked over to where he was sitting, asked if he was still looking to go to Anfield, he nodded vigorously and I put the precious little square permits to Liverpool's stadium on his desk and said, 'You're in luck.' Well, I've always believed what a friend gets is no loss.

So, almost eight years down the line, I wasn't going to make the same mistake. Cunningly, months ahead of the game, I put my name down on the holiday rota. It was okayed; I could go ahead and plan a week in

London, travel to the game in Cardiff and get back that same evening. At the time, I did all the Scottish football coverage for SHOOT! magazine, ghosting columns for John Greig, Tommy Gemmell and so on. I also wrote a monthly column for World Soccer and knocked out random features for Charles Buchan's Football Monthly and GOAL weekly. I knew all the guys at SHOOT!, but my only connection with the hacks on the other magazines was via the telephone, so I thought it would be a reasonable idea to hoover up a few beers with these guys and we could all put faces to names. What could go wrong? Some halfwits in Cardiff came close to turning everything upside down. Including me.

There was no way I was going to ask Alex Cameron for tickets for this match and run the risk of the plug being pulled. A friend of mine, Tony Roche, not to be confused with the former Australian tennis player of the same name, worked for one of the football magazines and was a good mate of Ian Rush. I told Tony I was travelling down to London and was planning on taking in the World Cup-tie at Cardiff. 'I'll get you tickets,' he offered, generously and helpfully. 'Leave it to me.'

Did you know Ian Rush had five brothers? I didn't until I took my place in the row behind the Welsh goal in the first-half that fateful evening. The Liverpool legend had very kindly supplied the tickets to Tony who passed them onto me. Yes, you've guessed, I was smack in among the Welsh fans. The Scotland support was at the other end of the ground, seemingly miles away. My friend and I, with tartan scarves all too visible, were in among the enemy. I looked along our seating arrangement and I saw one Ian Rush lookalike. Sitting beside him was another. Then another. Then another. And then, finally, another. Believe me, they all looked as though they were wearing Ian Rush masks; the nose, the moustache, everything. I had to ask the guy sitting nearest me, 'Are you, by any chance, related to Ian Rush?' 'Sure thing, he's my brother,' he answered. I didn't have to ask the other four Ian Rush clones.

It's history now how the game panned out. The Welsh, with Ian Rush leading the attack, deservedly took the lead early in the first-half through Mark Hughes and, unbeknownst to the supporters, there was drama in the Scotland dressing room during the interval when Aberdeen goalkeeper Jim Leighton had to admit he had lost a contact lens. That came as a surprise to his club manager at the time, Alex Ferguson, who was Jock's assistant, because he had no knowledge of his goalie having defective eyesight. Alan Rough was told to get on and that left Jock with only one substitute, Davie Cooper.

I saw Scruff, one of the nicest blokes you'll ever meet, racing towards the goal right in front of me at the start of the second-half and could only imagine Leighton had picked up an injury. Anyway, the game restarted and I have to say here and now that Ian Rush's brothers were as passionate about their country as any of the lads with the Tartan Army up at the other end. They yelled, cheered, gesticulated and booed with the best of them. My friend and I must have seemed just a tad conspicuous with our neck gear, but no-one said anything. Big Jock put on Davie Cooper for Gordon Strachan with twenty-nine minutes remaining. ('He started out making great decisions and he went out making a great decision - taking me off!' said Strachan years later.)

With ten minutes to go, Scotland were awarded a penalty-kick. Apart from two isolated and vulnerable figures among the frenzied Welsh support, that end was suddenly enveloped in silence. Cooper had to score. If he missed, Scotland would not be presented with the opportunity to get to Mexico the following year. A goal would knock out Wales and would set up Scotland for a two-legged play-off with Australia to determine which nation would take its place among the elite in the 1986 World Cup Finals. There was an eerie hush as the Rangers man stepped forward and then, with a swoosh of his cultured left foot, he placed the ball merely inches beyond the fingers of the outstretched Neville Southall. I couldn't help myself, I went ballistic. To be fair to the Rush brothers, they must have been bitterly disappointed, but they ignored the two cavorting Scots in their midst. Scotland held out for the remaining nine nerve-shredding minutes to book their encounters with the Aussies.

As Ninian Park slowly emptied, I sat with my companion to allow the area to clear. Tony Roche was due to have a quick interview with Ian Rush before returning with us to London. He asked me to hold back and the three of us could get the train to Paddington. No problem. That situation altered fairly dramatically about fifteen or so minutes after the final whistle. At that time, by the way, I did not have a clue about Big

Jock's situation.

As I stood in the quiet of Ninian Park, I could see a gang of blokes making their way slowly round from the end that had been occupied by the Scottish support. They didn't look too friendly. They were burning Lion Rampants and St. Andrew's flags, tartan scarves and anything that looked remotely associated with Scotland. The bright thing would have been for me and my mate to get out of there pronto. I decided to stand my ground, I wasn't running away from these cretins - the good old Glasgow upbringing coming to the fore. I noted that not one of these pyromaniacs was actually wearing Welsh colours. It dawned on me they might just be a motley collection of thugs out for trouble and, unfortunately for me and my friend, they were heading in our direction. Inexorably, the knuckle-draggers edged closer to us, still setting alight flags and scarves and anything the Scottish fans had left behind or had taken from them.

Inevitably, they came to a halt in front of me. They looked at my Gordon tartan scarf and one stepped forward. I'm 6ft 2in tall and, hard to believe today, but I was fairly fit those many moons ago. This bloke was about 5ft 8in, so he was on a loser if he attempted to look me in the eye in a staring contest. His mates congregated around, fairly menacingly, I have to say. I must have been on the Braveheart pills that day because I realised things could turn extremely nasty and the odds didn't favour me or my pal. I'll always remember this guy's words. He sounded more Croydon than Cardiff. 'What have we got here, Jock? Nice scarf. I'll be having that.' He motioned his hands towards my scarf when I whispered in his ear, 'Touch that and I'll boot your fuckin' balls round your neck. I'll get a doing, but you're going with me. Understand?' Remarkably, he stepped back. For a moment or two, there was a stand-off; my heart was hammering away under my shirt. Then he said, 'I can't be bothered with no exercise tonight, Jock.' Then he and his cronies kept walking round the ground heading towards the exit at the far end. I kept my eye on them until they disappeared out of sight.

'Christ, that was close,' said my pal. 'What did you say to that guy?' I repeated my words of wisdom and my mate said, 'Fuck's sake, Alex, are you trying to get us killed?'

I checked my watch and reckoned Tony Roche would have had time to interview Ian Rush, so I started to make my way round to the same exit the Alex Gordon Fan Club (Cardiff Branch) had taken five minutes or so beforehand. I needed to go to the loo, so I told my pal to hang on as I went to the toilet, which was plunged into darkness. 'You really are looking for trouble, aren't you, Jock?' I had walked straight into the flag-burning entourage again. I said nothing, but I have to say I did cut short my lavatorial duties before I got out of there sharpish; I wasn't going to push my luck twice in the same night.

We walked round to the front entrance of Ninian Park and it was obvious something was not right. A footballer I knew came up and said, 'Big Jock's collapsed.' We milled around with possibly another twenty or thirty inquisitive supporters. Tony appeared and informed us Big Jock was in a bad way. That's all he knew. Just at that point, a small ambulance, siren blaring, swept up to the door. 'It's serious,' said my friend, who knew a thing about medics.

I remember Andy Roxburgh, who would become Scotland manager after the Mexico Finals, walking past me, looking deathly pale. Across the road from the front entrance at the ground was a field with a small wooden fence. Roxburgh stopped there, leaned forward and looked as though he was throwing up. I asked a few media guys what was going on. Everything was sketchy, but there was little doubt that whatever was taking place only a few feet away inside Ninian Park was, indeed, critical.

We had to leave at that point to catch our train back to London. The mood was strange in the corridors as we made the journey. There was little celebrating; news had reached the fans that something had occurred with Big Jock. Days before mobile phones, my friend. We spent just over two hours completely ignorant of Big Jock's death. We arrived in Paddington and I raced to grab the first available public telephone. I got through to the Record Sports Desk to be told the news; Jock Stein was dead, possibly of a heart attack. To put it mildly, I was stunned. I told my friend and Tony grabbed another phone and began making calls.

About forty to fifty Tartan Army members were walking through the station. As I came away from the bank of telephones, one asked, 'You heard anything about Big Jock, pal?' I relayed the sad news. That guy immediately told the other supporters and a few of them simply burst into

101

tears. It was one of the most surreal moments of my life.

The following day, I received a phone call at our hotel from Phillip Rising, Editor of World Soccer. He could delay that month's publication by twenty-four hours if I could get a spread to him by early afternoon. To be honest, it was the last thing I wanted to do. However, I borrowed a typewriter and some paper from reception at the White House Hotel on Euston Road and I knocked out the piece. It was all a bit of a blur, but I managed to get through it. I remember finishing the piece by using the line, 'When will we see his likes again?' Phillip organised a taxi to have the copy picked up and taken over to his offices at Onslow House in Saffron Hill across London. We made the deadline and the article appeared a week later. I didn't know it at the time, but World Soccer put the eulogy up for an award among European football magazines and I won in the specialised category. Later, I received a scroll written completely in Italian. I haven't got a clue what happened to the scroll or what it said; it really didn't matter.

When will we see his likes again? Jock Stein … and the end of an era

Cardiff, Wednesday, September 10 1985 is a location, day and date that will live with me forever. For all the wrong reasons, I'm afraid.

Part Three

Stars of stage, screen, pitch and papers

Chapter 20

Simply smashing

The mesmerising world of newspapers presented many mysteries for a fifteen year old not long out of school. When I first joined the editorial at the old Noon Record, I was more than a little puzzled at one recurring theme.

There was a window in the Daily Record sports writers' room that seemed to be smashed and repaired on a regular basis. I was beginning to wonder if the newspaper's resident glazier wasn't doing a reasonable job with a particularly feeble piece of glass. On Monday it was in place; on Tuesday it was in bits; on Wednesday it was repaired; on Thursday it was smashed to smithereens. This went on for about a month. It was a puzzle worthy of the attention of Poirot.

Eventually, I had to get to the bottom of the conundrum. Why was that pane of glass smashed, restored, smashed, restored almost on a daily basis? The answer, of course, was obvious.

One veteran hack took me aside. 'That's where the sports subs play cards at night.'

That didn't provide the entire answer. I asked again.

'Well, there's a bloke who comes down from the switchboard and joins in with the sports guys. Okay?'

'Not really.'

'Well, the bloke's normally half-pissed and continually loses. That's unfortunate, but, even worse, he never pays up.'

'And?'

'Well, he gets his head put through the window, doesn't he?'

'Just about every night?'

'Aye, you would think he would learn his lesson, wouldn't you? Always sits in the same seat, too.'

Chapter 21

Shoot! It's Kenny Dalgleish

Poor old David Gregory was probably one of the first Englishmen to be given the run-around by Kenny Dalglish. Gregory was the Editor of SHOOT! football weekly magazine when it came to life in 1969 and, two years later at the age of seventeen, I was doing the bulk of their Scottish material.

I was working as a sub-editor on the Daily Record and rarely got the opportunity to write original copy, apart from covering games on a Saturday. I had bought the first edition of SHOOT! and it was avidly devoured along with three other weeklies, Goal, Soccer Star and Jimmy Hill's Football Weekly and two monthlies, World Soccer and Charles Buchan's Football Monthly. It's interesting to note that SHOOT! and Goal both sold around 220,000 copies each in 1971. Stunning sales figures. Anyway, it was joy unconfined in the Gordon household when all six titles came out in the same week. (It didn't take much to keep me happy.)

I got in touch with David Gregory at the magazine's Farringdon Street offices in London. 'Are you interested in any contributions?' I asked. He said he would look at anything I sent him and enquired if I had anything that would 'do a good spread'. Off the top of my head, I said I was working on a feature about the emerging players at Celtic and Rangers, players such as Kenny Dalglish, Lou Macari, Derek Johnstone and Alfie Conn. I was going to call the article 'The Young Firm'. Gregory said, 'I love it. Send it right away, will you? I'll clear two pages for it. We need the copy by the end of the week. Send it to the address in the mag and mark it for my attention. Okay?'

That three-minute telephone conversation opened a huge door of opportunity for me. It gave me the chance to originate editorials, as opposed to edit and rewrite in the Record. The copy was done that afternoon, put in the post with a couple of first class stamps on the envelope and posted off to London. A day or so later, the SHOOT! Editor phoned me and told me he was delighted with the piece. He asked me what was coming next and that was the beginning of a whole new ball game for me. I had the best of both worlds: production in the Daily Record and the freedom to express any writing talent I may have possessed in a weekly football magazine.

Bang on the money ... a young Kenny Dalglish.

Kenny Dalglish had a whirlwind start to the 1971/72 season and, remarkably, scored in three successive Celtic victories over Rangers, twice in the League Cup and once in the league. I managed to obtain a phone number for him; he lived with his parents in the Milton housing scheme in Glasgow at the time. I put a call in to the new 'Wonder Bhoy', as he was already being acclaimed in the press. I asked him if he was free to do an interview. He readily agreed and I told him SHOOT! would pay the princely sum of £5 for an exclusive 'first person' piece. Kenny was happy to go ahead and we chatted for about half an hour or so. I wrote up the interview and posted it immediately. I got in touch with David Gregory to let him know the feature was on its way. 'Brilliant,' he said, 'I'll clear another spread.'

I was delighted until I saw the magazine. A sub-editor in London had inserted an extra 'e' in Dalglish's surname, making him a more English-orientated Dalgleish. His first-ever magazine interview and it looked as though the lad didn't know how to spell his own name! Subs, as you have may gathered by now, can be wonderful or woeful; some can make or break a story. How about the sub on an English newspaper who received the match report on England's goalless draw with Scotland at Hampden in 1970? The scribe wrote the intro, 'This was much ado about nothing.' The sub, clearly not a fan of the works of Shakespeare, changed it to, 'This was much ado about nothing-nothing.'

The misspelling wasn't the problem, though. Kenny wanted his cash. I had explained to him that it would take a while for it to be processed by the accounts department and it might take up to a month for the cheque to arrive. I think Kenny gave it a week before he phoned me. I told him payments were out of my hands and would be dealt with by the staff in London. Helpfully, I passed on David Gregory's office telephone number. About a week later, a harassed SHOOT! Editor called me. 'Who is this Kenny Dalglish person?' he asked. 'He's never off the phone looking for his money. Please tell him it's on its way as swiftly as we can arrange it.'

Kenny got his fiver and, ironically, he became a columnist for the magazine when he joined Liverpool in 1977. Actually, he could have been what was known as a 'star writer' in SHOOT! three years before that, but knocked back the offer. David Gregory wanted to have a Celtic and Rangers columnist in his magazine, alternating week by week. I think the cash was around £20 and, as I've said in an earlier chapter, John Greig was happy to contribute the Rangers angle.

Kenny, though, knew what Scotland captain Billy Bremner got for his column in SHOOT! and he wanted the same cash as the Leeds United player. I believe Billy received something in the region of £80 back in the mid-seventies - not bad cash for what would probably have been a thirty-minute phone call from a reporter once a week. I telephoned David Gregory, who was, by this time, well aware of the name Kenny Dalglish, without the extra 'e'. The Editor asked me to tell Dalglish about the logistics of the situation. Billy Bremner's column was in the magazine every week and the percentage of sales in England was astronomical compared with that of Scotland. I realised all this, of course. Dalglish wouldn't budge. Eventually, Danny McGrain agreed to do the column.

When I was writing the book, D*enis Law: King & Country* (available at all good bookshops!), I came across this gem of a quote from Matt Busby after he had signed the Aberdonian from Italian side Torino for Manchester United in 1961. Negotiations were protracted before Denis signed. 'There's a lad who knows the true value of his worth,' said the legendary Old Trafford manager. Law, of course, was the original and, for me, the only King of Scottish football. Kenny Dalglish came close.

It appeared they had more than just incredible footballing ability in common.

(Just to set the record straight, Kenny could also be an incredibly generous individual. In 1996, I was on the Mike Galloway Benefit Committee after the ex-Celtic player's career ended following a car crash. Kenny not only agreed to play in the game for free, he moved his family into a hotel in Glasgow for the weekend and picked up all the expenses.)

Chapter 22

Hughie Taylor-made for memories

My parents could have clubbed together and bought me a brand new E-Type Jaguar, but no Christmas would have been complete without *The Hugh Taylor Scottish Football Book*.

That was the ultimate festive treat; the gift that was first to be enthusiastically ripped from its shiny Xmas wrapping and devoured page by page. First, a quick glance at the action photographs and, then, every article scrutinised while marvelling at the Great Man's dashing prose. I discovered early in my professional life that Hughie (no-one ever called him Hugh or Shuggie or Shug) was every bit as colourful as his lavish, magnetic writing style.

Look up 'irrepressible' in the Concise English Dictionary and there's likely to be a photograph of Hughie, moustache immaculately trimmed, smiling back at you. My old pal was blessed with the gift of being able to assemble words in such a compelling fashion that there is no doubt he could have brought a game of chess to vibrant life in print. No easy task, I would have thought.

Before I joined the Daily Record in 1967, I would always volunteer to go shopping for my mother every Saturday morning. It was my ritual to take the list from my mum and head off for the nearest shops at Croftfoot. I used to run - no-one jogged in those days - all the way downhill from Dougrie Road to the nearest shops. It would take me around twenty minutes, but almost double that coming home. Apart from having to climb the fairly steep hill, I was a wee bit distracted because I would be scouring that day's edition of the Record. A must-read was Hughie's hilarious Saturday Sports Bag where he interacted with the readers and answered their letters with his usual panache and tongue-in-cheek style. He was a god among sportswriters, as far as I was concerned. To actually work alongside him when I was only fifteen was simply awesome. To drink with him was equally daunting.

Hugh Taylor hands over the Player of the Year shield to Morton's Andy Ritchie in 1979

Hughie Taylor was a complete one-off. I loved the wonderful yarns he used to spin and he always insisted they were true. I always took his word for it. Hughie's capacity for strong drink was phenomenal. Look that word up in the Concise English Dictionary and, once again, there's likely to be a photograph of Hughie, dark-rimmed specs askew, peeking back at you.

I recall one evening when we were having a snifter in Dick's Bar on the Broomielaw. It was a pub with a real eclectic mix of customer, but a lot of journalists had long since commandeered a huge part of it after the Daily Record and Sunday Mail moved from Hope Street to Anderston Quay in the early seventies. It was an unusual little howf with an entrance in York Street and another around the corner on Clydeside.

I was there when a punter, obviously the worse for wear, just about collapsed in the York Street side entrance. John Dick and his son Alan would never tolerate drunkenness in their establishment. (Well, maybe they looked the other way every now and again with a wayward journalist.) Anyway, this poor guy had no chance of getting served. 'Out!' shouted John. The bloke squinted at John through a booze-induced haze and instantly realised there was little point in pushing his case. He turned around and made a sharp exit. About a minute later, he entered through the Broomielaw door. 'Out!' exclaimed John again. The guy tried vainly to focus and slurred, 'Do you own every fuckin' pub in this city?'

There was one memorable night when Hughie was going for Olympic Gold in downing the shorts. He had finished his shift around 5pm and had obviously worked up a voracious thirst. I arrived around 9pm after the first edition was safely going to press. Hughie was howling at the moon. There was never any trouble with Hughie when he was snorkelling in bevvy; he just became even more animated and humorous. John and Alan Dick realised there was no chance of aggro when the Record's ace sports reporter decided to give the ball a right good dunt.

I was in the loo when Hughie lurched in and went straight for the cubicle. It was obvious he was indulging in a technicolour yawn, yodelling into the big white telephone. Hughie emerged, dusted himself down, splashed his face with cold water, turned to me and said, 'Well, Alex, that's enough of the whisky for one night.' He paused and added, 'I think I'll go onto the vodka now.' And he did, too.

Hughie was hauled over by the traffic police on another occasion on his way back from a meeting at Rugby Park. I had to laugh when our man was continually labelled as a Celtic fanatic or a Rangers diehard. Hughie was a Kilmarnock supporter. Strangely, no-one ever accused him of having an allegiance to the Ayrshire outfit. This particular evening, Hughie was ordered to lock up his car and was taken to the cells in one of the local cop stations. Hughie was not too pleased. In fact, he was outraged.

'I want my lawyer,' he demanded.

'Who's your lawyer, sir?' asked one of the policemen.

Hughie identified his brief and added, 'You must know him; he's a Kilmarnock director.'

'Oh, yes,' said the cop. 'He's in the cell next door. Good night over at

Rugby Park, was it?'

I hope I don't upset anyone with the next little anecdote concerning this incorrigible human being. Every year around Christmas time, the Daily Record and Sunday Mail used to hold an Editorial Ball at a plush Glasgow Hotel. I attended these so-called gala evenings although I was never a massive fan of looking like an elongated penguin with an over-large bow-tie. I would sit at the Record Sports Desk table and on this occasion I was parked beside Hughie and his companion. I was calling her Mrs Taylor all night. When there was a lull in proceedings, a colleague sidled over to me and said, 'Christ's sake, Alex, stop calling her Mrs Taylor,' he whispered. 'That's not his wife. That's his girlfriend.'

To be frank, I was astounded because I had only ever seen Hughie with this female in tow at all the functions we attended. Years later, after Hughie's wife sadly passed on, he actually married his long-term girlfriend. Then, at another Editorial Christmas Ball, there was the bold Hughie turning up with ANOTHER lady on his arm. Now, remember, Hughie, at this stage, wouldn't be blowing out the candles on his sixtieth birthday cake again and was heading for his bus pass.

'Hughie, what's going on?' I asked, trying to disguise the incredulity in my tone.

He looked at me, grinned and delivered yet another immortal line.

'Son, you've got to have something on the side.'

Chapter 23

Buchanan and gunfire in New York

Ken Buchanan is such a resolutely charming and thoroughly likeable guy it is impossible to believe he used to knock people senseless for a living.

Back in 1989, I had the pleasure and privilege of spending a fair bit of time with Scotland's legendary boxer. I was gathering fresh material for a three-parter for the Sunday Mail and I have to say I really enjoyed his company. Here is one of the tales in his own words.

'The song tells you New York is a wonderful town. You could have fooled me! Most of the time I have been there people seem to be getting shot, mugged or threatened.

'In September 1973, I was due to fight a Puerto Rican named Chu Chu Maleve at Madison Square Garden. A few hours before the fight, I was involved in a face-to-face confrontation with a burglar who was going through my room at the Slater Hilton Hotel. I chased him down to the foyer, dived on top of him and there was an almighty scramble. He produced a gun from somewhere and the pistol went off during the struggle before he was chased out onto the street where he made his getaway.

'Casually, I picked up the abandoned revolver near the reception desk and was immediately aware that there were several policemen and security guards in the foyer. Where were they when I needed them? I couldn't fail to notice that they were all armed to the teeth and their guns were pointing at yours truly. Thankfully, there were a few eyewitnesses around to reassure the cops I was not a gun-toting robber. The hotel tried to hush up the story. I don't suppose it would have looked too clever in their brochures as a forthcoming attraction. They said the burglar had used a toy gun.

'Oh, really? A chunk of plaster was blasted out of their ceiling when

115

the 'toy' went off.

'It was only afterwards that I fully realised what could have happened. Anyway, I still beat Malave. That was the important thing!

'And I'll never forget the occasion when I was in the Big Apple again for another fight when I went out for a jog in Central Park with former world welterweight champion Emile Griffith. We were jogging along, minding our own business, when I heard this voice at my side. I looked round and there was this guy running alongside us. I hadn't a clue what he was saying, but I did recognise what he had in his right hand ... A GUN! I didn't stop to ask him if it was a toy.

'Emile and I simply decided to speed up our gentle jog to a frantic sprint. Baffled New Yorkers were treated to the sight of two world champion boxers racing past them as fast as our heels would carry us. Interesting town, New York. Not too sure about the wonderful!'

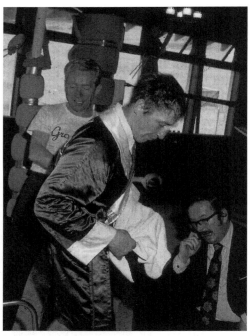

Ken Buchanan in New York with his father Tommy while my alter ego, the Daily Mirror's Frank McGhee, sits this one out

Chapter 24

Lost in Gloomfield

How many times have you heard someone ask a football reporter, 'Were you actually at the game?'

Yes, I accept some of the so-called 'expert' views from the inhabitants of the press box don't always coincide with the man in the stand, but I have to admit that most of the reporters have, in fact, been in attendance when the game has been played.

There are exceptions, though.

I was at Broomfield one chilly winter's afternoon - I must have done something to upset the Sports Editor - for an Airdrie v. Hearts game in the old First Division back in the late sixties. No-one ever volunteered to cover a game at this particular ground. The natives, normally, were restless. The antiquated main stand looked as though it had been put together by Chad Valley and the whole place belonged to a long-forgotten and unlamented century.

Reporters had to pick up their telephones from a dilapadated wee hut beside the stand and then you had to run the gauntlet of the deranged to get to your seat in the press gantry. I have to say Airdrie supporters must have been at the end of a very long queue when the Good Lord was handing out senses of humour. 'Hey, you, gie's that phone, I want to call my brother in Melbourne,' was a regular muttering from one of the local worthies every matchday. I don't suppose he ever worked it out that he had no place to plug the damn thing into. You had to get there early to make certain you did get a socket in the press box that was actually in working order. Never an easy task, I'm afraid.

On one such assignment at Gloomfield, as it was known to most of the press, a Sunday Mail news reporter by the name of John Sullivan turned up about fifteen minutes after kick-off. I knew Sully covered a football game every now and again to top up his blue drinking tokens. By the look of him, Sully had had a hard night. Maybe, even, a harder morning. 'Okay, son? Have I missed anything?' I reassured him it was still goalless as I prepared to hand him the team lists.

He was almost nodding off, when he turned to me, did his best to focus and asked, 'Is this Gayfield?'

I thought I had misheard. 'Gayfield? No, this is Broomfield.'

'Is that not Arbroath?'

'No, that's Airdrie.'

'Is that not East Fife?'

'No, that's Hearts.'

'So it's not Gayfield? It's not Arbroath? And they're not playing East Fife? Are you sure?'

'Positive.'

The horrible realisation dawned on the newshound. 'Fuck,' he said. 'I might as well go back to the pub.'

He left his phone behind. I don't suppose he was going to need it for the rest of the day.

Chapter 25

Pat Roller and the angry World Cup superstar

An extremely agitated Scotland international footballer was on the other end of the line.

Clearly, he was not happy with the Daily Record and my ears were on the receiving end of a ferocious verbal bashing.

'Calm down,' I implored. 'What's the problem?'

'What's the fuckin' problem?' came the vehement response. 'That bloke Pat Roller's the problem. I want to speak to him. Get him on the phone. Fuckin' now!'

Back in the sixties and seventies, the Record ran a daily news column called 'Pat Roller - Looking For Trouble'. Basically, a news reporter would trawl around the police stations of Glasgow for some up-to-the-minute crimes; arrests for street fights, pub brawls, break-ins, car thefts, that sort of thing. It was actually a very good idea and soon practically everyone knew the name 'Pat Roller' and the slogan 'Looking For Trouble'.

But Pat Roller had enraged this footballer. Apparently, he had written a story about the players recording the 1974 World Cup song before the finals in West Germany that summer. There was a hint that some of the players were not happy about the cash they were to be paid. That didn't sit well with this particular individual. And he was going to let Pat Roller know all about it.

'Put that guy on the phone,' spluttered the footballer, who, it must be said, was a household name and a recognised world class performer.

'There is no Pat Roller,' I said.

'Aye, there fuckin' is. I've got the paper here. It says Pat Roller. I want to speak to this bastard. This story's a lot of shite.'

'No,' I protested. 'There is no-one called Pat Roller ...'

'Aye, there fuckin' is. It says so right here in the paper.'

'No, would you wait a minute?' I asked. Now the character on the other end of the line was never liable to crash the Mensa ratings, but I was well aware he wasn't the bluntest tool in the box, either. I wondered if his sense of humour had taken a detour.

'Put the two names together,' I said. 'What do you get?'

'What are you fuckin' talking about? Get that bastard Pat Roller on the phone. Now!'

'Patroller,' I said. 'That's why he's called Pat Roller. He is a patroller patrolling the streets of Glasgow looking for news stories. Get it? Pat Roller? Patroller?'

Silence.

'Aye, right,' came the response a moment or two later, the penny dropping, I hoped. 'So there is no Pat Roller, eh? Well, who the fuck is Pat Roller? His name's in the paper right here. It says Pat Roller. Let me talk to this bastard.'

I felt my life ebbing away; this was going to be a long conversation.

'Anyone can be Pat Roller,' I said. 'Any news reporter can get that job on any given evening. Fred Bloggs could be Pat Roller. Joe Smith could be Pat Roller.'

More silence.

'I don't get this. Do I have to speak to this Bloggs guy? Or this Smith bloke? Listen, I want to speak to Pat Roller.'

There were occasions when I wondered if I had chosen the right profession. This was most of them. Maybe I should have taken up bull-fighting. Or catching bullets between my teeth. I tried again. 'Pat Roller is just a made-up name. It's like Garry Owen in the racing pages ...'

'This has got fuck all to do with Garry Owen. I want to speak to Pat Roller.'

'Please listen before one of us snuffs it,' I said. 'I can't let you to speak to Pat Roller because there is no Pat Roller. Believe me, I would let you speak to Pat Roller if I could, but it's not possible.'

'You newspaper guys always cover up for each other.'

'I'm not covering for anyone. Pat Roller is patroller. Put the names together.'

Silence.

'Aye, okay. I'll leave this message with you. Tell Pat Roller that if I ever meet him he should be prepared for a boot up the bollocks. Okay? You tell him that.'

I surrendered. 'I'll do that.'

The line went dead.

And I hoped there was no-one out there unlucky enough to be actually called Pat Roller who would meet the acquaintance of this angry footballer any time in the near future.

The Pat Roller hunter sings out of tune – but which one is he? Scotland's 1974 Top of the Pops wannabes are (back row, left to right) Kenny Dalglish and Tom Forsyth; front: manager Willie Ormond, George Connelly, Erich Schaedler, Jim Holton, Donald Ford, song writer Bill Martin (half-hidden), Willie Morgan, Denis Law, Sandy Jardine and Danny McGrain.

121

Chapter 26

Garry Owen rocking in the roller

When I joined the Daily Record Sports Desk in early January 1968 - about a fortnight before my sixteenth birthday - I was introduced to this marvellous, red-faced, cheery little Aberdonian called Alec Duncan. He was better known to horse racing fans by his pseudonym, Garry Owen.

My dad thought I had hit my personal klondyke. I have never been a gambler and, in any case, there would be every likelihood I would lose in a one-horse race. My old man liked a flutter, nothing extravagant, just a couple of bob here and there. But, with his son now working at the Record Sports Desk, I could get the info straight from the horse's mouth, so to speak; a direct line to a fortune.

I made the mistake of mentioning this to Wee Alec. He gave me a tip for a horse running the following day - 'a cert', he said. I relayed the message to my dad and, sure enough, the nag romped home. The same scenario twenty-four hours later. And the day after that. Three tips, three wins; Garry and my dad were on a roll.

I think at that early stage my old man had kicked off dreams of early retirement and British Rail could stuff their job. Then disaster. An entire week without a win. Wee Alec was most apologetic. He said, 'Please tell your father I wouldn't be sitting in an office in Glasgow working all sorts of hours if I really could pick out a winner every day. I would be a professional gambler and my home address would be somewhere in the South of France.' The message got across and all my father's thoughts of quitting anti-social shifts at Polmadie Railway Works were instantly shelved.

It was impossible not to like Wee Alec. Every Friday in life, Garry Owen, 'Scotland's No.1 Racing Tipster', and Hugh Taylor, 'Scotland's No1 Sportswriter', two absolutely wonderful characters, would race through their copy and repair to the Copy Cat pub for early snifters.

My shift started around three o'clock, so by the time Alec and Hughie returned from the pub after about four solid hours of guzzling whiskies and vodkas, they were both just a tad unsteady on their toes. No-one turned a hair; this was Friday and it was their day. Jack Adams was the Sports Editor and he was often heard to say, 'I'm seriously thinking about taking every Friday off.' The editorial would shake with the screeching Doric tones of Wee Alec shouting, 'Don't you tell me what to do, Jack Adams!' I can still hear those words to this day.

As you would expect, Alec Duncan, in his guise of Garry Owen, knew everyone there was to know in horse racing. He was courted everywhere he went; horse owners looking for a bit of publicity for their investment, trainers seeking a mention, bookies wanting their name in lights, that sort of thing. Wee Alec did a great juggling act to keep everyone happy.

There was a Glasgow Turf Accountant - I've often wondered about that official tag - who went out of his way to woo Wee Alec one day. The bookie was a chap called Kenny McLean and he had several shops in Glasgow and was looking to expand. On this occasion, he turned up at Hope Street in his brand new gleaming white Rolls-Royce. I've got no idea how much it cost, but I had the notion it might have been the price of a reasonable-sized bungalow back then.

It was the last word in motoring elegance. Kenny opened the door for Wee Alec and was only too proud to show off the genuine leather interior of the vehicle and the latest in gadgets. James Bond would have envied that car.

Anyway, they took off for their destination with Kenny reassuring Wee Alec the champagne was on ice in a special compartment at the back of the Rolls. They were travelling over the Fenwick Moor when the bookie offered the racing 'expert' a cigar; a genuine Havana. It was so big that Wee Alec told me later he almost fell off the end. Kenny pointed to the cigarette/cigar lighter, another of the lastest mod cons. My pal accepted the Havana, took out the lighter, lit the cigar, rolled down the window and threw the apparatus out of the car. Kenny spluttered, 'Alec, what are you doing? That cost about £100!'

Wee Alec merely smiled. 'Oops! Old habits.'

Chapter 27

Oliver Reed, the ex-nun, the streaker and the porn star

Drinks are on me ... Oliver Reed

There are some thankless tasks in journalism, but, surely, nothing can even begin to compete with the one that was lumbered on my old mate Hugh Farmer, News Editor of the Sunday People back in the days when that newspaper had a genuine presence.

Hell-raiser Oliver Reed was invited to Glasgow by BBC Scotland bosses in 1982 when they were making a series called *Sin On Saturday*. Bernard Falk was to host the show and it was due to run for eight weeks. The theme was based on the Seven Deadly Sins and an eighth programme was scheduled to round everything off with an assortment of celebs agreeing to discuss their thoughts and air their views on all sorts of misdemeanours.

Reed was due to appear on the first show covering Lust. Someone, in their infinite wisdom, had put him in a line-up alongside a former nun, busty streaker Erica Roe and porn actress Linda Lovelace, she of *Deep Throat* infamy. (No jokes about 'They've all got it infamy,' please.) There was also a rock band who would perform a little ditty entitled, *Pump Me With Your Love Gun.*

Each episode was scheduled to run thirty-five minutes and would be aired at the back of 11pm. There were pre-recorded musical inserts, but, crucially, the actual debate about whichever sin was under discussion was to be beamed live. Oliver Reed. Late Saturday night. Live TV. Ex-nun. Busty streaker. Porn performer with a penchant for fellatio. Rock band. Anyone see a problem on the horizon?

Big Ollie was known to be volatile after a bevvy. He was once forced to leave the set of a Channel 4 chat show called *After Dark*, arriving drunk and attempting to get friendly with feminist writer Kate Millett, muttering the unforgettable phrase, 'Give us a kiss, big tits.'

One of my favourite stories about this joyously potty character came long before his break in movies. He was working as an orderly at St. Helier Hospital in Carshalton where his duties mainly involved collecting the recently departed and taking them to the mortuary. Bored witless one evening, he climbed into a coffin and persuaded a nurse to pull down the lid and wheel him into a lift containing a group of medical students. In his best Boris Karloff impersonation, he groaned, 'Let me out. I'm alive!'

The wild man of celluloid duly arrived in Glasgow in the early afternoon to be greeted by Farmer and myself. The News Editor had roped me in just in case things 'got a bit hairy'. Hugh had arranged an interview with Ollie while a friend at the Beeb urged the extremely capable newsman to 'keep an eye' on the actor. Much easier to persuade a ravenous lion to give up his supper and let you walk free.

Ollie, after previous visits, had a fair idea of what Glasgow was all about. Or, at least, he knew where he could get a small libation. Hugh insisted on taking him somewhere in the region of the former BBC HQ at

Queen Margaret Drive in Glasgow's west end. 'Keep him out of the pub,' Hugh was ordered. 'Make sure he doesn't get a drink.' Aye, right.

Within minutes of our taxi arriving at its destination, Ollie was off like a bride's nightie heading towards Byres Road while the harassed Hugh was fumbling with change to pay the cabbie. 'Get after him, Alex!' screamed my friend.

I took off in hot pusuit. All I could see was his coat billowing out from behind him as he sprinted full-pelt down the road, dodging in between bewildered pedestrians in the process.

I could hear startled citizens asking, 'Is that not that actor bloke?' Quickly followed by, 'And why is that guy chasing him?'

Ollie, making the best of his head start, disappeared off the radar. Hugh, not built for speed, eventually caught up with me. We shared an inkling the man who once played a werewolf in an early movie (and appeared quite at home continuing the role throughout the remainder of his life) might attempt to find succour in a bar somewhere nearby. We searched all the usual haunts. No sign of Ollie. He had vanished. Like errant schoolboys, we reported to the TV people to inform them we had 'misplaced' their star guest.

What seemed like an interminable period passed and panicking bosses at the Beeb were about to begin hacking at their wrists when, extraordinarily, the actor appeared in the studio about an hour before the show was about to go out live to the nation. He was adamant he was 'perfectly fine' and insisted in being escorted to the Green Room for some 'hospitality' before joining the other guests. Not a good idea.

This was it; the big moment. 'Five ... four ... three ... two ... one. You're on!' The credits rolled and Bernard Falk's face was a picture as he introduced the ex-nun, the streaker, the porn star and a bleary-eyed Oliver Reed. Ollie, clearly, had enjoyed himself in some snug off Byres Road and maintained a steady and determined progress towards oblivion in the Green Room. If you were being polite, you would have said he was inebriated. If you were being accurate, you would have said he was as drunk as a skunk.

Throughout the programme, host Falk did his absolute best to avoid Ollie, who was desperate to join in the discussion of that evening's topic. Eventually, Ollie saw an opening when the former nun hesitated in answering a question.

'LUST!' boomed Ollie. 'LUST! It's such a wonderful word, isn't it?' He then proceeded to stretch the word. 'LLLLLLLLUUUUUUUSSSSSTTTTTTTT! Marvellous word.'

He was about to go again when Falk broke in. 'Right, thank you ...'

Ollie froze in time. He was sitting forward in his chair, his arms outstretched and was just about to mouth 'LUST' one more time. The camera followed Falk, but Ollie was clearly seen in the background continuing to adopt the same frozen pose; his lips pouting, his eyes bulging. Not even a particularly stirring rendition of 'Pump Me With Your Love Gun' could save the show with a dishevelled, leering Ollie in full flow. Unfortunately, despite Falk's finest efforts, it descended into drunken farce.

The series lasted only two more shows - about covetousness and envy - before the plug was pulled. Sadly, gluttony, due to star Fanny Cradock, was never aired.

A Beeb boss summed it up. 'It could have been worse. Imagine what might have happened had Ollie had been on the same show as a Fanny.'

Chapter 28

A real rum do

Sub-editors on national newspapers tend to be fairly peculiar people. I don't mean 'peculiar' as in funny, but 'peculiar' as in odd. I should know, I was one for more years than I care to remember.

Who else would want to go to work in the dark, miss the daylight hours, and go home with the moon waiting to greet them? If you worked constant backshift - and these were the normal hours for these folk - you had something in common with a certain count from Transylvania.

To a lot of people, a sub-editor is just one promotion away from the title of Editor. Not so. A sub, as they are known in the industry, is one of the people in at the sharp end. When I began at the Daily Record in the sixties, there was a huge semi-circular desk that must have housed at least twenty News subs. No-one had a specific desk. Directly in front of them in the middle was the chief news sub-editor and he would be assisted by his deputy. There was a copy taster who would collect the stories, from the news reporters and the wire services, and he would compile them in order of importance. The copy would then be handed to the backbench, the Editor and his many helpers; deputy, assistant, Night Editor, etc. Immediately behind them was the Art Desk which normally housed about four guys who drew up the lay-outs for the news pages.

So, if you were a sub-editor on a daily newspaper in the sixties, there was every chance your hours were 3pm to 10pm or 5pm to 1am. You really did become a creature of the night. I had a pal who worked as a Sports sub on the Evening Times and his problem was that his shift started at 5am and finished around two o'clock in the afternoon. Three pints of lager later, he would be plastered and normally in bed by 6pm.

The really lucky national newspaper subs were the folk who populated the Features Desk. Mainly, they could work normal office hours, i.e. 9am to 5pm. It made sense; there was little need for a Features sub to be in the editorial at midnight on a Monday putting together a story that wouldn't appear until Thursday's paper. A lot of what they did, showbiz interviews, TV listings and the like, could be handled days in advance and that left the 'live' on-the-day stories for the Sports and News Desks.

Every now and again, a personality would have the temerity or thoughtlessness to die outwith the hours that suited the Features subs. If only Elvis had conked out in the morning as opposed to the late evening. How dare he? On these occasions, the Features subs worked at pace and more than a few proved more than capable of a swift response to a breaking story. Two of the anonymous guys who could operate at speed were Alastair Murray and Jim Murray (not related), both good friends, but they much preferred some breathing space not afforded to subs on the other desks. So, late feature stories all appeared to be penned by someone by the name of Tony Head. The Murrays, working with wire copy most of the time, made a star out of that bloke. Of course, there was no Tony Head; it was an anagram for On The Day.

So, now we have established that all subs are a tad unconventional, given their choice of occupation, may I introduce you to a newsman by the name of Bill Swanson? I didn't really know this rather odd guy from Edinburgh. He would arrive at the News subs' desk, a huge haversack over his shoulder - goodness only knows what he had crammed in there - and simply sit down, rarely converse with anyone and just get on with his job. He was quite a talented headline-writer, as I recall. One of his best was about a hospital patient who was in a bit of discomfort days after undergoing a routine operation. An x-ray showed the surgeon had left a small piece of equipment inside the stomach before the patient had been stitched up. 'THE FORCEPS SAGA' was Bill's offering and I, for one, thought it was pretty smart.

But I often wondered why Bill drank on his own during his break in the Copy Cat. We would head for the 'doocot' and he found a space at the lounge bar well away from his colleagues. This happened night after night for years. Now I've been blessed with a great sense of smell; there would have been little use of God gifting me a hooter that rivalled that of Rod Stewart (in a head-to-head, I'm not sure who would win by a nose) if it didn't serve its purpose. As far as I was aware, Bill hadn't been cursed with a substantial body odour problem and he was a popular enough character, if, maybe, a wee bit withdrawn.

One night, as I was celebrating the countdown to my twenty-first birthday, I decided to do a bit of detective work. I was filled with bonhomie, or it might just have been bevvy, when I confronted him at the bar. I really had to get to the bottom of this.

'Bill,' I asked, 'why do you always drink on your lonesome? What's the problem?'

'No problem, Alex,' he answered. 'It's just the way it is.'

'Why?'

'Trust me, it's for the best.'

'Let me buy you a drink. I'm twenty-one in a couple of days' time. Let's celebrate.'

'If you don't mind, I'll just stick to my own. Thanks all the same.'

I wasn't having any of it. 'I insist, Bill, let me get you a drink. What's your pleasure?'

'Are you sure?' asked the newsman.

'Absolutely positive. I've never bought you a drink in my life, let me buy you one tonight.'

'Are you definitely sure?'

'I won't take no for an answer. Call it up.'

Bill drained his tall glass, called over Wee Anna, barmaid extraordinaire, and pushed it in front of her. 'Usual, please, Anna,' he said.

Anna picked up the glass and said matter-of-factly, 'Seven dark rums and a Coke coming right up,' she said.

In an instant, the mystery of why Bill had no drinking partners was solved.

Chapter 29

Mo Johnston: the lying game

There has been some amount of drivel written and spoken in the many years since Mo Johnston signed for Rangers on July 10 1989. Quite rightly, it has been labelled the most sensational transfer in the history of Scottish football. Also, it proved, without any shadow of a doubt, that some folk are fairly expert at speaking with forked tongue.

A lot that has followed the remarkable deal has been an avalanche of lies, nonsense and baloney. Honesty has been booted around like a burst ball. I'm so sick and tired of all the hoo-ha, I think it's time I set the record straight. What you are about to read is the absolute truth. I will happily go to any court in the land and swear on oath that the following is 100 per cent accurate. Put me through any polygraph test and I'll come through the other end without a blemish.

I was Sports Editor at the Sunday Mail at the time of the drama and I was receiving all sorts of messages from many excellent contacts that the Johnston deal for Celtic from French club Nantes was on the rocks; there was no mention or hint of Rangers at the earliest outset. Celtic manager Billy McNeill, of course, had already paraded the player in front of the press at Parkhead and a beaming Mo was caught on film saying, 'Celtic have come in for me and I'm delighted to be joining them.'

All well and good, but still a lot of my friends - 'people in the know' - were flagging up that it was far from a done deal. Mo sat with one of his mates in the Love Street stand on Saturday May 13, when a Joe Miller goal gave Celtic a 1-0 victory over St. Mirren on the last day of the league season. The following Saturday, I believe Mo was in the stand at Hampden when Miller netted the only strike of the game to hand Billy McNeill's men the Scottish Cup, upsetting old foes Rangers, who were chasing a domestic treble after lifting the Premier Championship and the League Cup earlier in the season.

Apart from the actual football, two separate incidents occurred that May day I found very interesting. On my way through the Hampden car park before the game, I was pulled aside by someone I knew who worked for Radio Clyde. There was no reason for him to indulge in any claptrap. He said, 'There's a problem with the Mo Johnston move. We can't nail it, but I think there might be something in it for you.' I thanked the guy. In fact, that wasn't the first time I had heard something along the same lines, but, of course, we were constantly reassured by Celtic that everything was in order. They had paid a deposit of £400,000 and the fee - in the region of £1.2million - had been agreed with the French club and everything was fine and dandy.

After the Scottish Cup Final, I made my way back to the Sunday Mail offices at Anderston Quay with colleagues Don Morrison and Dixon Blackstock. Later that evening, I received a call at the desk from a very well-placed Rangers mole. He told me Graeme Souness was absolutely livid after the defeat. That hardly surprised me. I was also told the Rangers manager had screamed about having 'Something up my sleeve that'll rock Celtic'. My informant from within that dressing room also revealed Souness had said, 'They've got a shock coming.' I was well aware that the Rangers manager possessed a volcanic temper, but he did not spout hot air for the sheer hell of it. Now I was intrigued. What was the 'something' he had up his sleeve? Or, more accurately, the 'somebody'?

Souness, talking twenty years after the historic event, admitted he was ignorant of the fact Johnston had any thoughts of returning to Scotland from France until he noticed the news in the papers and the player wearing a Celtic top and being cuddled by Billy McNeill. He told my old newspaper, the Daily Record, 'I had no idea Maurice was coming back until I saw that.'

I believe him. At the same time, I had also been informed FIFA, the world governing football body, were investigating racism and religious bias in the game. Rangers, with their archaic refusal to sign Roman Catholics, may have been about to come under investigation. A club in Chile, Universidad Catolica, were also about to be scrutinised for their practice of only signing Catholics. FIFA, I was assured, were about to act and they had the ultimate powers of withdrawing playing licences and shutting down football clubs if they determined such stringent action was required.

That may, or may not, have been a coincidence of timing. What was certain is that Graeme Souness was a man who would not have been frightened to break with Ibrox tradition. As he said, 'I was married to a Catholic, my children were christened Catholics. I was brought up in Edinburgh. Every day I walked with a Catholic friend to school. It was never an issue in our house. I was brought up by very level-headed, right-thinking parents. Maybe I was naive, but religion just wasn't an issue with me.'

So, the timing was right to go for Mo Johnston. Back to Souness, 'It wasn't just signing a Catholic; it was a Catholic who had played for Celtic. It was a double whammy.'

Souness recalled the moment he saw the opportunity to seize the player from under the noses of his club's fiercest rivals. 'I came down the stairs after a game at Ibrox and Bill McMurdo (Johnston's agent) was leaning against a radiator. I said, "You should have told me Maurice was thinking of coming back." It was a throwaway line. I turned to walk away when he said, "Why? Would you be interested?" I stopped in my tracks and turned back to talk to him.'

If that is accurate - and I have absolutely no reason to doubt the word of Souness - that conversation must have taken place at Ibrox on Saturday, May 13 after their last league game of the campaign, a 3-0 defeat from Aberdeen. That was the same day Johnston was in Paisley watching his 'new' club Celtic. So, what happened between Saturday May 13 and the Scottish Cup Final a week later? I have no doubt Souness would have acted quickly after his meeting with McMurdo, who, as a well-known Rangers fan, would have given him every assistance in brokering a deal for his client.

One of the first to be told of Souness's idea of signing Johnston was his assistant manager, Walter Smith. According to Souness, 'It took the wind out of his sails. He was stuck for words, but, after about a minute, he was fine and he thought it was a great idea.'

If my information is correct, and I have no reason to think otherwise,

Souness then drove home to Edinburgh, taking a slight detour to have a word with chairman David Murray. By Souness's own admission, 'At first, he just went silent, but again, within a minute, he, too, thought it was a great idea. They both knew that if Rangers were to be accepted as a proper football club, it couldn't have this ridiculous situation hanging over it.'

As Rangers prepared for the Hampden final, Souness secretly flew to Paris for a meeting with Johnston. Souness is now on record as saying, 'I persuaded him to sign for Rangers. I had played for Scotland with him. I had a relationship with him. It was relaxed and there were no difficult moments. It was an exciting time in Glasgow and he wanted to be part of it. He was a Scottish international, we needed a striker and he would complement what we had at the club.'

At least, we now know the 'something' Souness had up his sleeve when he hit the roof after the defeat at Hampden. But there were weeks of denials ahead before the press conference at Ibrox and the unveiling of the player almost two months after the Scottish Cup Final. What happened in between was highly intriguing. If the curse of Pinocchio for telling porkies applied to certain human beings, we might have had to build an extension onto the planet to cope with all the rapidly growing noses. I'm sure more than a few rainforests could have been saved if there had been no requirement for immediate and extended nasal structures. You could have built an entire Viking fleet out of one individual's prominent conk.

The telephone calls wouldn't go away. I met with friends and it was the main topic of conversation. The enquiries we were making were all getting batted back at us. I wasn't convinced and arranged to go over to Celtic Park one morning to meet a club executive. I won't embarrass him by naming him and he has nothing to do with the club these days. I asked if I could see some of the paper work concerning the transfer of Mo Johnston from Nantes to Celtic. Very helpfully, the documents were fished out of a desk and placed in front of me. I wasn't too bad at French language at school, but I had left Mr Cosgrove's 3A class in May 1967 and this was June 1989. A few bouteilles de Sancerre had been chucked behind my Adam's Apple between then and now. I hoped I didn't sound like Inspector Clouseau as I read from the document.

It was like an old-fashioned parchment with a wax seal. Basically, what I could decipher was that this document was an 'Agreement to a Transfer' and not a 'Transfer Agreement'. It appeared this piece of paper from Nantes Football Club was merely granting permission for Celtic to talk to their player. It meant Celtic's officials were not breaking any rules while approaching a player who was still under contract with another club. Of course, that is illegal and known as 'tapping'.

I was told there was another document from the French team acknowledging receipt of a deposit for their player. I left Celtic Park later on that day with my suspicions well and truly alerted. It was time for the Sunday Mail team to do some good old-fashioned sleuthing. We hit a barrier of lies. I can well understand some folk being sworn to secrecy, but some of the subterfuge that we encountered was simply outrageous. Dealing in balderdash appeared to be a specialist subject for some characters. The situation at the time was simple: Mo Johnston had changed his mind about signing for Celtic, 'the club he always adored as a school kid'.

What seems to have been forgotten over the years was the fact FIFA did intervene in an effort to sort out the mess. They examined the paper work and threw their considerable weight behind Celtic; Mo Johnston was their player, as far as they were concerned. I believe the £400,000 that had been paid up front and had been banked by Nantes swung it in Celtic's favour. The French club were satisfied with the deal and now awaited Celtic's settlement of the balance. Mo didn't have a leg to stand on. He threatened to quit football if he was forced to play for Celtic; a staggering metamorphosis in such a short space of time.

Billy McNeill, I was reassured by the man himself, was quite prepared to call the player's bluff. I can tell you the Celtic manager would have threatened to put Mo Johnston out of football. With FIFA's backing, Johnston would not have been allowed to play in any country under their auspices. The only people who could bail out Johnston were the guys on the Celtic board. They went against their manager's wise advice, cobbled together a statement that basically indicated that if 'the player does not want to play for Celtic then we don't want him.' The sigh of relief from Mo Johnston and around Govan must have thundered around Europe.

135

Celtic called off the transfer - and the rest is history.

Blues Brothers ... Mo Johnston and Graeme Souness

Right up to the very end, there were lies, lies and more damned lies. Around that time, I spent a Friday evening with a friend of mine - let's just call him an 'entrepreneur' - having dinner at the Granary in Shawlands. Everyone I met that night wanted to tell me about Mo Johnston signing for Rangers. The following morning, I asked Don Morrison to put in a call to Ibrox. 'Let's get this sorted once and for all,' I said. Don duly did so and I heard him talking to someone in authority at Rangers - not Graeme Souness, I hasten to add. Don replaced the receiver and said, 'Well, that guy doesn't seem to think Mo Johnston will ever be allowed anywhere near Rangers. He's just said, "Remember the traditions of this club and, if we were going to break them, it wouldn't be for that individual."' (Actually, he didn't use the word 'individual', but I'll leave it to your imagination to insert what you believe would be appropriate and more likely.) Don added, 'He seemed quite emphatic.'

It seemed like a rehearsed line from the guy within Ibrox I have chosen not to embarrass by naming him. Frankly, I didn't believe him. I asked Don to telephone Bill McMurdo. Again, I listened to the call. Our Chief Sports Writer came off the phone again. 'He has just said, "It's a complete fabrication – you could run that story for ten years and it still wouldn't be true."' That didn't sit well, either. To this day, Don, one of the most honest blokes you are every likely to meet, stands by that recollection.

A couple of days after the categorical denials and weeks of ducking and diving from some prominent characters, Mo Johnston was wheeled out at Ibrox as a Rangers player on Monday, July 10 1989.

Quelle surprise! I didn't reel back in astonishment.

Chapter 30

Ad-libbing with the Sherry

Gordon Stephen won't be a name that is well-known to newspaper readers. That's a pity, because 'Big Stevie' was one of the most colourful characters I ever met in almost half-a-century in the old inky trade.

'Big Stevie' lived for three things: his job on the Daily Record Racing Desk, Rangers and booze. Definitely not in that order. He was a throwback to a golden era in newspapers when flamboyant individuals were allowed to flourish. For me, 'Big Stevie' was Richard Burton, Oliver Reed, Richard Harris, Peter O'Toole and Lee Marvin all rolled into one. He was the Racing Desk's very own charismatic rebel. He was in his sixties when he was still living at his parents' home in Lambhill, Glasgow. 'Big Stevie' never got married and rarely talked about the lack of female company, but I got the impression he had been hurt earlier in life and, thereafter, vigorously concentrated on his profession, football and bevvy.

I loved the guy. He would get up from his chair every evening bang on six o'clock and, in a booming voice, announce, 'That's me away to shift my car, Alex. Back in a moment.' Everyone on the editorial floor knew 'Big Stevie' had never driven in his life. He headed straight for the Copy Cat and would return, suitably refreshed, about an hour later. 'It's a bugger trying to get a parking space down there,' he would say without a hint of irony.

In truth, 'Big Stevie' over-indulged in the firewater. I never signed up for any temperance society, but I didn't touch spirits and my colleague could sink them at a rate of knots Messrs Burton, Reed and Co. would have surely applauded. Or even envied. Such recklessness comes at a price, of course. 'Big Stevie' landed in hospital. I visited him a few times and, on one occasion, I dared to ask him about his alcohol consumption. Needless to say, he never bothered about unit limits. What he revealed in his reply surprised even me, considering I had been working with him for about twenty years.

His shift would normally start around midday, but, every morning, he would link up with a very fine Features writer by the name of Donald Bruce. They had Rangers and booze in common. They had found a drinking den - it was known to them as the 'Gentlemen's Quarters' - off Blythswood Square that didn't appear to bother with licensing laws. 'Big Stevie' and his mate would spend an hour or so in this establishment before walking down to the office. They would check everything was going according to plan before heading for the Copy Cat. I would start work around 2pm and 'Big Stevie' would return to the Racing Desk around the same time. And then he popped in and out 'shifting his car' as the evening wore on. Do you know I never saw him even tipsy? Not once. And the booze did not interfere one jot with his ability to work diligently and professionally.

Actually, 'Big Stevie', and I mean this as absolutely no disrespect to anyone working on racing sections, could have done so much more in newspapers and could have been a household name if he had wished. I was aware Sports Editor Jack Adams would have made him his deputy any time he got the nod, but 'Big Stevie' was happy with his lot.

As he lay in his hospital bed, 'Big Stevie', with a beetroot red face that betrayed his fondness for spirits, came clean about his boozing. 'The doctor told me I had to be frank and honest,' said my pal. 'Otherwise, there was nothing they could do for me. I told him the truth. I was above board about the bottle of vodka I drank every morning.'

'Big Stevie' might have detected my jaw bounce off the floor of the ward at this point. I knew nothing about a bottle of vodka; I didn't even realise he touched the stuff.

'I also told the doc about my little excursions to the Copy Cat. Hard to quantify, but I would probably do in a bottle of whisky. Maybe more; who was counting?'

I was astonished. And then came the coup de grace.

'I ad-libbed on the sherry,' confessed 'Big Stevie'.

There is a bitter sweet ending. This relentlessly-remarkable character made a full recovery and, a few years later, accepted an early redundancy deal. It saddens me terribly to admit we drifted apart after I joined the Sunday Mail in 1987. Our paths rarely crossed and we didn't keep in touch as we might have done. That breaks me up a little, but I'm sure 'Big Stevie', wherever he is, knows there will always be a place in my heart for him.

Gordon Stephen was a special big guy.

Chapter 31

Time's up, Ally

Time, Ally, please

A shrewd observer once remarked, 'Ally McCoist is such a lucky beggar he could fall in the Clyde and come out with a salmon in one pocket and a Rolex in the other.'

The Rangers icon would probably put the fish to a good use, but God only knows what he would do with the time-piece. Ally's famous quote is, 'This is the earliest I have ever been late.' Trust me, he is up there among the worst time-keepers I have ever met. And Martin O'Neill wasn't too clever, either. What is it about Old Firm managers?

Back in 1989, as Scotland looked ahead to the following year's World Cup Finals, Umbro, the sporting manufacturing giants, got in touch with the Sunday Mail as they were preparing to launch their latest range of gear for the football extravaganza in Italy. They were looking for nationwide publicity and it was one of those deals that dovetailed beautifully with the ambitions of the newspaper and the goods people. Umbro wouldn't have to shell out big bucks for colour coverage over two pages in the biggest-selling paper in the country. And the Sunday Mail would get an excellent spread with the added bonus of free goodies to give away in a readers' competition. It was known as 'cross-fertilization'; never an expression I particularly cared for as it conjured up too many bizarre images.

Everything was put in place and it was arranged for Ally to model the latest Umbro creations, with a couple of lovelies on hand to add a bit of glamour. What could go wrong? The studio was booked, the photographer made sure he had film in his camera, the gorgeous girls were poised and ready to pout. Everything was geared for one o'clock on a Tuesday afternoon, allowing Ally the opportunity to get his morning training session out of the way. The allotted time came and went. Two o'clock, as well. And then another hour. It became obvious there would be no show from the Rangers player.

Remember, these were the dark days before mobile phones. An agent telephoned eventually to make some sort of excuse for the AWOL personality. Let's try again on Wednesday. Studio arranged, photographer poised to snap, the models wearing their best lip gloss. All that was required was a cheeky wee chappy with the ready grin. Another wasted day; another phone call; another excuse. 'Ally's terribly sorry, but something urgent has just come up. Blah blah blah. How about Thursday?' Okay, let's try for third time lucky. In moments such as this, I was thankful - and relieved - I worked for a Sunday newspaper. At least, we still had time on our side.

Everything was good to go once again; studio, snapper, stunners. No Super Ally. Now we were getting pushed for time. A full centre spread had been set aside for the photo shoot and by Thursday evening there were two blank pages in the newspaper's 'dummy'. On these occasions, it's too easy to suck out the fillings from your teeth. I spoke to the agent and told him we required Ally to be at the Sunday Mail offices BEFORE training on Friday which would normally begin around 10am. Was it possible? 'Yes,' I was told. 'No', would have been more accurate. Once again, everything was set up, everyone was in place with the exception of Ally. There may have been very good reasons for the player's non-appearances, but there comes a time when you resort very swiftly to Plan B.

Umbro added another two gorgeous puckering girls and thought the best idea would be to have the four Pamela Anderson-lookalikes model the range without a footballer in sight. I believed we still needed a sporting personality to front the photographs, another reasonably photogenic individual to strut his stuff with the quartet of nubiles. Who would do that job? Who could be trusted to turn up at such late notice? The name came to me like a bolt of lightning. By the end of Friday afternoon session everything was in the can. The photographs had been taken, Umbro were delighted, the newspaper was happy and everything was hunky dory with the world.

I knew Frank McAvennie wouldn't knock back that assignment.

Chapter 32

The pop singer and capital punishment

It was June 1990 and newspapers were smack in the middle of the Edinburgh uproar with Hearts chairman Wallace Mercer being accused of trying to buy Hibs. There was a real stooshie in Auld Reekie, as Scotsport legend Arthur Montford might have observed.

On the day the controversial tale broke - and I swear this is an absolutely true story - I was sitting by a roadside café just outside Marbella, sampling a cold afternoon ale and taking in the sights. Again, these were the days before mobile phones and I was blissfully unaware of what was happening back at the ranch. At that particular moment, I wasn't too inclined to even attempt to show an interest in anything outside this so-called 'millionaires' playground'. (If that had been the case, I would never have been allowed within one hundred miles of the border.)

Anyway, I was sipping away with a contented air when the bar owner appeared at my table. He was a Scot called Andy Marshall and, as luck would have it, his daughter, Donna, was a secretary at the Sunday Mail.

'Alex, phone call for you,' he said. 'It's the office.'

Now, what are the chances of that? 'You're joking?' I spluttered. I admit there might have been a rather loud expletive in the middle of those words.

'No, honest,' he said, with a completely straight face. 'It's Charles McGhee and he needs to talk to you urgently.'

What did Humphrey Bogart say? 'Of all the gin joints in all the world.'

However, I realised it had to be serious if our Deputy Editor, an extremely accomplished operator who had my overwhelming respect, had put in the call. He knew I was in the Marbella area and Donna, God bless her, had volunteered the information I might be partaking of a beverage in her father's bar. As if ...

Anyway, Charles revealed the news of the sensational happenings in Scotland's capital city. He knew of my friendship with one of the Hibs directors and asked me if I wouldn't mind making a few calls. Andy, very kindly, allowed me the use of the pub's only telephone for half an hour and I called my colleague back with a couple of quotes. That done, Charles was satisfied and asked me if I could be found at the same number at the same time tomorrow.

'I've promised to go snorkelling with the girlfriend,' I said. 'All day.'

He knew it was a lie.

Now, back from holiday and sitting at the Sports Desk, I had a rather excited reporter on the other end of the telephone.

'I think I've got a real scoop on the Hibs/Hearts situation,' he said.

At last, I hoped, we might draw a line under this ongoing farce. 'Go on,' I urged.

'Have you heard of the American singer Del Shannon?' he asked.

Admittedly, the question did slightly knock me out of my stride, but I said, 'Yes, of course. *Runaway*, *Hats off to Larry*, *Little Town Flirt*. That guy?' I knew my early sixties music courtesy of my elder sister Betty, a fan of Elvis, Fabian and all those Rockabilly-type guys.

'Aye, that's the bloke,' confirmed our eager reporter. 'I've just met him in a hotel in Edinburgh. He's over looking at some venues for his next British tour. I've been introduced to him and he's just told me he's keen to buy Hibs. He's got a spare million quid or two and he wants to invest it in a football club in Britain. Wonderful story, eh?'

I have to say this revelation took a moment or two to digest. Once I had regained a semblance of composure, I'm afraid I had to pour some cold water on the notion that one of America's great singer/songwriters was just about to take his seat in the directors' box at Easter Road.

'Don't think it's going to happen, mate,' I said.

'Why not?' queried the reporter. 'He told me he's interested and he's definitely got the money.'

'Del Shannon put a rifle in his mouth back in February in California and blew his head off,' I replied.

'Christ! You sure?' asked our incredulous hack, who had been completely duped by some irritating imposter.

'Apparently, Del had been suffering from depression and the Prozac wasn't working,' I assured my colleague.

'Wow! How depressed can you get?'

I refrained from mentioning anything about grey old Edinburgh on a damp February afternoon and the possibility of Hibs getting turned over by Queen of the South ...

Chapter 33

Big George, Chuck and a chariot race

Working in the newspaper industry for close on half a century has ensured I have had more than my fair share of powwows with a wide assortment of rogues, villains, charlatans, rapscallions and scoundrels. However, enough about politicians.

Undoubtedly, one of the most remarkable individuals I have ever met was a character by the name of George Mulholland. He was an enormous bloke, originally from Maryhill, who made a small fortune in the steel construction business working on the skyscrapers that began dominating the Toronto skyline in the early sixties.

George was one of those daredevils whose expertise was toiling away a thousand feet or so above sea level. 'There are only four types of people who do that for a living,' he told me once. 'Scots, Irish, Red Indians and lunatics.'

He insisted, 'It was seen as a sign of weakness or cowardice if you went about your duties wearing a harness. We would throw red-hot rivets up something like one hundred feet and the Red Indians would lean out without any safety equipment and catch them in a bucket and immediately fit them to a girder. The rivets slotted in better when they were still glowing. I thought about starting my own company and calling it "Jock, Paddy and Cochise". Had a nice ring to it.'

I was first introduced to George by my former Daily Record colleague Ken Gallacher, a fine sportswriter, back in the early seventies. George was fanatical about two things in life: Rangers Football Club and beer (possibly not necessarily in that order). He met up with Ken while the Ibrox club were touring in Canada one summer and they immediately struck a friendship that endured over the years. Given his chosen profession, it would be reasonable to assume George never turned up for work nursing a hangover.

I was amazed when he told me he didn't drink at all in Toronto, where he lived eleven months of the year. He would time his visits to Scotland to coincide with the end of the football season, the Scottish Cup Final, the now-defunct Home International against England at Hampden or Wembley and the Scottish Football Writers' Player and Manager of the Year awards ceremony. In those four weeks in May, George more than made up for his abstinence in Canada. Really, he should have carried a Government Health Warning. Livers were in for severe punishment when George was in town.

George, who looked like a cross between Fred Flintstone and a Giant Redwood tree, would start his drinking spree early in the morning over breakfast at his Glasgow 'lodgings', normally the old Albany Hotel in Bothwell Street, continue through lunch and meet up with some of the more foolhardy among the Daily Record sports staff in the evening when we went for our break, normally around 9pm after the first edition of the newspaper was rolling. We would go at it hammer and tongs for about an hour in the Off The Record pub beside our offices. A tidal wave of alcohol was consumed before we wandered back to the Sports Desk to somehow get out the later editions.

'See you in the Press Club,' George would say cheerily and some of us, including me, were daft enough to keep the date at the late-night drinking establishment in West Regent Street in Glasgow city centre. Back then, it was difficult to find a place selling booze after the 10pm shutdown. The Press Club often came to the rescue of thirsty newspaper hacks, lawyers, doctors, surgeons, dentists and other ne'er-do-wells.

George always travelled business class. He would save for eleven months in Toronto and do his best to spend the lot in the four weeks he was in Glasgow. He was a marvellous storyteller, too, and there was one he relayed to me over a few beers that I will never forget.

Apparently, George was flying out of Heathrow one morning bound for Toronto. The plane was packed as he took his seat beside a striking-looking gentleman with chiselled features and jutting square jaw. George didn't want to stare, but he recognised his fellow-passenger after a few squints.

'Charlton Heston?' he enquired. The movie star, smiled, said, 'Yup,' and shook George's hand. 'You're Scottish, huh? You can call me Chuck.'

Charlton Heston, real name John Charles Carter, was fiercely proud of his Scottish ancestry and was a member of the Fraser clan. It was no surprise he named his first-born son Fraser in recognition of his Scottish roots. I've read his autobiography, *In the Arena*, and it's peppered with tales of his descendants and his love of Scotland.

In fact, an agent for the actor got in touch with the Daily Record News Desk back in 1983 when Charlton was preparing to celebrate his sixtieth birthday on October 4. The Hollywood legend was eager to have a Scottish theme and he gave his agent the name of one particular personality he really wanted to attend his big day. The agent got a phone number for the Daily Record, Scotland's national newspaper as it proudly portrayed itself, and put a call in to the main switchboard where he was transferred to the News Desk. 'Can you help this American guy?'

The news reporter accepted the call and asked, 'How can I be of assistance?'

The agent identified himself, told him what it was all about and said Charlton Heston was insisting on this character coming to his birthday bash, all expenses paid.

'Who's the lucky chap?' asked the reporter. He was told the name.

'I'm afraid that's going to be a little difficult,' he said.

'Really? Chuck will be disappointed.' He added quickly, 'Look, if it's cash, there's nothing to worry about. Chuck will meet any appearance fee. All flights and accommodation will be first class. Nothing will be spared.'

The reporter sighed. 'No, it's got nothing to do with money.'

'What's the problem, then?'

'Rabbie Burns died in 1796.'

'Gee, really? Didn't know he was unwell. Chuck will be sorry to hear that.'

Anyway, back on the Jumbo, George and Chuck were getting on

famously. Gravel-voiced George was laying it on porridge-thick, sounding even more Scottish than he normally did.

'Glad you got rid of the beard, Chuck. Didn't do anything for you.'

'Oh, Moses? Yeah, very good, George.'

'You know, Chuck, you were one of my first sporting heroes. I thought you were brilliant in Ben-Hur. You and your white Egyptian horses in that chariot race with that actor Stephen Boyd. What was his name in the movie?'

'Messala,' answered Heston, happy to reminisce about the 1959 Oscar winner. 'You know, George, Marlon Brando, Burt Lancaster and Rock Hudson all turned down the Ben-Hur role?'

'Really? They wouldn't have been as good as you. That role was made for you. You were Ben-Hur.'

'Why thank you, George. Another drink?'

And so it went on until the Jumbo touched down in Toronto. They were now the best of friends, exchanging addresses and telephone numbers. They picked up their luggage and Charlton Heston said to George, 'Let's go to the bar. Let's have a couple of drinks before we say farewell.'

George had to decline the invitation. 'Sorry, Chuck, but that bunch of guys over there are waiting for me.'

'Bring them with you, George,' said Heston. 'Let's ALL have a drink.'

George rubbed his ample chin and said, 'That wouldn't be a good idea, Chuck.'

'Really? Why not?'

'They bet big money on Messala.'

Chapter 34

Hurricane snookered

A few of my colleagues enjoyed a game of snooker at the Press Club in Glasgow after they had completed their shifts at the Daily Record, normally beyond midnight. I discovered, to my dismay, it was yet another sport at which I was absolutely useless.

Mike Davidson, the newspaper's superb Sports Production Editor, fancied himself on the green baize and, with the little appreciation I had for the game, I have to say he looked the real deal with a cue. I used to wind up Mike constantly by insisting snooker was not a sport, but merely an irrelevant pastime; a parlour game, at best.

The game really took off during a time in the seventies when football was off the air following a row with the TV companies over cash. Snooker and darts were suddenly promoted to take the place vacated by the beautiful game and interest rocketed. Everyone wanted to be Steve Davis or Jocky Wilson; well, maybe not as boring or as overweight, but most pub-dwellers were quick to have a go with the cues and arrows. (I wasn't too bad at darts, but, for some obscure reason, my game disintegrated normally after my sixth or seventh pint.)

I recall an evening when Mike and I went up to the Press Club on West Regent Street. As usual, we went through for a beer, bypassing the snooker room, and Mike stuck up his quid at the bar to be next on the table. An hour passed and my mate was getting a bit edgy, obviously requiring his snooker 'fix'.

'Peggy, tell them to get a move on in there, will you?' asked Mike of the helpful barmaid. Another thirty minutes went by and Mike was getting more than a little frustrated. 'Peggy, give them a nudge, will you?' After another half-hour, Mike said, 'Right, that's it - I'm going through to get rid of those guys. Who the fuck do they think they are commandeering the table all night?'

One of them was an Irish bloke called Alex, better known as Hurricane Higgins. It was 1972 and he was the reigning world snooker champion.

It didn't stop Mike from telling him to bugger off.

Chapter 35

Brief encounter

As luck would have it, I was strolling through the Sunday Mail editorial early on a Saturday morning in May 1984. I was 'next door' doing my shift for the Sunday People when I wandered along to have a chat with some of my Daily Record colleagues who were doing stints for our Sunday sister.

It was the week before that great tribal gathering known as the Home International against England at Hampden. Apparently, there had been a deluge of fake, very authentic-looking, tickets on the market and Strathclyde's finest were getting more than a little anxious. I was chatting to one of my mates when Editor Endell Laird came over to the Sports Desk. 'Has anyone here got a ticket for next week's match?' he asked. Alex Cameron had furnished me with a pair only half an hour or so earlier. 'I've got two,' I said, 'but I'm not selling.'

'Oh, I don't want to buy them, Alex, I just want to get a photograph of one to stick on our front page. You can trust me, I'll get them right back to you.'

I trusted Endell - three years later he would take me from the Record to the Mail - and I handed over the precious briefs. I got them back shortly afterwards and I thought that was the end of the matter. The Sunday Mail did, in fact, publish an image of the Scotland v England ticket on their front page the following day. Unfortunately, they did so with the ticket number clearly visible; these days they would be airbrushed out as a matter of course. Not back in 1984, unfortunately. Early on Sunday morning, I received a call from Alex Cameron.

'Where on earth did the Mail get that ticket?' he asked.

'From me,' I answered innocently.

'Good Lord, that was one Ernie Walker passed onto me; it was part of his private stash. Now questions are being asked all over the SFA.'

Ernie 'Ayatollah' Walker

Oops. Ernie Walker, of course, was the secretary of the Scottish Football Association and here was one of his allocation of tickets appearing on the front page of a national newspaper with the serial number clearly visible and a headline roaring, 'BEWARE FAKES!'

I have to say, the SFA supremo had done nothing untoward, but this little revelation did highlight just how close he was to the Chief Sports Editor of the Daily Record. Thankfully, it blew over, but I learned a lesson that day. Keep your eye on the ball, I told myself.

I didn't really know Ernie Walker, who was a guest of Alex several times over the years at what was known as 'The Pie In The Sky', the executive canteen on the top floor of the newspaper building. When I became Sports Editor at the Sunday Mail I was given official clearance to join in with the great and the good upstairs. I never went once; a pint and a pizza in the Copy Cat were far more enticing. Anyway, Scottish football's supremo was often around the newspaper editorial and we met on several occasions although we never got around to exchanging addresses for Christmas cards.

However, I think I crossed him once. I had worked on a few Scotland international programmes and practically wrote the entire magazine for the Rous Cup match against England at Hampden in May 1985. Richard Gough scored the only goal that storm-lashed afternoon in Mount Florida and, later that evening, I found myself in the delightful company of Howard Kendall, who was manager of Everton at the time, in a pub called Cafe Zazou in Glasgow's York Street. The champagne was flowing and everyone was happy. I didn't realise it at the time, but that would be the last international programme to which I would contribute anything. I was dropped without an explanation. I wasn't even on the substitutes' bench.

Could it have been coincidence that I had dared to criticise Ernie Walker in a World Soccer column shortly after that? I disagreed with something he said and made it clear in print. I heard a whisper Ernie - christened 'The Ayatollah' by my pal Bertie Auld - had read the column and wasn't best pleased. I've no idea if he spat out the dummy, but I do know that was that door closed forever on that particular venture. Do you know something? I would have written the same article, word for word, even in the knowledge I would get the elbow for airing my views.

Mind you, I would have thought the SFA secretary might have become accustomed to criticism by then.

Chapter 36

Let there be light

Jack Middleton was a legendary photographer with the Glasgow Herald and Evening Times and known to all as a 'character', that fabulous all-embracing expression that sat so comfortably on this particular chap's shoulders.

My good friend George Wilkie was his long-suffering Picture Editor at the Herald when he ordered the snapper into the office for an early shift in late December one year. George recalls, 'We all knew Jack liked a good bucket and sometimes didn't know when to stop. Heaven forbid! However, I had a job that had to be done that morning and I didn't want him turning up smelling like a distillery.'

'The newspaper used to run an annual competition to find Miss Junior Evening Times. Some kid would get dressed up in all her finery, have her hair done at some top-class salon, be presented with a bouquet of flowers and be awarded a sash to wear on the big day. We would then take her to George Square where she would get her photograph taken to coincide with the Christmas Lights being switched on. So, I told Mid, as he was known, to make sure he was on his best behaviour. I didn't want him breathing on the wee lassie and knocking her out cold with stale whisky fumes.'

George was delighted when Mid turned up, sane, sober and set to go.

'Everything was going according to plan,' said George. 'The wee girl looked a treat and was so excited about her big day. Mid made a fuss of her and off they went to George Square to await some dignitary pushing the button to light up Glasgow city centre. Mid was there in plenty of time, but, unfortunately, the hospitality in the City Chambers seemed to be going on a bit too long. No-one appeared in a rush to kick-start the ceremony.

'Mid was not known for his patience. He was getting a tad irritated and slammed his photographer's case down on a raised platform. The case landed straight on top of a rather large button. Suddenly, to rapturous applause from thousands of spectators, George Square was illuminated; the Christmas Lights bursting to life. Mid took his pictures and beat a hasty retreat.'

It was never recorded what the Lord Provost and his guests thought when they looked out of the windows of the hospitality suite at the City Chambers to discover Glasgow city centre bathed in neon.

Chapter 37

Verbal assault and pepper

Rangers signed an Icelandic midfielder by the name of Therolf Beck in November 1964. He had made an initial impact at St. Mirren and that prompted the Ibrox club to snap him up for a nominal fee.

My old mate Alex Cameron loved telling the story about the player who was nicknamed 'Totty' by his new team-mates. The player did not have permanent residence in Scotland at the time and, as was the way of things, Rangers arranged for him to stay with a family in lodgings near Ibrox until suitable permanent housing could be located. Unfortunately, 'Totty', try as he might, did not have a good grasp of the English language. However, he did pick up a word or two from his colleagues during training.

On his first day at his new temporary lodgings, 'Totty' was introduced to the family; mum, dad, two sons and a daughter. He would get to know them a little better when he returned after training for dinner. The family set the table and the children were warned to be on their best behaviour in front of their guest, a famous Rangers footballer. The mother duly placed the soup starter in front of 'Totty' and provided for the rest of her family. All was going well until the Icelander attempted some broken English.

'Hey, you, bastard, pass the fuckin' salt.'

The mother apparently came to after a large shot of brandy.

Chapter 38

Smash-hit Goram

It was around 7pm on a Saturday night in the Sunday Mail editorial and the streets edition of the newspaper had already rumbled off the presses at Anderston Quay. It was time to take a breather after the hectic activity and to begin planning for the next edition heading for Aberdeen and surrounding areas.

The telephone on my extremely untidy, paper-strewn desk burst to life. 'Pest!' was my first thought. The amount of nuisance phone calls on a busy Saturday was enough to drive any man to strong drink. (Not that I ever needed an excuse. I'm still convinced I was the profit margin in The Copy Cat.)

I always smile at the recollection of the story I was told about one of my Sports Editor predecessors at the Sunday Mail, Adrian Hannigan, snapping after receiving his umpteenth interruption one Saturday. No matter how many requests were made to our switchboard to block these calls, the operators still fired everything through to the desk. Punters wanted to know what had won the fifth at Perth, what was the score with so-and-so, was Freddy Flypogger running at Shawfield that night? Everything and anything. Believe it or not, I was once asked this gem, 'How many haystacks are there in Wales?' Honest.

Comedians Andy Cameron and Frank Carson would often make midweek calls to the Record when they were on tour. Needless to say, they were not inquiring about the results of the same team from Glasgow. Remember, too, mobile phones were not around at the time. Information was not instantly available at your fingertips. And, at least, Andy and Frank knew the direct number to call.

Adrian Hannigan, one particular evening, had obviously had enough. He cracked.

'What do you do for a living?' he snarled at the caller.

'Oh, you're a plumber? Good for you. Give me your phone number and I'll phone you every five minutes and see how you like it. Okay?' And with that he slammed down the receiver.

So, when the instrument of extreme irritation buzzed yet again that evening, I couldn't help myself. 'Pest!'

I changed my mind as soon as I detected the voice of the individual on the other end of the line. It was a well-known Rangers player, a Scottish international and a genuine legend at Ibrox.

'Have you got anything decent on your back page?' he enquired.

'We've got a couple of reasonable tales,' I replied, adding swiftly, 'But I'll happily listen to anything you may have to tell me.'

The guy on the other end of the line never once asked me for a payment for a tip-off; not once. I knew he was a wealthy enough individual, so he wasn't looking for a quick buck. Money was never an incentive. I had known him for years, going back to my Daily Record days, and we got on well enough. He would do me a favour and I would return the compliment when I was in a position to do so. When I would offer cash, he would always answer, 'Buy me a pint the next time you see me.'

I was intrigued. 'Okay, what's so important that you need to get off your chest?'

'You should have been in our dressing room at the interval,' he laughed. 'It was like a scene from Apocalypse Now.'

Rangers had played Aberdeen that afternoon and had won 3-1 after being a goal down at half-time. I encouraged him, 'Okay, go on.'

'Well, you know The Goalie (Andy Goram) doesn't particularly like criticism from anyone?'

'Aye, your man will go toe-to-toe with anyone, we all know that.'

'Well, he laid into Nigel Spackman. Came close to knocking him cold. Two or three punches and Nigel was flat on his back, almost sparko. The physio had to revive him.'

'And what had Nigel done to incur the wrath of The Goalie?'

'He asked for it; he really did. Roy Aitken had just put the Dons ahead and Nigel made 'the wanker' hand gesture to Andy. That was a mistake because Andy was raging at losing a goal in the first place, but it was obvious Nigel thought he should have done better. Nigel then repeated the gesture and Andy looked as though he was about to do his impression of The Incredible Hulk, bursting through his goalkeeper's jersey. He thought he was being made to look a fool in front of 50,000 fans at Ibrox. He was fuckin' furious, to say the least. The half-time whistle went and Nigel was one of the first in the dressing room with The Goalie moving up the tunnel faster than anyone has seen him in their life. I swear steam was coming out of his ears.'

This is getting interesting, I thought.

'In the dressing room, Andy grabbed Nigel by the throat and threatened to kill him if he ever repeated those actions. Thankfully, the other players got in the middle of them and managed to quieten things down - for all of about three seconds. Nigel must have had a death wish today. He then called Andy "a fat bastard!" And that was when the whole place went up. The Goalie came out throwing punches from all angles. I thought it might be a good idea to watch this one from the safety of the exits. Nigel went down in a heap.'

At this point I checked the team lists and noted that Spackman had, in fact, played the entire second-half. I didn't think my Rangers mole was into over-exaggeration. I asked him about the miraculous recovery.

'The physio managed to get him back on his feet. He was a bit groggy, obviously. Who wouldn't be after being hit by a sledgehammer? Several times, too. But he insisted on going out for the second-half.'

'Anyone else witness this? Any doors lying open?'

'No, just the people who should have been in the vicinity.'

It was a good tale, a rammy in the Rangers dressing room at half-time and a player almost knocked unconscious. It was all explosive, readable stuff, but there was one problem, as far as I was concerned. Where on earth did I get that story? The dressing room was the sanctuary of Walter

Smith, his backroom team, the players and the bloke who made the tea. Who was my spy? The tale had to emanate solely from that area. I could run the story all over the back page. The story was authentic, I had absolutely no doubts about that, and, of course, it would have carried the banner EXCLUSIVE line. It is always highly satisfying to leave your rivals trailing in your slipstream on the following day's newsstands. It's easy to be tempted to publish and be damned, as they say. However, you have to think fast in these situations, despite the heady lure of massive headlines and a fabulous story.

I would have expected Rangers to immediately play everything down, possibly deny the entire incident had ever taken place. The players would have been asked, or ordered, to back up the official line. I would have been isolated and, fairly obviously, I wasn't a member of the dressing room to witness the fracas that day. One thing I wouldn't have done would be to name my informant. That was never going to be the merest of possibilities. It was an absolute non-starter. I prided myself on never revealing the names of my sources of information. I lost count of times I had been threatened by chairmen, directors, managers and even players about giving up the names of sources. I never did. For me, it wasn't an option. I'm far from being Peter Perfect, but that was a line I wouldn't cross.

I needed some corroborative evidence. Check and check again was the mantra with which I had been brought up. I could have phoned Walter Smith, of course. Don't think I would have got too far with that line of enquiry. I had a contact number for Andy Goram, but I didn't fancy *The Goalie* coming at me like a combined harvester. Nigel Spackman? He was hardly likely to want to go into print about being bounced around the dressing room by a team-mate. I realised, alas, I, too, would hit brick walls everywhere.

My Rangers mole had acted in good faith to give me a back page story. Clearly, he hadn't thought it through. Or maybe he trusted me never to finger him, if you pardon the expression. (We got on well, but maybe not THAT well.) However, to get myself off the hook all I had to do was name a name. I would have been in the clear and the spotlight would have swung elsewhere. And I wasn't prepared to do that. Undoubtedly, it would have soured relations with Rangers. Writs could have flown around like confetti in the wind. To be honest, I wasn't too bothered about that. We had many runs-ins with Rangers - and Celtic and just about everyone else, too - and we still kissed and made up. Eventually.

If I could have found another way of backing up the dressing room story, I would have run with it. Sadly, I couldn't. My only link to the story was the player who had spilled the beans.

That was in August 1992. The whole incident is told in Andy Goram's excellent autobiography *The Goalie*, co-written with Iain King, which was published in 2009. I could have had the tale all over the back page of the Sunday Mail seventeen years earlier. But someone would have paid a very heavy price. And it wouldn't have been me. A career at Rangers might have turned out slightly differently if that story had seen the light of day.

And you will never guess the identity of my Rangers Deep Throat!

Chapter 39

Press passes - part one

The latest recruit at the Daily Record's news desk didn't resemble the stereotype of a reporter. There was no obligatory shirt and tie for a start, but no doubt someone would drop a word in an appropriate ear at some stage in the near future.

The rookie wore a Fair Isle sweater over a rough denim shirt, brown baggy knuckle-cord trousers and well-worn tan brogues. At least, the novice on the editorial floor possessed a 'sensible' haircut that would have pleased the bosses. They frowned on newsmen representing the paper, knocking on doors of the public while looking as though they were rejects from the Rolling Stones. The newcomer had hair shaved into the wood.

After an hour or so, the eager apprentice was told a taxi was downstairs waiting to take them to a police station in the West End to pick up a 'collect' story; a routine tale of a burglary or some minor misdemeanour. It was a worthwhile exercise for the latest acquisition to the news staff. After grabbing a pen, notepad and bag, the reporter went to the back door to be picked up by the cabbie.

'You're a new face,' said the taxi driver. 'Where are you from?'

'Dundee,' he was informed.

'A wee word, if I may. If you go around with a handbag like that in Glasgow people will think you're a poof. What's your name, anyway, son?'

'Valerie,' she said.

*

It was more than just a shade advantageous that Anna Smith, the superb former chief news reporter of the Daily Record, was blessed with a cool sense of humour.

Anna, now an extremely fine and prolific writer of the Rosie Gilmour crime novels, was pitchforked into the minefield of a News Desk populated by a pile of hard-nosed greybeards on Scotland's biggest-selling daily newspaper.

One day, after another heavy session at the ever-demanding coalface of information-gathering, Anna made her way along the second floor editorial to grab an elevator to aid her escape.

The lift doors opened and a stranger asked, 'Going down?'

'My goodness, sir,' remarked Anna. 'We haven't even been formally introduced.'

*

Being the thoughtful bloke he was, Jack Adams would often invite me along when he was going for lunch with a celebrity. 'It will let you see that they are human beings in real life,' he would say.

One day, we picked up Rangers skipper John Greig, one of the most famous footballers in Scotland at the time, as we headed into the city centre to source an eaterie.

As the taxi was heading up Hope Street, Jack spotted a poor soul struggling with crutches, his right leg heavily encased in plaster. 'Hey, Greigy,' he said, 'is that not the guy who was playing against you the other day?'

The Ibrox legend immediately responded, 'Don't think so. He can still hobble, can't he?'

*

Martin Wright was a guy with one of the best jobs in newspaper; he was a glamour photographer.

I suppose it is difficult to frown when you've spent all day clicking away at an array of voluptuous beauties in various stages of undress. So, when Martin was mugged walking along the Broomielaw one dark evening on his way towards the city centre, he couldn't help laughing at his assailant, who actually relied on a walking stick and was wearing a camouflage jacket.

'You can't run, but you can hide,' said Martin.

*

Stan Shivas was a chief features writer par excellence. I would have happily paid to work alongside this flamboyant character, with his spectacular reminisces of a bygone age in journalism.

No-one ever saw Stan with a notepad. Remarkably, he would utilise a cigarette packet for interviews that could somehow, magically, stretch to about sixty paragraphs across a full spread in the Daily Record.

We were having a couple of refreshments in the Copy Cat one Saturday afternoon in 1979, after Stan had just returned from collecting a whole list of 'exclusive' interviews with the star cast of a movie being made in Kent of an Agatha Christie whodunnit, *The Mirror Crack'd*. My pal, who never used a tape recorder, was talking about some wonderful stuff he had unearthed in conversations with the likes of Elizabeth Taylor, Tony Curtis, Kim Novak and Edward Fox. He was a bit puzzled, though, about the antics of one of the major names in the cast.

He observed, 'As soon as filming finishes, he begins walking in a very odd manner. His voice even changes, almost falsetto. I've even seen him doing embroidery in between 'takes'. It's very mystifying.'

It was another six years before Rock Hudson, after months of speculation over his sexual preferences, died of AIDS.

*

There was a strict jacket, shirt and tie rule at the Glasgow Press Club.

It was probably written in ink, with a quill and implemented when Queen Victoria was still on the throne. If you weren't properly attired, there was no entrance to the establishment. And there were no exceptions. It was just as well there was no ruling on trousers, or the Alexander Brothers would have been barred for life (missed opportunity there, methinks).

One evening, in 1971, a formidable lady called Peggy was in charge. A crowd of about twenty very thirsty guys appeared at the door seeking admission to the club.

Peggy checked them out and was totally unimpressed by their lack of neckwear.

'You can't come in here,' she barked in her strictest tones.

They tried to protest, but Peggy stood firm.

'No chance,' she insisted. 'On your bike.'

Beaten, they had to hold up their hands in surrender. Johan Cruyff and his Ajax teammates filed silently back down the stairs.

After dismissing Celtic in the quarter-final, the laid-back Dutchmen won the European Cup two months later, beating Greek side Panathinaikos in the final at Wembley. They would successfully defend it for the next two years.

Bet they were glad they never had to try to get past Peggy again, though.

*

It would be reasonable to assume that most operators working in a national newspaper's editorial would possess even a minimal grasp of geography. Not one sub-editor in the Daily Express back in 1977.

Scotland had just beaten Wales 2-0 at Anfield on the evening of October 12 to book their qualification spot in the 1978 World Cup Finals in Argentina. A huge front page x-reference the following morning screamed ...

'RIO HERE WE COME!'

There was a bit of a purge at the Daily Record and Sunday Mail in the eighties, when the powers-that-be decided to investigate the alcohol consumption of both editorials.

The 'caring' bosses were eager for their employees to undergo medicals; the bill to be picked up by the Mirror Group. It was a ruse, of course. They didn't really care if an individual was near death's door; they merely wanted to identify the serious bevvy merchants.

Jim Blair, a gifted and very individualistic sports writer, was one of the first to go for a medical.

'Do you drink?' asked a nurse.

'Aye, I'll have a large gin and tonic, please,' he answered.

*

Former Celtic star Paddy Crerand won a European Cup medal with Manchester United in 1968, and now has his own show on MUTV. But he's a dangerous man to sit beside when he is doing his co-commentary on matchday.

Reporter Stewart Gardner was covering a pre-season game against Yokohama Marinos live on air when he said, 'He's a hard man to mark.'

'Whit?' asked Crerand in his best Gorbals tone.

'He's a hard man to mark,' repeated the reporter.

'Oh, thank God for that,' gasped Paddy, 'I thought you said something else instead of mark.'

The Scot is seen as a bit of a cult down Old Trafford way.

*

John Lees was as thin as a rake and about 6ft 6in tall. He looked like a well-dressed Hen Broon with a grey wig. He was a senior executive on the Daily Record backbench when I first joined the Sports Desk in 1967.

One evening, when I was left to man the fort while my colleagues took their break at 9pm, the daunting figure of the editorial gaffer loomed over me. He held a page proof, put it down in front of me and said in a very proper Kelvinside manner, 'Get rid of the flies' arseholes, please.' Then he strode back to his desk.

Flies' arseholes? What the hell were flies' arseholes? This was a journalistic term I hadn't encountered in my few months in the job. I looked at the page proof. I scrutinised it. I turned it upside down. Reversed it. I hadn't a clue. I didn't want to appear naive or ignorant, so I did not question Big John's orders. Nor did I want to disturb my work mates as they indulged in their nightly pursuit of attempting to drink the Garrick pub dry.

What was I to do? Flies' arseholes? I had a pal, Jimmy Miller, who worked on the Art Desk. Casually, doing my best not to attract the attention of John Lees, I meandered over to Jimmy. 'What the fuck are flies' arseholes?' I asked in hushed tones. What was this secretive journalistic 'in' phrase? I was informed by my mate and, a lot wiser, I returned to my desk to carry out my instructions.

How was I supposed to know that flies' arseholes was the term for small head pictures?

*

Bruce Camlin was the Daily Record's Deputy News Editor at the time and was far from satisfied with a report that was being filed about a fire in a manse outside Oban.

He grabbed the copy-taker's earphones and yelled down the receiver at the rookie reporter, 'This stuff is fuckin' dull. Put some fuckin' colour into it.'

The nervous news reporter came back on with a fresh story five minutes later. 'There was a big red fire in a black night in Oban when the

169

grey manse was set alight. The bright red fire machines arrived outside the green gates ...'

*

One of Robert Maxwell's many little foibles was his insistence on his editorial executives looking youthful and vibrant. Despite being one himself, he wasn't too keen on old fogeys.

I don't suppose anyone should have been unduly surprised one morning when one of his toadies, who had appeared quite comfortable with his greying thatch for years, suddenly appeared with Adolf Hitler-like jet black hair. No mention was made of the startling metamorphosis of his barnet at that morning's editorial conference, but I don't suppose he was too happy when I christened him 'Sooty'. He never remarked on the dramatic transformation of his follicles.

Just as well Cap'n Bob didn't reveal a hankering for executives to paint their face purple, wear lederhosen and take up Swahili as their language of choice.

*

The workers in the Caseroom department enjoyed partying. If there were any who doubted this fact, their notions were surely laid to rest after one particular boisterous Christmas night-out. Alas, the rowdy celebrations got too much for a retired compositor, who was also laid to rest a few days later.

After a booze cruise round the hostelries of the city, the lads eventually fetched up at the old haunt of The Montrose. The lumpy stuff - Christmas Dinner to you and me - was swiftly dispensed with as the newspaper contingent felt compelled to dive into their individual vats of alcohol. By the time they reached The Montrose they were all heading for Jupiter.

The singing, dancing and bevvying continued in the lounge until someone noticed Large Lionel, his age pegged at around the mid-seventies, wasn't exactly participating in the joyous fracas. In fact, Large Lionel, sitting in a corner seat and propped up against the wall, wasn't doing too much at all, including breathing. Large Lionel had passed on.

An ambulance was called and the Caseroom veteran was carted off. If his fellow-workers were devastated by his demise, they hid it exceptionally well. By the time I arrived at the pub later that evening, the party was still in full swing. I was informed of Large Lionel's final farewell.

One of the Caseroom guys told me sombrely, 'Lionel always was a tight-fisted old git. He would do anything to get out of buying his round.'

*

Lachie Kennedy was a Daily Record news reporter whose true love in life was DIY. Lachie, a lovely chap, was a bloke to avoid at the bar in the Copy Cat. If you were trapped by the newsman you knew you were about to learn, inside an hour, how to assemble a castle, strip the Waverley from stern to bow, or varnish the inside of a chimney pot. Lachie was the DIY enthusiast's idea of a DIY enthusiast. What that guy couldn't do with a screw driver.

One day, a veteran army photographer arrived in the Copy Cat. He had just flown back from the Falklands and was waiting for a reporter to arrive to arrange an interview. He was still in his best BDU (Battle Dress Uniform), all the camouflage combat gear, the huge military boots, the beret pulled down tight onto his aviator sunglasses. He had two 'Long Tom' cameras strapped across his chest, looking for all the world like machine guns. This guy could have just stepped out of *Platoon*.

Lachie entered the pub, glanced at Action Man who gave the impression he had been in the thick of it in Goose Green twenty-fours earlier, moved to the bar, ordered his usual pint of heavy and took stock of the situation.

'You should see the queues outside B&Q in Kirkintilloch,' he said.

*

171

A veteran sports reporter from Edinburgh was asked to cover a boxing bout at Glasgow's Kelvin Hall for TV. He was sitting ringside as he set the scene for a heavyweight fight between a black American and a white British opponent.

'The boxers are easily identifiable,' reported the experienced hack to the viewers. 'The American has a white stripe down his shorts.'

*

Celtic had just beaten Rangers 1-0 through a goal from Joe Miller in the 1989 Scottish Cup Final and, after returning from Hampden, I was working on the second edition of the Sunday Mail. The back page headline was *Joe Cool*, and there were two large photographs to supplement the words; one of Miller scoring the goal and another with ecstatic manager Billy McNeill and Co holding aloft the trophy.

I received a phone call from a pal by the name of Ricky, who is best described as Glasgow's answer to Arthur Daley. My mate, a well-known Celtic supporter, had seen the first edition and asked if he could have the picture of Joe Miller's goal. I trusted Ricky completely, so, of course, I told him, 'No chance!' The copyright belonged to the Mirror Group and I could envisage that snap copied a thousand times, shoved into dodgy frames and on sale at the Barras the following day. Ricky was persistent. 'Honest, Alex, I've got no intention of doing such a thing.'

Eventually, I relented. Ricky appeared at the back door of the newspaper building about five minutes later and I passed on the photograph. 'This isn't going to reappear in frames all over Glasgow tomorrow, is it?' I asked. 'You've got my word,' he said. 'I'll get it back to you next week.'

It got to around nine o'clock in the evening and, needless to say, I had worked up quite a thirst. All the editions were rolling along on schedule and I told my deputy, Alex McLeod, that I was nicking out for an hour to The Montrose. It was a fairly unique Glasgow hostelry because it was frequented by both sets of the Old Firm support; the Celtic fans in the lounge and their Rangers counterparts in the bar. And never the twain etc.

I walked into the lounge that evening where I knew Ricky would be in attendance. It was bedlam. It looked as though the Celtic end at Hampden had decanted into this one area. The owner, Jim Cullen, had erected a massive marquee in the car park, safe in the knowledge it was a no-lose situation. Either half of his boozer would be celebrating that night. There must have been about four hundred fans in the place. And I believe every single one of them was wearing a T shirt proudly displaying a large image of Joe Miller's winning goal. They even had the words 'JOE COOL' emblazoned across their chests.

Everywhere I looked I saw that damn picture. If it had been a commercial venture, the photographer who took that snap could have retired there and then and would probably be rubbing yachts with Roman Abramovich somewhere exotic in the Med to this day.

Ricky fought his way through the throng and handed me a T shirt. 'And you thought I was going to put that picture in a frame,' he chided.

Chapter 40

Chic Murray: the best bar none

Chic Murray ... natty bunnet, deep pockets

Chic Murray was one of my favourite comedians. You had to be in sync with his lateral thinking, or you would be left just a tad bewildered. 'Are you very small or are you just standing far away?' See what I mean?

'I call my wife "dear" because she has horns on her head.' Or 'I was walking over the Kingston Bridge the other day and there was a chap in the Clyde yelling, "I can't swim ... I can't swim." I said, "I can't play golf, but I don't shout about it."' Or 'I was walking down Sauchiehall Street. I knew this because I kept putting one foot in front of the other.'

All wonderful stuff if your head's not plugged in properly. So, naturally, I thought the material was fabulous.

The genius that was Chic Murray is no longer with us, of course, and I'm sure he wouldn't mind me making this observation. As he might have put it, he appeared to have an impediment in his reach - especially when there was a bar somewhere in the vicinity.

Back in the seventies, seemingly from nowhere, Chic began appearing in the Off The Record pub around the back of nine o'clock most weeknights. That coincided with the Daily Record Sports Desk evacuating to that particular watering hole once we were satisfied the first edition was rolling off the presses at Anderston Quay. In normal circumstances, there would be about three or four thirsty hacks making their way to my pal Gerry McCabe's smashing wee howf.

We were having a few beers at the bar one evening when in walked the irrepressible Chic and straight into our company. 'Hi, lads, a wee half when you've got a minute.' No preamble. He would ask us the usual questions about sport and football, in general. No-one wondered about the stranger in our midst as we all assumed he must have been an acquaintance of one of us. The drinking, and, trust me, it could be a ferocious hour, took us to ten o'clock. That was the break over, and we headed back to the editorial to put together later editions. 'So, that's the norm, lads?' asked Chic. 'Nine till ten? Interesting.'

The following night, we were back at the bar and in strolled Chic. 'Fancy meeting you guys here,' he said, left eyebrow arching upwards. 'A wee half when you've got a minute.' The following evening, the same script. 'We can't go on meeting like this. A wee half when you've got a minute.' An action replay twenty-four hours later. No-one said anything for fear of offending Chic's 'chum', but it was rather obvious he wasn't reciprocating on the booze-buying front. He wasn't playing the game; he wasn't getting his round in. I think one of us made a joke about 'short arms and deep pockets', but Chic didn't crack a light. This went on throughout the week. Eventually, one of us asked, 'Who owns Chic?' No-one took responsibility.

A quick bit of investigative work was called for. It transpired a relation of Chic - I think it was an editorial secretary - had joined the Daily Record and had casually mentioned to her uncle the nocturnal daily feverish drinking habits of the thirsty hacks on the Sports Desk. The comedian lived in the west end of Glasgow at the time and could take the quick train journey to Anderston station and walk the short distance to Off The Record.

After a while, the guys on the Sports Desk were contemplating clubbing together to hire a bouncer to throw Chic at the bar when it was his turn to get a round in.

We were sure Chic would see the funny side.

Chapter 41

Explosive stuff in the Copy Cat

Over the years at the Daily Record and the Sunday Mail, editorial staff were routinely warned to be on their guard. There was always the alleged threat of the building being blown up by the IRA, UDA, SFA, AA (probably the Automobile Association AND Alcoholics Anonymous) and all sorts of so-called terrorist organisations.

I'm sure even Women Against Tiddlywinks were unhappy with the newspapers over some perceived insult. It was almost a daily occurrence that 'today's going to be the day' when our workplace was going to be blasted to smithereens and everyone with it. Strange how you take little things like that in your stride.

One afternoon in the 'doocot' of the Copy Cat - the nearest pub on the Broomielaw beside the newspaper building at Anderston Quay - there was the usual scrum of journalists around the podium. The 'doocot' was actually designed for the use of the residents of the hostel around the corner, while the pub planners had conjured up a vast and more luxurious lounge for the newspaper workers. So, being the odd people we are, we headed for the smallest area in the hostelry and our friends from next door got the more spacious and opulent settings of the lounge.

Hopefully, this won't surprise you, but three guys I thoroughly enjoyed sharing a pint and a blether with were blokes from the hostel called John The Pipe (don't ask), Little Michael and Harry. Three excellent characters with some truly wonderful tales to tell. They fitted in well to the editorial's madcap coterie.

The 'doocot' could probably comfortably hold around fifteen people. On any given afternoon, it would usually be packed with about fifty. These were the bad old days when smoking was allowed in pubs and how my colleagues enjoyed that freedom. As a non-smoker, I didn't quite match their enthusiasm for shoving a weed in my face and puffing away merrily like a steam train, before immediately replacing it with another. The walls of that particular part of the establishment had to be repainted about three or four times a year, and I had to get a mortgage to cover the cleaning bill for my clothes.

I guess we all knew that the large, raised circular table at which we gathered wasn't actually a podium. A podium, technically, is a raised platform upon which a person may stand. However, someone had christened it a podium and the name stuck. Anyway, it was another quiet afternoon in the doocot (which wasn't actually a doocot, either) with the wee tucked-away area resembling something out of fog-filled Victorian London. Jack The Ripper could have run amok in there and no-one would have noticed.

The drinks, as usual, were flying around at a steady rate. Jokes were being told, confidences being broken and backs being stabbed, the habitual passing of time for most of my colleagues. It would be fair to say they all enjoyed their daily bit of teetle-tattle. 'I'll have a gin with a little dash of character assassination, please.'

Oh, how I miss those days of whine and neuroses.

Gordon Blair, known simply as 'Yogi', was a good friend of mine and that guy could get you into all sorts of trouble. 'Yogi' and I often covered the same game on a Saturday - he did a shift for his dad John at the Sunday People and I would normally get the gig from the Daily Record, Sunday Mail and Sunday Mirror. Our normal haunts were Morton, Kilmarnock, Airdrie, Motherwell and Falkirk. Lord help those quaint little airts and pairts of our wonderful country when Yogi and I were joined by Jim Blair, no relation to Gordon, when he was working for the Evening Times. Jim was known as 'The Sundance Kid', so when we three hombres were in town it wasn't a bad idea to batten down the hatches.

Please allow me to break in here for a moment just to underline once again how off-the-wall journalists were back then. We had a political writer called Stewart McLauchlan and he resembled Jack Nicklaus just a little. So, of course, he was nicknamed 'Golden Bear'. His assistant was a bloke called Alasdair Buchan, whose dad Norman was a prominent Labour politician. Alasdair was known as 'Boo Boo'. Two great lads, as I recall. Anyway, if Stewart, Gordon and Alasdair arrived in the pub at the same time, strangers in the boozer may have been a little curious as to why the rest of us went through the ritual of loudly welcoming the trio with the a rapturous, 'Hello, Golden Bear! Hello, Yogi! Hello, Boo Boo!' (You don't even want to know about the four female writers who answered to 'Hubble, Bubble, Toil and Trouble'.) Told you we were odd.

In 1976, 'Yogi' joined the Daily Mirror in London as their Showbiz Editor and quickly became a frequent visitor - well, mainly when there was a 'y' in the day - to the White Hart pub in Fleet Street. It was known as 'The Stab' to the newspaper workers. The pub had a little lounge round the corner and it was christened 'The Stab In The Back'. Yes, I'm afraid to admit, a few of my colleagues were just a tad two-faced. I was brought up with the mantra that it was better to have a true enemy than a false friend and that has stuck with me all my life.

'Yogi', who later moved into PR and represented personalities such as Dennis Waterman and Freddie Starr, would tell me stories about his London colleagues attempting to shaft each other. He always insisted, 'In London, they use scalpels; in Glasgow, it's machetes.'

Anyway, on this particular afternoon around the podium, it was no different from any other as reputations were being shredded and egos shattered. Suddenly, though, the clamour died down as the door to the doocot opened just a few inches and a small green spherical-like object was thrown into the middle of our part of the boozer.

'GRENADE!' screamed someone.

I've never seen the place empty so quickly. Bodies were climbing over each other, wildly overweight individuals were vaulting the bar, elbows were pushed into faces as out-of-condition hacks fought to get out the door and others dived behind chairs as the 'grenade' rolled inexorably towards its destination. It came to a halt at the podium. For whatever reason, in an instant, I was convinced it was just a joke; a sick one, maybe, but I believed it was a hoax. Either that, or I was about to become what was known as a 'two-mile job'; my head found two miles from my torso. Possibly, I had been working in newspapers too long to be taken in. I had the 'doocot' virtually to myself as I picked up the 'grenade'. It was a kid's toy, but it certainly did look like the real thing. I gave it a shake just to make sure.

My colleagues slowly made their way back into the pub. 'We knew it was a fake,' they chorused, as they wiped the sweat from their brows and a few were overcome by the urgent desire to visit the loo. I smiled, but a thought did occur later on that evening in the cold light of day. What if it had been a real grenade? Some organisation could have wiped out a fair chunk of the Daily Record and Sunday Mail editorials at a stroke without having to go anywhere near the actual newspaper.

It wasn't worth thinking about.

No-one ever did own up, but I'm sure I detected a larger than usual smile on the lips of John The Pipe that day ...

Chapter 42

The Godfather, Guff and Gowf

Robert Duvall promised Ally McCoist the bright lights of Hollywood. Instead, Wee Ally had to settle for the second-hand floodlights of Broadwood.

In 2001, it appeared that the Rangers legend, having conquered everything put in front of him on the football fields of Scotland, had set his sights on becoming a celluloid superstar. And Robert Duvall, of *The Godfather* fame, was the Svengali who was about to mastermind the remarkable transformation from red cards to red carpet.

Duvall was confident he could catapult McCoist towards movie stardom, firing his name onto the gigantic billboards alongside Brad Pitt, Johnny Depp and George Clooney. The film providing the magic carpet to a glittering new career was to be called *A Shot At Glory*. A wee team called Kilnockie, from a small fishing town, was about to gatecrash the big-time after winning through to the Scottish Cup Final where they were to meet, of all clubs, Rangers. It was a tale of inspiration and aspiration laced with romance. Duvall hoped it had all the ingredients of a money-spinning blockbuster.

In truth, alas, it was a Tinseltown turkey, a movie that went straight to the toilet. If they had billed it as a comedy and given Duvall's role to Leslie Neilson it might have stood a chance. There was never a hope in hell of a meeting with Oscar at the Academy Awards later that year.

However, the making of this clunker did provide some genuine moments of fun as Duvall, whose character Gordon McLeod was apparently based on a mixture of Jock Stein and Bill Shankly, starred alongside Michael Keaton, the 1989 version of *Batman*, and Dundee's own Brian Cox; no, not the nerdy know-all, but the veteran of such movies as *The Bourne Identity*, *Day of the Triffids*, *Scooby Doo and The Samurai Sword* (voice only).

181

Many extras were involved in the 'exciting' match scenes when the Knockies, as they were known, were on their march towards the national stadium for their day in the sun. Most of the scenes were shot in Crail, Fife, and several stand-ins were players from Raith Rovers, including future Celt Didier Agathe. Manager John McVeigh also got a role as a coach. It had all the makings of a smash-miss.

One of the extras was a footballer with a First Division club who, unfortunately, was inflicted with a dreadful stutter. It couldn't have helped his career much considering he was a goalkeeper. One night Duvall wined and dined the players at a hotel in Dumfries. It was an overnight stay with some footage being shot the following morning. The veteran actor reminded everyone that it was important to be on set at the appointed hour. Everyone nodded in agreement; they had an epic to make and they were ready to play their part.

Duvall said his goodnights just after 9pm and was already halfway up the stairs leading to his room when a voice cried out from the lounge where the players were mingling.

'Hhhhhey, Rrrrobert, is that yyyou aaaway fffor a wwwee ... wwwee ... wwwank?'

Duvall smiled back and then continued his progress to his room. To this day, it's quite possible he still hasn't a clue what he was asked.

And I'm sure the American was scratching his head on another occasion when the Knockies were due to do some film work at Partick Thistle's ground at Firhill. Here's how Chic Charnley, one of the Jags' all-time greats, told the tale when I co-authored his book, *Seeing Red*, in 2009.

'Amazingly, the Hollywood icon ended up in the heart of Possil one morning when no-one could get access to the ground. A lady called Brenda was the keyholder and she hadn't turned up one day. It appeared no-one else had a key. John McVeigh, who, of course, had actually managed Thistle, had the solution. "I know where Brenda stays in Possil. I'll drive over there just now and pick up the keys." Duvall, rather surprisingly, agreed to join John in the drive through Glasgow. They duly arrived at the close where Brenda stayed and Duvall must have thought he was back in the Bronx. There was graffiti everywhere as he and John made their way to Brenda's door. They rang the bell. No answer. They rattled on the door. Still no answer.

'Suddenly, there was a voice coming from the stairwell above them. A young boy peered down and asked, "Are you looking for Brenda?" "Aye," said John. "You've just missed her, mister. She left about five minutes ago." The lad must have been a fan of films because he actually recognised Duvall. "Hey, are you that wee fuckin' actor?" queried the urchin. Duvall agreed he was, indeed, that "wee fuckin' actor". John and the movie legend were walking out of the close when they heard the plea from behind them, "Gonnae lend me a tenner, pal?"'

Grade Z listers ... Ally McCoist and Robert Duvall

Duvall arrived alongside Billy Connolly for the Scottish Football Writers' Player and Manager of the Year award night at the Glasgow Hilton in May that year. I was standing at the bar with a few friends before waiting to take our seats. One of the guys in my company was a former executive of *Scotsport*, which, at that stage, was the longest-running sports show in the history of television. I'll spare the chap's blushes, but, trust me, this is a true story.

He had been going on endlessly about how much he loved the movies of Robert Duvall. *Lonesome Dove,* an acclaimed western mini-series in the late eighties, was one of his all-time favourites. Apparently, my friend had the DVD, with a running time of 384 minutes, and had watched it on countless occasions. He hoped to meet Duvall that evening to have a quick word and perhaps even, if he was fortunate, an autograph.

'Your time has come,' I told him at one point. 'The Great Man has arrived.' Duvall had entered the lounge and looked like a fairly approachable bloke. 'On you go,' I urged. 'You'll never get a better chance to meet your hero.' My mate threw back his whisky, straightened his shoulders and said firmly, 'This is it.' Then he practically marched in the general direction of the actor. I watched as the scenario unfolded. They met and shook hands. They chatted for a moment and then my friend stepped back abruptly, turned and walked towards the bar, looking completely crimson-faced.

'What's the problem?' I asked.

'I don't believe it,' he said. 'My all-time screen hero, too.'

'What went wrong?'

'I only called him David, didn't I?'

Unfortunately, my mate was also a golf nut and, in particular, a massive fan of a former world No.1 from Jacksonville, Florida. His nickname was Double D. His parents, Mr and Mrs Duvall, alas, decided to christen their son … David.

Chapter 43

Fish and the four-letter word

Fraser Elder was working as a journalist on *Reporting Scotland* when he was asked to take a camera crew to Peterhead to cover a story that was creating a bit of consternation with the fishing community. Apparently, there had been the construction of a coal-fired power station in the vicinity of the harbour and some particles were dropping out of the chimneys onto the trawlers as they brought in that day's catch.

Fraser, known to everyone in the trade as Fraz, duly travelled north from Glasgow to the port and was surprised when there wasn't a single vessel in sight. 'We hung around for about an hour with nothing happening. Then a trawler came into sight. It was like something out of *Para Handy*. We were all delighted; at last we could do an interview.

'This craggy-faced old chap berthed the trawler and then hauled himself up a ladder to the harbour's surface. I asked him if he had any objections to giving *Reporting Scotland* an interview to get across his side of the story. He was only too happy to talk. And I mean talk. I asked him about the smoke belching out of the nearby chimneys. He ignored the question.

'He pointed to the boat. He said, "That's ma two weans there helping me, ye ken. That's Jamie there and his wifey has just got hersel' pregnant. And that's Wee Ewan and he's just bought himsel' a new motor. We need the money, ye ken. And we go oot in a' sort of weather to get the very best fish. We've got the best haddock and we've got the best cod, ye ken. And then we tie up here at the harbour and that's something we've been daein' fur years wi' nae problems. Noo, though, we've got a' this soot and stuff coming oot yon chimneys and it comes ower here and lands oan oor catch. And the fish're fucked."'

Fraz called a halt to the interview. 'I'm sorry,' he told the trawlerman, 'we can't have that word on television.'

'Whit word would that be?' asked the fisherman innocently.

'Fucked,' replied Fraz. 'We're not allowed to say "fucked" on television. Can you use another word, please?'

'Aye, okay, Ah ken other words.'

'Right.' said Fraz. 'We'll need to start filming from the start. Okay?'

'Aye, fine, nae problem, ye ken.'

Fraz asked the question, 'How are these chimneys interfering with your catch?'

Once more, the trawlerman ignored the question. He started off again, pointing to his sons on the boat. 'That's ma two weans helping me, ye ken. That's Jamie there and his wifey has just got hersel' pregnant. And that's Wee Ewan and he's just bought himsel' a new motor.' It was word for word perfect. Then he came to the end of the monologue. 'Noo we've got a' that soot and stuff comin' oot yon chimneys and it comes ower here and lands oan oor catch. The fish're fucked.'

Fraz blinked. 'You've just said "fucked" again. We can't use "fucked" on the television. I told you that.'

'Christ, did I say "fucked" again? Ah'm awfy sorry,' said the contrite fisherman.

Fraz looked at his watch. Time was against them. The cameraman told him the film would have to get to the Aberdeen studios to be developed before it could be transmitted. These were the days before videos, remember.

Fraz took the trawlerman aside. 'Okay, we'll give it one more go. We want to give your side of the story, you understand? But, please, for God's sake, don't use the word "fucked" again. Remember, don't say "fucked".'

'Right, Ah ken,' said the interviewee. 'Don't say "fucked", Callum,' he said to himself. 'Nae "fucked", okay?'

Fraz began the interview for the third time. Once more, he tried to cut to the chase, but Callum was having none of it. He pointed to the boat. 'That's ma two weans helping me, ye ken. That's Jamie there and his wifey's got hersel' pregnant. And that's Wee Ewan and he's just got himsel' a new motor.' And so on until that last sentence. 'Noo we've got a' this soot and stuff comin' oot yon chimneys and it comes ower here and lands oan oor catch. The fish're fucked.'

Fraz went ballistic. 'For fuck's sake stop saying "fucked", will you? We can't use that fuckin' word. I've told you.'

The BBC guys gave it another go. And another. It appeared Callum just couldn't finish a sentence without the word "fucked".

Fraz pulled him aside for the sixth time. 'This is the last time we're going to do this, okay? We're running out of time. It's now or never. Okay?'

The trawlerman nodded. 'Right, Callum, don't say the word "fucked". They cannae use that in Glesca. Nae "fucked."' Callum composed himself. 'Right Ah'm ready.'

Fraz dutifully asked him the original question and, once again, the trawlerman launched into his monotonous monologue. He pointed to the boat. 'That's ma two weans helping me, ye ken. That's Jamie there and his wifey's got hersel' pregnant. And that's Wee Ewan and he's just got himsel' a new motor.' Then came the moment of truth. 'Noo we've got a' that soot and stuff comin' oot yon chimneys and it comes ower here and lands oan oor catch.'

There was a dramatic pause before the trawlerman took a deep breath and continued. 'And the fish're ...' He struggled for the word. He took another stab at it. 'And the fish're ...'

'Fucked?' offered Fraz helpfully before he could stop himself.

Chapter 44

Small talk with Bertie Auld

Bertie Auld was sitting opposite me across the lounge table in the Georgics Bar at the Millennium Hotel in Glasgow sometime in March 2008. I was 'ghosting' his autobiography, *A Bhoy Called Bertie*, and I have to say it was an enjoyable and exhilarating experience. Wee Bertie, a genuine legend, had just so much to tell and I was getting it all down on paper. They say there is a book in everyone; in Bertie's case there is a library.

Bertie Auld ... with the European Cup and his brilliant autobiography *A Bhoy called Bertie*

I don't use a dictaphone and I have never been taught shorthand, so when I've conducted interviews, I've always relied on a 'bullet' word in a sentence. With some main words jotted down, I've always found it possible to go back and construct paragraphs. Probably not too conventional, but it works for me.

I realised with Bertie around I was going to get through more than one or two notebooks. The Celtic icon is a born storyteller. Anyone else in the Georgics Bar around the time of putting the book together must have wondered what was going on at our table, normally one tucked right in the corner of the glass-fronted dining area. My wife Gerda and I were often doubled up with laughter at some of Bertie's tales - and, remarkably, we could even put some of them in his book.

On this particular day, I was searching again for a story that no-one knew about, a tale that had never been aired for public consumption. Trust me, that is no easy task when you are dealing with a guy such as Bertie Auld and you consider the amount of newspaper and magazine column miles that have been devoted to this colourful character during his days as a fantastic player and manager. He was never camera shy, either. So, roughly twice weekly, we would meet and pour over the anonymous good old days. 'I've got a good one no-one has heard before,' said Bertie. 'Did you know I used to drive a taxi for a living?'

'No,' I answered. 'When was that?'

'Oh, I had just left Partick Thistle after my second stint as boss,' answered Bertie. 'It was 1986 and I found myself out of a job for a wee while. Nothing was opening up for me on the football front. I was only forty-eight and wasn't quite ready for the pipe and slippers. I wanted to keep active and someone suggested taking up taxiing.'

'How did you get a licence?' I asked, scribbling away in the notebook.

'Oh, that was no problem,' said Bertie. 'I actually got one back in the sixties in my early days with Celtic. I thought it might come in handy. I sat another exam on the quiet and I was good to go. Obviously, I wanted to keep it all hush-hush. I looked out the biggest bunnet in my wardrobe and plonked it on my head. I found the longest scarf I could wrap around my face about six times. I always wore a jacket where you could push up the collar. Liz, my missus, would have had difficulty recognising me.'

'And you got away with it?' I was astounded. A Lisbon Lion driving a taxi around Glasgow and no-one twigged? And especially such a famous face, too.

'Aye,' said Bertie. 'I admit I was a wee bit apprehensive about my knowledge of the streets because, although I had passed my exam, I was still a bit in the dark about all the changes in the city. Obviously, there was no such thing as sat-nav in those days, either. I joined the taxi rank outside Queen Street and I couldn't believe my luck when I got my first hire. I helped this old lady in with her shopping and I was so happy when she asked me to take her to an address in Maryhill, my old stomping ground. I was delighted. So, I drove her to her front door and looked at the meter and told her what it cost. She said nothing.'

'And?' I asked.

'Well.' Then, she spread her legs wide apart and said, "Can ye no' just take it oot of this, driver?"'

'What?'

'And I said, "Have you not got anything smaller, missus?"'

End of interview.

Chapter 45

Looking down the barrel of a gun

It didn't just look like a shotgun; it WAS a shotgun. The possessor of the firearm also gave a firm impression he knew how to use it. He was about six foot tall, stockily built, longish, greasy black hair, a mean smile and dead eyes. He wore a dark suit, top button of the light blue shirt undone with a gaudy floral tie on display. The shotgun was tucked into an inside pocket of his ankle-length, thick tweed herringbone overcoat. He looked as though he had stepped out of an episode of *The Sweeney*. Where were John Thaw and Dennis Waterman when you needed them?

Standing beside him was a genuine world famous former Scotland international footballer. He has passed on now, but I would prefer not to name him for two very good reasons. I have no intention of besmirching his character. And his pal might still be around with his shotgun.

It was a Saturday evening in January in the mid-1980s and I was standing with Hugh Farmer, News Editor of the Sunday People, in the lounge bar of The Montrose pub in Carrick Street on the Broomielaw. Thankfully, there was no sign of Oliver Reed on this occasion.

We had both finished our shifts for the day and, as ever, believed we thoroughly deserved a beer or three for our efforts. I had a meeting in the city centre later that evening, so I had an hour or so to kill (not the most appropriate word in the circumstances). The lounge and the bar were largely deserted. It was the lull after the festive period and people were either skint or tuckered out. Or both. I was sipping what I believed to be my well-earned pint of lager when I saw my friend looking over my shoulder. 'Christ,' he muttered. I looked round to see the ex-footballer sauntering in with the heavy. I knew the former player and I liked him, but it would be fair to say he carried a little baggage around with him. If you were being kind you would term him a 'loose cannon'.

He strolled up to where Hugh I were at the top of the bar and exchanged the usual pleasantries - 'Happy New Year', 'How are you doin'?' - all that sort of stuff. He introduced his mate as 'Wullie'. I knew the ex-player drank Rum and Coke, so I ordered up a large one and was surprised when Wullie asked for an orange juice. 'He's got to remain sober,' said the former footballer; let's call him 'Andy'.

It was then Wullie casually opened his overcoat to proudly show off the shotgun. I believe that action could be interpreted as a conversation stopper. There's not an awful lot you can say in the circumstances, is there? 'Oh, what a nice shotgun. Did you get it for your Christmas?'

My friend and I gulped down our lager. 'Andy' chuckled. 'Wullie and I might have a wee bit of business to attend to later on this evening.'

Now journalists, by nature, are normally inquisitive folk; it comes with the territory. Others might simply refer to us as being 'nosey bastards'. On this occasion, though, neither the News Editor nor myself desired any more information. 'Andy', however, was eager to tell us more.

'My missus has been having it off,' he said matter-of-factly. 'She's been getting shagged bandy by this bloke.' ('Andy' mentioned a name and a profession, but I can't divulge either. To do so would be to provide too many pieces in a jigsaw that could be put together fairly effortlessly by some people out there. And I've got kind of used to this breathing lark.)

'Oh, really?' I heard myself saying.

'Aye,' answered 'Andy', 'and that bastard's going to pay. Wullie's no' a bad shot with that thing from close range. Could blow someone's todger to bits.'

Nods all round from me and my friend. We had popped into a quiet, wee boozer for a couple of pints on a Saturday night and now it looked as though we would be participating in the Clydeside's version of High Noon. That wasn't in the script. Wullie nonchalantly sipped at his orange juice; not a care in the world.

'Aye, I think this bloke'll need to be taught a lesson,' added 'Andy'. 'He can't slip my missus a crippler and expect to get away with it. No chance. Aye, something will have to be done about that. Nobody messes with my missus.'

I almost laughed. This guy could have screwed for Britain in the Olympics and we would have been guaranteed a gold medal. He had been putting it about for over a decade. At the height of his fame - and, believe me, this bloke was right up there with the best of them - no-one could have guessed at how many females he was getting through on a daily basis. As they say in the trade, the guy enjoyed his 'Nat King'. And now he was clearly affronted that his long-suffering wife had had enough and decided to enjoy herself and indulge in some sins of the flesh. Let ye who is without sin etc. I came close to smiling. The realisation that 'Andy's' mate Wullie had a shotgun inside his coat made sure no grin was forthcoming.

'Shocking,' I heard myself saying.

'Aye, you can say that again,' said 'Andy'. 'Fuckin' liberty. I gave her everything she ever wanted and this is how she repays me. The bloke's a lot younger than her, as well. A fuckin' toy boy, is that what you call these guys? He'll be a fuckin' toy boy with a high-pitched voice when we're finished with the little bastard.'

Wullie nodded, grinned and opened his overcoat again just to reassure us all that the shotgun, obviously armed and ready to go, was still contentedly residing in a safe place.

Thankfully, 'Andy' drained his Rum and Coke and began buttoning up his jacket. 'Time to go,' he said.

Three little words. Three little welcome words.

'You sure you don't want another?' asked my friend. I could have used Wullie's shotgun on my mate myself.

'Andy' pondered for a moment. 'No thanks,' he said. 'I might as well keep my wits about me, too. Don't want to miss the fun.'

And with that the pair headed for the exit of The Montrose pub. My mate and I looked at each other. 'Did that really happen?' I asked. The News Editor nodded and said, 'I heard nothing. I saw nothing.' Noses were being kept clean. Or, at least, they weren't being broken.

I scanned the newspapers over the next few days, hoping not to come across a story about someone having their crown jewels blown in the general direction of Kingdom Come. It was with genuine relief to me that no such tale hit the headlines.

An unsuspecting lover of an ex-footballer's wife would have been mightily relieved, too. If only he had known.

Chapter 46

Tales from the bedroom

'I had sex with a famous footballer the other night. How much will you pay me for my story?'

It was Tuesday morning, a couple of minutes beyond ten and it wasn't the normal start to my working week as Sports Editor of the Sunday Mail. I had heard the telephone's demanding buzz on my desk as I walked into the editorial. 'David McKinney,' I thought, wrongly. David was a schoolteacher who was desperate to break into newspapers and he was always first to ring on a Tuesday to see what game I would be sending him to at the weekend. Jokingly, I used to say, 'Please give me a chance to get my jacket off, David, and have the first sip at my coffee. Could you hang back and telephone about half-past ten?' However, despite my pleas, the enthusiast was normally first on the blower on that given day. Not this time, though, unless he had undergone a drastic change of sexual preferences and voice alteration since I had last seen him the previous Friday.

'Pardon?' I asked the mystery caller, trying to shake loose the cobwebs of two welcome days off.

'I had sex with a VERY famous footballer' - I noticed his status had been upgraded over the past few seconds - 'and I want to sell my story. How much is it worth?'

I had received similar telephone calls in the past, of course, but, as a rule, the switchboard normally put them straight through to the News Desk. The footballer in question got extremely lucky on this occasion. I was keen to discover the footballer's identity. She told me and added, 'See, I told you he was VERY famous, didn't I?'

Over the years I got to know that a fair percentage of these 'revelations' were merely pranks from pests with nothing better to do. The female on the other end of the line did not sound as though she was related to Hans Christian Anderson. The name of the player made sense, too, because I knew he had 'a bit of previous', as John Thaw used to say in *The Sweeney*. I gave her a bit more attention. I looked for more details.

'When did this happen?'

'Saturday night,' she shot back. She had either rehearsed this entire conversation or she was pretty sure of her facts. I decided it was the latter.

'Where did this take place?'

'His house,' she said and gave me an address. That was hardly any sort of proof because she wouldn't have required the skills of a code breaker to get that information; a multitude of Glasgow cabbies would have had that knowledge.

'You do know he's married?'

'Oh, aye, lovely looking girl, too. I saw the wedding picture on their mantelpiece.' Suddenly the plot was thickening. How on earth would she know of the location of such a photograph? Maybe she was related to a painter and decorator, an electrician, a plumber, a heating engineer, a joiner, a carpet fitter, a window cleaner, Uncle Tom Cobley? Someone who could have described the living room. It was possible, just possible. I told her that.

'Naw, naw,' she said, 'I don't know any of those people. I saw it for myself.'

'And you're saying the sex was consensual?'

'Eh?'

'You weren't forced to have sex?'

'Naw, naw, nothing like that. It was right good; he wasn't bad, at all. I'll tell you everything - if the money's right.'

'I'm afraid it will be your word against his,' I said, thinking of the footballer, who was more than just a passing acquaintance. 'He'll take you to court, you know. He'll sue you and you'll lose. You don't have any proof, do you?'

Thankfully, there were no mobile phones with built-in cameras back then.

'I'll tell you what his bedroom looks like, if you want. I can tell you every detail; the type of curtains he's got; big, brown velvet hideous-looking things, the colour of the carpet and the duvet, the type of bed.' She seemed pretty assured. 'I even had a sneak look in his wardrobe. Do you want me to tell you what's in there? And I looked in the wife's side, too. I can tell you everything.'

'It's still your word against his, I'm afraid. We would need proof, something like photographs, perhaps?' I knew that was highly unlikely and, thankfully, so it proved. I was also aware this female could quite easily pick up a telephone and put a call into another newspaper. The footballer might not have had a guardian angel on that particular editorial floor. 'Look,' I said, 'I'll need to run this by my Editor and he doesn't start until midday on a Tuesday. Do you want to give me a number and I'll call you back?' She wasn't too keen on divulging that information. 'I'll call you before one o'clock, right?' she said. 'You tell your Editor he'll get a right big story, but the cash has got to be right. I'll tell you EVERYTHING. I know what this is worth.'

It was far too early to talk about sums of money and, in any case, that might just encourage the caller to start wondering how she was going to spend her new-found wealth. 'Okay, I'll be here,' I said and gave her my direct number. I couldn't take the chance of her being mistakenly routed through to the News Desk and everything kicking off big-style. I had three hours to get to the player in question and relay what I had just been told. I left a message for him and he called me at the desk just before noon. He was his usual cheery self until I informed of my early-morning caller.

'She can describe your living room,' I said. 'She can tell me what your bedroom looks like. What sort of curtains have you got?'

'Brown velvet, why?'

'She's on the button.'

'Aye, but she can see them from outside, can't she?' This guy had the ability to think on his feet.

'True, but unless she carried a set of step ladders around with her, I doubt if she could tell me the colour of your bedroom carpet, what sort of bed you've got and the contents of your wardrobe. I take it you left her alone at one point?'

'Aye, just for a second. Nature called.' He realised he had been rumbled.

'It was just a bit of fun, I thought the lassie knew that. The wife was away for the weekend, I had a few drinks and one thing led to another. You know how it is.'

'Why didn't you take her to a hotel?' I asked reasonably.

'You kidding? I'm running out of hotels. I thought it was only a matter of time before someone spotted me. Christ, I thought I would be safe at home.'

'Clearly not,' I replied. 'Okay, we're going to have to establish an alibi for Saturday night. Who do you trust who won't give you away?'

Instantly, he mentioned the name of a team-mate. 'He was away shagging and told his missus he was spending the weekend with me,' he said. 'Told her my wife was away for a couple of days and I was afraid of the dark or something daft like that. Will that do?'

'Get your stories straight and I think you'll be okay,' I reassured him. 'She's just another bird on the make.'

The kiss-and-tell female duly telephoned me just before one o'clock. I told her the footballer was with a colleague all weekend and they would swear to it. It was their word against hers and she had no chance of proving anything. They might even sue her.

'Bastards,' she exclaimed. 'You can't fuckin' trust anyone these days.'

Chapter 47

Wise guys

There are a lot of wise guys among the footballing fraternity. And I'm not talking about the Cosa Nostra characters with the habit of carrying violin cases around with them. I'm actually referring to smart arses.

No doubt you have heard the one about the reporter asking the footballer for a quick word and getting the response 'velocity.' Hilarious. Some actually believe they are sport's gain and academia's loss. Don't get me wrong, please. I have been privileged to spend a lot of time in the company of managers and footballers and, mainly, I have enjoyed myself. I'm happy to break bread with a lot of these people. There are some, though, with whom I have spent time and it has been as pleasant as coping with toothache. You ask a simple question and you get some tortured, convoluted answer.

Decades ago, I was doing a question and answer piece with one footballer for SHOOT! magazine and it was all the usual mundane stuff. Then I asked him what sort of home he lived in. Straightforward poser, I would have thought. 'What do you mean?' came the reply. 'A mud hut by a stream? A barn? A treehouse?' Maybe he was bored. I know I was. Mind you, he did live in Airdrie, so there was a possibility that one of the three choices might have been correct. (Sorry, good people of Airdrie; I'm still carrying scars from covering games at Broomfield.) We later found out it was a two-bedroomed semi-detached.

'What sort of car do you drive?' I asked, by now expecting some daft, awkward reply.

'You mean my dream car? The one I really want to drive?'

'No, the one you currently own?'

'Not my dream car, then?'

Eventually, after a bit of to-ing and fro-ing, it turned out to be a Ford Cortina. And so it went on. This bloke is now a youth team coach and I have to say I pity the kids who have got to decipher his verbal nonsense on a daily basis. I'm delighted to say he has never been invited onto *Match of the Day*. Gordon Strachan, Pat Nevin and this bloke? Perish the thought.

My old pal Jim Blair was working for the Daily Record and was invited over to Fir Park on the day Brian McClair was unveiled as a second-time around Motherwell player by proud owner John Boyle in 1998. McClair, as you may know, once studied mathematics at Glasgow University before his career in football took off. He's a bright chap and likes to let folk know it. The press conference was coming to an end when Boyle asked if anyone else had another question for Brian.

Blair, at the back of the room, piped up, 'Aye, I've got one. Brian, what's the capital of Peru?'

I would have paid good money to hear him answer Reykjavik.

Chapter 48

Anonymous among the lions

It's Monday, March 19 2007, and I'm propping up the bar of the Iron Horse pub in Glasgow's West Nile Street with four of football's most illustrious names; a quartet of the existing eight Lisbon Lions, the Celtic team that swept into the history books by winning the European Cup on a gloriously sunny day on May 25 1967 in Portugal's beautiful capital city.

Billy McNeill, Tommy Gemmell, Bertie Auld and Jim Craig have all turned up for an 11am meeting before I take them round the corner to an excellent little Italian restaurant, O Sole Mio, in Bath Street for what I planned to be a mass interview over lunch.

The legendary foursome agreed to have a chat for the forthcoming *Lisbon Lions* book I was writing with them to commemorate the 40th anniversary of their epic triumph over Inter Milan. As can so often happen, it was a throwaway line, this time from Tommy Gemmell, that led all five of us to the city centre hostelry that March morning. Tommy used to call the Iron Horse our 'HQ'. He worked for financial consultants a goal-kick away from the pub, while my old offices at 7 Day Press were directly opposite. Every now and again, I would receive a phone call. 'Fancy a pint in HQ?' Who could turn down a sporting icon? We would meet at the top of the bar - known as the Celtic End, apparently - and just shoot the breeze about nothing in particular as we put the world to rights.

One day I asked, 'What have Celtic got planned for the Lisbon anniversary?'

'Oh, this and that,' said Tommy. 'Big meal at Celtic Park and a few autograph-signing sessions.' He thought for a moment before adding, 'We're doing a few specials for you guys, too, in the Press. One of the newspapers is going to do a twenty-page pull-out. It's before-and-after stuff; the players as we were back then and up-to-date interviews and pictures as we are now.'

'I hope they're paying you well,' I said.

'Not a penny,' answered Tommy. 'We'll just do it for the PR.'

'The last team in the world that needs good PR is the Lisbon Lions,' I said in earnest. I also realised that the newspaper doing the special so-called giveaway would earn a fortune in advertising revenue. It wouldn't be too difficult to sell space in such a vehicle and a lot of companies would be only too delighted to jump on board. So, the newspaper would rake in a few quid while in all probability putting on sales that day and the Lisbon Lions wouldn't receive a brass yazoo. Didn't seem fair.

A bulb went on above my head.

By complete coincidence, I had received an email that very morning informing me that a publishing house in Edinburgh were welcoming submissions on any subject from journalists. I was given a name and a direct telephone number that might come in handy in the future. They say everyone has a book in them and I had written *Celtic: The First 100 Years* with Macdonald Publishers to celebrate the club's centenary in 1988. On that occasion, I was contacted and offered a contract and was happy to accept. There was a snag, though. As I was Sports Editor at the Sunday Mail at the time, I had to receive special permission to pen the book. 'The Sunday Liam' theorists would have had a field day and the Editor might have knocked me back. However, when it was revealed who owned the publishing house in London, I got the go-ahead. A certain Robert Maxwell also had Macdonald Publishers in his stable and suddenly all problems were obliterated. So, nineteen years later and following a chance remark from Tommy Gemmell, I thought it was time to double my literary output as far as the book world was concerned.

'Hold on a minute, Tommy,' I said as I fumbled for my mobile phone. I called my office and Craig Swan, now doing an exceptional job on the Sports Desk of the Daily Record, answered. He had taken down the phone number of the Edinburgh publishers and passed it on. I telephoned a chap called Campbell Brown, MD at Black and White Publishing. Unfortunately, he wasn't in the office, but a girl called Janne Moller took my number and promised to get him to call me back.

'A penny for them,' said Tommy.

I had quickly formulated an idea in my mind that I could pull everything together and offer the eight Lisbon Lions a chapter each in the book, while providing a lot of the editorial myself. I just needed to get a price from Campbell Brown, if, of course, he was interested. If the money was on the button, I would then be in a position to divide it up equally among Tommy, Billy McNeill, Bertie Auld, Jim Craig, Bobby Lennox, Stevie Chalmers, John Clark and Willie Wallace. To be absolutely honest, I wasn't that interested in making a buck myself which would probably have put yet another frown on the face of my bank manager. I knew I could do this as a favour for eight guys who had given me so much pleasure while I was growing up. I thought it was only right and proper that the lads got a couple of quid from such a book. Would the price be right? And would the publishers be interested? I told Tommy I would get in touch as soon as I heard anything.

Sure enough, later that evening, Campbell Brown telephoned me. Yes, he was interested and he would give me a financial figure in the morning. There was one massive obstacle, though. Campbell, as you would expect, wanted the book in the shops well in time for the May 25 anniversary. Basically, I had a fortnight to write at least 80,000 words. 'Can you do it?' asked the publisher. 'Of course, I can,' I answered with a fair bit of bravado while swallowing hard. I was still running 7 Day Press which really was a seven day operation and I couldn't afford to take my eye off that particular ball. I was also taught that only God was omnipresent. So I had a bit of a task on my hands.

The money was agreed the following day and the players were happy enough to play their part, so all that was required now was for me to conduct eight in-depth interviews, switch on my computer and write at least 80,000 words in two weeks. As simple as that. Campbell later called the task 'Herculean' when I sent the last chapter at precisely 11.46am on Monday April 2. I didn't argue with his assessment. Getting out of bed every morning at five o'clock, writing as swiftly as I could, getting to my office at 7 Day Press for around ten and then coming home about four to continue writing the Lions book really wasn't my idea of heaven. I wondered if that guy Willie Shakespeare ever encountered these problems.

So, that explains why Tommy, Billy, Bertie, Jim and I were in a

Glasgow pub on a crisp March morning in 2007. I reckoned if I could sit them down over lunch and take all sorts of notes then I would be halfway there. I knew Stevie Chalmers, Bobby Lennox and John Clark would be available at another time. Willie Wallace could have been problematic, though - he lived in Queensland in Australia! Tommy and Wispy, as Willie Wallace is known to everyone, had continued to keep in touch with each other over the years and I was assured I would be furnished with a phone number. These things rarely go off without a hitch, though. Tommy hadn't been informed that Wispy had recently moved house and had a new number. I had deliberately left Wispy to the last while writing up the other seven. I couldn't do the book without Wispy's chapter and we were running out of time. Eventually, Tommy, after a bit of Columbo-type sleuthing, provided a number and, believe it or not, I did the interview while Wispy was preparing a barbeque in sunny Oz. It was chucking it down in Glasgow at the time.

However, back at the Iron Horse that morning to kick off the book, I was aware there was a bloke at the bar who looked as though he had been celebrating big-style. The pub opened at 8am and had a licence to sell alcohol with a breakfast. I often wondered how much of the croissants ever got in the way of that first pint. Each to their own, I suppose. As a journalist, most outsiders believe I started the day with whisky in my Corn Flakes. Not true; it's vodka. Joking!

Anyway, this guy at the bar must have been first in the pub that day because, just over three hours later, he was more than just a tad merry. He shuffled along the bar and I noticed the Lions were all doing their level best to avoid eye contact. I guessed they must have appeared in this movie more than once.

Our inebriated 'friend' stared hard at Billy. Then he spoke, well, slurred really, 'You're Billy McNeill, aren't you?'

Billy, ever the gentleman, answered, 'I am that, sir.'

'Billy McNeill,' said the guy. 'Well, well.' Then he looked at Jim Craig. He focused hard. 'You're Jim Craig.'

Jim smiled back and nodded. 'That's me.'

Our chum at the bar was on a roll. He squinted at Tommy. 'You're Tommy Gemmell.'

'Got it in one,' replied Tommy.

'Billy McNeill, Jim Craig, Tommy Gemmell.' He shook his head. Then he looked at Bertie. 'You're Bertie Auld.'

'The one and the same,' laughed Bertie.

'Billy McNeill, Jim Craig, Tommy Gemmell and Bertie Auld,' he said. Then he fixed me in his gaze. He looked a little perplexed, just a shade puzzled.

'And who the fuck ur you?' he asked.

Chapter 49

Bomb scare at Ibrox

It was the start of the Eighties and Rangers had just beaten Hearts at Ibrox in a game of very little consequence. There was nothing to get too excited about during a fairly humdrum and predictable encounter. The real action came after the game, though.

A full-scale alert spread quickly round the ground when one of the Rangers cleaning staff came across a suspicious and odd-looking device tucked away behind a seat in the Broomloan Road stand. He immediately reported his discovery to the police, giving details of a black box with a wire protruding from the top. The police authorities immediately called in the Bomb Squad to deal with the matter. Next, they were told to clear the stadium. Oblivious of all the excitement going on around them, sports reporters continued to file their match reports from the press box.

I received a telephone call at the Sunday Mail from a friend within Ibrox to give me an advance warning. My immediate thought was to get in touch with our match reporter, Don Morrison. His line was engaged. I realised he would still be relaying his report, so I quickly raced to the copy takers' room to ask who was dealing with the Rangers v Hearts game. I managed to break in and talk to our guy. 'The police think a bomb has been planted at Ibrox,' I said. 'Get out of there as quickly as you can. Spread the word.' Ever the professional, Don said, 'I've only a few paragraphs to go, so I'll just finish, okay?'

I then told the Editor that this could be a genuine 'hold-the-front-page' moment. (By the way, I never heard that order said once in all my years in journalism.) The next thing to do was wait. I had an office number for Rangers director Hugh Adam, a true old school gent. I took a chance and put in a call. Hugh answered.

'What's happening?' I asked urgently.

'Oh, the panic's over,' said Hugh. 'It wasn't a bomb, thank goodness. The Bomb Squad weren't required, after all.'

So, what was this menacing-looking apparatus that had created so much anxiety?

Drinking at football grounds was, of course, banned after the riot following the Old Firm Cup Final at Hampden in 1980. One shrewd fan, though, had come up with a cunning plan.

The 'bomb' was merely a hollowed-out transistor radio with a half-bottle of whisky put in its place. The wire? Nothing more sinister than a straw.

Chapter 50

Snap happy

Henry McInnes was a photographer who was forever searching for a different angle on a snap. He was a marvellously-skilled creator and innovator when you stuck that Pentax in his hands.

He had the ability to accept a mundane task and turn it into a work of art. I was always in awe of his imagination when it came to conjuring up images that made you look twice. If you ask me to take a photograph of a pie and Bovril, that's exactly what you'll get - a pie and Bovril. Wee Henry would accept that as a test, before going off to produce something that wouldn't have looked out of place hanging on the walls of an art gallery.

We were having a chat in the Copy Cat one day and I asked him what we were to expect from today's gem of ingenuity via his lens.

'I've got to take a couple of photos of a new range of tartan ties that have been produced by some firm in Edinburgh,' he said.

'How do you make that look exciting?' I asked, stifling a yawn.

'Oh, I'm going to a model agency that specialises in babies,' replied Henry. 'I'm going to get a pile of ties, knot them, get the kids in their birthday suits, place them in some sort of formation and put the ties round their necks. Then I'll just keep snapping away and see what goes in the can.'

'Kids, eh? Could be troublesome, all that puking, yelling, peeing, bawling and falling over. Have you any experience of children?' I enquired.

'Sure, I have,' said the intrepid snapper. 'I went to school with hundreds of them.'

And there was the occasion when award-winning actress Glenda

Jackson was in town and had agreed to an interview and photo-shoot at the Glasgow Citizens' Theatre. She was in the foyer of the playhouse and halfway through the feature when she halted in mid-sentence and asked the reporter, 'Oh, dear. Is your photographer unwell?'

There was Henry, relaxing on a sofa, legs curled up, gently cuddling his camera and sound asleep. Only his soothing rhythmic snuffling gave any indication he was still with us.

That said, once he awoke from his impromptu slumber, Henry sizzled off an array of first-class images that supplemented the feature in the Sunday Mail a couple of days later. It's unclear, though, if his Rip Van Winkle impersonation in any way convinced Glenda Jackson she should take a different career path.

She gave up acting shortly afterwards to become a Labour MP in 1992.

Chapter 51

Jim Baxter, Celtic star

Quite rightly, Jim Baxter is recognised as a genuine Rangers legend. I suppose, then, that it may surprise more than a few that this strolling minstrel of a player once revealed to me that he would have happily played for CELTIC!

That may be tantamount to Billy McNeill admitting he wouldn't have minded turning out in the light blue of his club's fiercest foes. But Jim Baxter was never tainted by the unwelcome brush of sectarianism. The bloke from Hill o' Beath in Fife never got caught up in the madness that is the West of Scotland's so-called Great Divide. Religious differences meant nothing to him. Quite right, too.

I was Sports Editor at the Sunday Mail in the early nineties and I had met up with Baxter at his favourite hostelry, the Corona Bar, in Shawlands in Glasgow's south side. He was looking for publicity for the launch of his video and, with a circulation nudging one million, there was no better place to go. Jim Baxter a Celtic player? It was a marvellous throwaway line from an Ibrox Great and I realised immediately it would make a terrific back page splash in the newspaper. What a 'talker', as it is known in the trade, and it wouldn't have done circulation any harm. Could anyone be tempted to ignore a billboard that blasted, 'RANGERS LEGEND SAYS: CELTIC FOR ME!'?

'Do you realise what you're admitting?' I asked.

'Aye, of course,' smiled Jim. 'Why not? Name me any player who wouldn't have wanted to be in a side managed by Jock Stein. There won't be one. Denis Law. Billy Bremner. I would have been no different. If Big Jock had wanted me before I went to Rangers, I wouldn't have hesitated. He wasn't the Celtic boss at the time, of course, but if things had been on a different time scale I would have gone to Celtic. Of course, Rangers and their supporters mean everything to me and my first five years at Ibrox, from 1960 to 1965 when I arrived from Raith Rovers, were the happiest in my football career. I wouldn't change a thing. Celtic? Not a problem. If they had knocked on my parents' door first, I would have been off to the east end of Glasgow.'

I knew the dramatic repercussions of such an admission from a player adored and revered by the Rangers supporters. Undoubtedly, they would have seen it as a blatant act of betrayal by what they perceived as 'one of their own'. Headlines like that tend to stick and would have followed Baxter around for the rest of his days.

'I could write that story, Jim,' I said.

'Go ahead,' he replied, 'just make sure I get paid for it.'

'Not too sure it will do the sales of the video any good, though,' I pointed out. 'Rangers fans might think twice about buying it.'

Baxter rubbed his chin, grinned and chortled, 'Maybe use the story next year, eh? Just make sure I get paid for it.'

Until now, I have never been tempted to put those words into print. However, I feel compelled after recent chats with Billy McNeill and Mike Jackson about the Rangers player. Along with their Celtic team-mate Paddy Crerand, they were Baxter's three best pals in football. The Rangers hierarchy frowned on such an association, but Baxter, a free spirit, told them to get stuffed. 'It was my spare time and I could do what I wanted,' he said. 'I liked those lads and that was the end of it.'

Slim Jim, as he was known throughout his footballing days and, rather absurdly, beyond even after he had piled on the pounds, was a likeable chap, but he could undergo a startling character change in tandem with the flow of Bacardi and Coke. I'm not here to trample on anyone's reputation, but I think Jim's liking for alcohol and his serious disdain for physical work in training is fairly well chronicled. Otherwise, I think we can all assume he wouldn't have packed up playing at the age of thirty-one.

Jim Baxter never attempted to disguise his bitterness about the wages players with a mere fraction of his ability were picking up in the nineties. He was aware of his value and realised in another era he would have been a very wealthy man. Or, at least, a guy who had made bookies very wealthy. By his own estimation, he gambled away a minimum of around £500,000. Another £250,000 appears to be unaccounted for. A phenomenal amount of cash at the time.

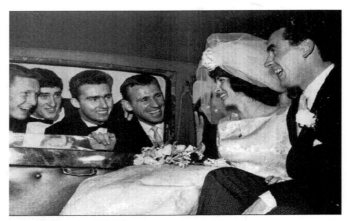

A Ranger in Paradise ... Jim Baxter (second left) was a great friend of Celtic rivals Billy McNeill, Mike Jackson and Paddy Crerand and is seen here at the wedding of their teammate John Colrain to Rosaleen in the early sixties.

When he was asked about the wage packets mediocre footballers were earning, he smiled, 'Aye, it would have been nice to have had one of those pay pokes every month. I would probably have gambled £50,000 a week rather than £100.' He meant it, too.

An old journalist pal, John Fairgrieve, a colossal talent who wrote award-winning features for the Daily Record and the Sunday Mail, collaborated with Jim Baxter on his autobiography, *The Party's Over*. It was a particularly well-written chronicle of one of Scotland's favourite footballing sons. I asked Jim about his thoughts on the book.

'Aye, I thought it was brilliant but for one thing.'

I was puzzled. 'What was that?'

'Oh, the title. I thought it should have been, 'THE PARTY'S JUST STARTED'.

Jim Baxter, after two liver transplants, died of pancreatic cancer on

April 14 2001. A constant visitor at his bedside was Billy McNeill. His funeral was held at Glasgow Cathedral. His ashes were scattered at Ibrox stadium.

Jim Baxter wouldn't have wanted it any other way.

Chapter 52

Freelance foul-ups

The Daily Record had a freelance sports reporter back in the sixties and early seventies called Bobby Allison. He was never going to win the Pulitzer Prize for his services to the printed word, but he was a steady and reliable character who never once let the newspaper down.

Back then, a good freelancer was worth his weight in gold. Some, of course, merely carried out the duties as a hobby while others, God bless 'em, took it very seriously.

I can still vividly recall one evening very early in my introduction to life on the editorial floor, when I was given a pile of evening games to sub-edit for the Record's first edition. It was hammered into me how important it was to get those massive presses running on time in the machine room hall in the bowels of our Hope Street building. There was a Highland League programme on this particular Wednesday evening and Sports Editor Jack Adams thought it wouldn't do me any harm to get the experience of six 'running' games, all about three inches deep across a single column. Any harm? I was almost climbing walls by the end of my shift.

Normally, you could anticipate the ground where you will get problems because the team line-ups didn't appear around kick-off time. That sets off the alarm bells. On this particular evening, though, everything looked as though it was going according to plan. However, there was no sign of first-half copy from one of the grounds. The teams were in, though, so our guy had definitely turned up. There was no way of getting in touch with the correspondent as there was no contact number at the ground.

Back then, you would get two or three pars at the interval, then an updated par halfway through the second-half and then a last par near the end to, hopefully, wrap it up. (Last-gasp winning goals were never welcomed.) The full-time result had to be in bang on time; there was no margin for error and time was of the essence. On these evenings, you knew you were skating on the thinnest of thin ice. Five of the match reports duly arrived, but there was no sign of the sixth. Frantically, I tried to discover what had gone wrong. No joy. We were forced to shove in a 'filler' instead of the game report which didn't look too clever, but, at least, it got the presses moving and ensured we would have a first edition out on the streets of Glasgow by 10pm.

Later on, I decided to phone our correspondent at his home number. Imagine my surprise when our freelance operator for that part of the Highlands picked up the phone. 'We've had to go without your match report,' I said. 'What on earth happened?'

I got the image of a laidback Fyfe Robertson-type character puffing away merrily on a pipe at the other end of the line. 'Och, aye, sorry about that, sonny,' he replied. 'Ah couldna get tae the phone, ye ken. Ah had a puncture oan my bike. Ah told the council to move that bloody telephone box closer to the ground, but they widnae listen. Sorry if Ah caused any inconvenience. Ah'll get the tyre fixed for Saturday's game. Good night, sonny.'

Welcome to the hectic hotbed of on-the-edge newspaper reporting, I thought.

At least, our friend in the north had some sort of excuse. What about the guy who didn't file at all from the Nottingham Forest v Leeds United First Division game at the City Ground on Saturday, August 25 1968? My colleagues at the Sunday Mirror were going doolally when their corr merely filed a two-word report, 'Game abandoned'. He failed to let anyone know that there had been a raging, out-of-control fire at half-time and the main stand eventually burned to the ground. A crowd of 31,126 had to be rushed to safety as flames licked around the timber of the old ground. Thankfully, no-one was injured. The Mirror guys were thinking about financing a hit on the freelancer.

When they eventually contacted him, I'm told all he said was, 'What's all the fuss? There was no game to report. You can't blame me for the fire.'

And people wonder why journalists take a dram.

Anyway, back to good old dependable Bobby Allison. He had a slight speech impediment and sounded a bit like Sir Alex Ferguson when he says, 'I was weally pwoud of my boys.' Yes, he had trouble with his 'r's. Ask him to cover a Raith Rovers Reserves v. St. Mirren Reserves game at your peril. One afternoon, he was filing his report from a Hibs match at Easter Road. He was phoning one of the copy-takers and everything was going just fine and dandy until he was asked for his Man of the Match.

He had a stab at it first time around.

'Sorry,' said the typist, 'I didn't quite get that.'

He tried again.

'No, sorry, Bobby, I can't decipher that.'

He had another go. Same response. 'Maybe it's a bad line. You want to spell it, please?'

That didn't work, either. Bobby eventually ran out of patience. 'Oh, fuck it, give the Man of the Match to Pat Stanton.'

Jimmy O'Rourke never knew how close he came to getting that accolade.

Chapter 53

Steve Murray and the pathetic thief

Billy McNeill was convinced he had outsmarted Brian Clough when he persuaded the Nottingham Forest boss to sell a young homesick Scot by the name of Steve Murray to Celtic for a bargain £50,000 in 1987.

A year later, at the age of twenty, the player's promising career was over after a sickening challenge in a reserve game against Motherwell at Fir Park on September 7 1988.

McNeill was in the stand that evening to watch Murray, no relation to the Celtic player of the same name who played for the club between 1973/76. A wild assault from an opponent left Murray writhing in pain. Billy maintains to this day the tackle on his young player was one of the worst he has ever witnessed. 'Scandalous,' was his description. One moment of recklessness had brought down the curtain on what could have been an exceptional career.

Years later, as we downed a couple of beers in the Off The Record pub, Billy looked back at that incident. He was genuinely emotional. 'Just like that,' he said. 'One minute, everything in front of him, everything to play for and the next, gone. I have absolutely no doubt that Steve Murray could have been a massive player for Celtic. He had it all; clever with good technique, an eye for a pass, a powerful engine and a genuine desire to succeed. I know Cloughie did everything to keep him at Forest, but the lad had made up his mind. He wanted to come home and, fortunately for us, it was Celtic he wanted to play for. You just wonder what might have happened for the lad if he had remained with Forest. Football can be such a cruel game sometimes.'

Billy and Bobby Lennox, who was the club's reserve team coach in 1988, were in court on Wednesday November 23 1993 to act as witnesses on Murray's behalf. The player settled the £900,000 damages action out of court. Murray became only the third Scottish footballer in history to sue an opponent, in this case Motherwell's Jamie Dolan. (Dolan, by the way, died of a heart attack at the age of thirty-nine in August 2008.) Rangers' Ian Durrant took a similar action against Aberdeen's Neil Simpson after an incident at Pittodrie in October 1988 and, five years earlier, Dunfermline's Jim Brown did likewise against St.Johnstone's John Pelosi. Murray's quote after the settlement was so sad. Describing the past five years, he could only say they had been 'terrible, murder.'

I met him just prior to the out-of-court settlement. He had undergone a series of operations, his leg was encased in a brace, he could only walk with the help of crutches and was unemployed. I had been asked to try to help put together a charity game for the player. If I could persuade the bosses at the Sunday Mail to get behind it, give it a bit of publicity and a push in the right direction, then the player might get a well-merited few bob. Of course, I was delighted to lend my support.

One thing that struck me about Steve, who was twenty-three at the time, was his unremitting good humour. Not once did he moan about his dreadful situation. Simply, he accepted it as 'the bounce of the ball'. You could only wonder what went through his mind in the moments he was on his own. No-one could have blamed the lad for dreaming of what-might-have-been.

Anyway, with a lot of people chipping in, we managed to stage a game for Steve at a ground of one of the Ayrshire Junior clubs. I was working the day of the match, but I was delighted to be told it had been a success and a few quid had been raised for a very worthwhile cause. A week or so later, I arranged to meet Steve for lunch. As ever, he was in good spirits. He was telling me about the game, not far from where he stayed in Symington, and how things had gone.

'I can't thank everyone enough for their generosity,' he told me with a real warmth in his tones. 'Please give the Sunday Mail readers a big thank you from me.' Then he smiled and added, 'There must have been someone at the game worse off than me.'

I wrinkled my brow and narrowed my eyes. 'How do you make that out?'

'I was away getting photographs taken with some of the players and the fans. When I came back someone had nicked my crutches.'

In moments like that, you really don't know whether to laugh or cry.

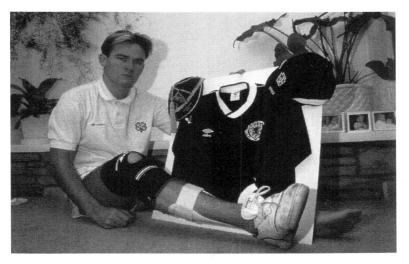

Steve Murray ... Celtic's Mr. Unlucky

Chapter 54

Scotland World Champions 1978 ... If only

'Make your fuckin' mind up. Are you a fuckin' goalkeeper? Or are you a fuckin' journalist?' The erudite Bobby Howitt, manager of Motherwell Football Club, had a way with words.

It was August 1968, I was sixteen years old and training with the Fir Park club. I had just played in a 3-1 win over Hearts in Edinburgh in a reserve game. So, the Motherwell boss, quite rightly, wanted to know the lay of the land. He was aware I was working constant back shift at the Daily Record and, in all honesty, it was impossible to combine both roles. I couldn't train in the evening, for a start. I told the manager, as he had thought so long and hard on how to frame his question, I would be sticking in at the newspaper.

Yes, before you say it, I know; as a goalkeeper I was a good journalist and as a journalist I was a good goalkeeper.

Quite remarkably, Motherwell also had another young goalkeeper on their books at the same time who worked at the Daily Express. That's an unbelievable coincidence, isn't it? His name was Keith MacRae and he was a year older than me. He was also a vastly superior last line of defence. I rated him higher than the other keeper at the club, Peter McCloy, who, of course, went onto play 535 games for Rangers after moving to Ibrox in 1970. I wasn't one bit surprised Manchester City shelled out £100,000 for Keith in 1973. I lost track of him when he went to the States in 1981 to wind down his career with Portland Timbers. The last I heard of him, he had married a Texas oil heiress. ('Lucky fuckin' bugger,' as Bobby Howitt might have said.)

Keith was still at Manchester City when I met him in the aftermath of Scotland's 5-1 mauling from England at Wembley in 1975. The Rangers goalkeeper, Stewart Kennedy, had a howler that dreadful afternoon. 'You would have done better than him, Alex,' observed Keith. It wasn't much of a compliment. A blind walrus would have been a reasonable alternative.

We decided to meet up later in the evening once we had changed out of our Bay City Roller outfits. We agreed to drink away some of our sorrows at a nightclub in Soho. It was a place called Samantha's, just off Regent Street. The bouncers were turning away anyone who had a shred of tartan about their person. Keith and I were booted and suited and lost our Scottish accents as we paid to get in. It was an interesting place and one very bizarre situation occurred.

Norman Rossington was an actor who appeared in movies such as *A Hard Day's Night*, with the Beatles, *The Longest Day*, with John Wayne, Richard Burton, Robert Mitchum and Sean Connery, and in three *Carry On* films alongside Sid James, Hattie Jacques and Kenneth Williams. I don't suppose many people can say they have worked beside Lennon and McCartney, 007 and the Rumpo Kid. That wasn't what concerned Rossington (not to be confused with the wonderful Leonard Rossiter of *Rising Damp* fame) that particular evening.

Apparently, his leather coat had been nicked and, for whatever reason, he pointed the finger at the 'two Jocks' at the bar, Keith and I. I didn't want to be too unkind, but I made the point my mate and I were both 6ft 2in. The actor was about 5ft 2in in stilts. Thankfully, the bouncers continued their search elsewhere. Personally, I would have rounded up all the Ronnie Corbett lookalikes and frisked them.

A year before my stint at Motherwell, my newspaper career might not have got off the ground at all. I had played for the Glasgow Schools Under-15s side against our counterparts at Dundee. My cousin Tommy Cunningham, two years older than me, was already making a name for himself as a centre-half with St.Anthony's in the rough and tumble world of the Juniors. He had been on trial at Birmingham City and St. Mirren before going to Partick Thistle. Davie McParland was manager of the Firhill club and he happened to mention he was looking for a young goalkeeper. Tommy informed him I had just played for Glasgow Schools and McParland immediately asked for my telephone number. One snag; my parents didn't have a phone. The chance was gone. McParland signed a youngster, just two months older than me, who went onto make a name for himself; a guy called Alan Rough.

Now if my parents had only invested in Sir Alexander Bell's invention back in the sixties, Scotland would almost assuredly have won the World Cup in Argentina in 1978. (Only joking, Scruff!)

Chapter 55

Derek Johnstone getting ahead of himself

Derek Johnstone's timing in the air was impeccable as he consistently sent soaring headers zeroing in on target with laser-beam accuracy.

Off the pitch, though, the man who scored 132 goals in 369 games for Rangers in the seventies and eighties wasn't quite so flawless. He quit football in 1987 after a short stint as manager of Partick Thistle and, with his natural charm, wit and excellent knowledge of the game, it was a certainty he would land a job in the media. Maggie Thatcher hadn't quite blown the unions apart at that stage and there wouldn't be an opening for Big Derek until he joined the National Union of Journalists. Changed days, of course, but, back then, those were the rules.

Derek was out in the cold until I proposed him for membership to the Union. Shortly afterwards, he phoned me to tell me he had a date to state his case to the NUJ panel. The meeting was due to be held in an upstairs hall at Sloans Pub and Restaurant in the Argyle Arcade. It was October 1987 and I got caught in a good old-fashioned Glasgow downpour as I, umbrella-free, walked along from the Daily Record and Sunday Mail offices at Anderston Quay. Drookit, I eventually caught up with Derek.

We had a quick beer at the bar before joining the many NUJ hopefuls in the hall. The script was fairly simple - you sat until your name was called and then the individual would make their pitch to the panel. An hour passed. And then another. Unfortunately, the roll call was not in any sort of alphabetical order, so you simply had to be patient. After about three hours or so, it was down to Derek and one other applicant for a coveted Press pass. Sure enough, the other guy got the call. We were last from about fifty wannabes. I wondered if there was a Celtic supporter on the three-man NUJ panel.

The bloke in front of Derek gave it his best shot, but was rejected because he could not provide proof that the required percentage of his earnings would be from media work. I believe it had to be around 50 to 60 per cent back then. No such problem for my Rangers chum because the way things had worked out, 100 per cent of his earnings would be through newspaper, magazine, TV and radio work.

After the last guy was dismissed, I noticed the journalists on the panel were putting all their stuff into their briefcases and were about to make their getaway. Luckily, I knew one of the NUJ bigwigs, a chap called Alasdair Downing, who worked as a news sub-editor on the Record. I raced to their desk at the top of the hall.

'What about Derek Johnstone?' I asked.

Alasdair sighed, fetched a ledger from his brief case and ran his finger down the list of applicants. No sign of a Derek Johnstone. 'Please check again,' I asked. Nope, no sign of the Ibrox legend. 'He must be in there somewhere,' I reasoned. I went back to where Derek was sitting and asked him for his notice from the NUJ. I had a swift scan of the contents.

He was only a month out; we were due in another four weeks. Thankfully, Alasdair and his colleagues must have taken a sympathetic view - I still looked as though I had gone down with the Titanic - and took Derek after close of play. And, thankfully, he got the Press card that evening and that was him up and running. So, yes, I'm partly to blame!

Mind you, my act of kindness has never prevented Derek from having a pop every now and again. I was with my wife Gerda at a Newspaper Press Fund Ball in the Glasgow Hilton some time shortly after the turn of the millennium. We were chatting in the lounge before we took our seats. I recognised a veteran women features' writer and thought I would say hello. Hopefully I am not being too unkind, but I think she started out in journalism when they were still using hammers and chisels to set their work in stone. Yes, she was THAT old.

Derek saw me chatting to this wonderful and, admittedly, ancient lady hack, nudged Gerda and said, 'I see Alex is talking to an old school friend.'

Chapter 56

Wet wet wet

The Sunday People Sports Desk in Glasgow was a nest of vipers. It was 1976 when the newspaper's Manchester Editor John Maddock flew up to Glasgow to meet me and make me an offer, as Don Corleone said, I couldn't refuse.

I had been working constant backshift at the Daily Record for nine years - I was now twenty-four - and Saturday was one of my two days off a week. Saturday was sacrosanct; if I didn't cover a game, I was free to go to a football ground of my choice, spend some quality time at home, listen to Spooky Tooth, Santana, Richie Havens, Isaac Hayes, Joe Cocker, Chicago Transit Authority, Howlin' Wolf, BB King on the turntable, catch up with some telly, a lazy day to just put my feet up, or perhaps even read a book.

Ian Gray, the former Sports Editor of the Sunday Mail, made a couple of excellent offers to work for the Record's Sunday sister, but I was never tempted. Then John Maddock came on the scene.

I liked the guy on sight and I quickly discovered he was a superb newspaper professional. John Blair was the main man for sports content in the Scottish edition of the paper. At that time, everything went via Manchester. The paper was put together and printed down there and flown up on a Saturday night alongside its stable mate, the Sunday Mirror.

I met John Maddock out of courtesy after John Blair had informed me the People were looking for someone to take care of business in the Glasgow office on a Saturday. Basically, I would be required to make sure all the main games were covered and copy phoned in on time, while putting together reviews for the old Second and Third Divisions. I was also to be on hand to receive half-time film from two of the games that would be covered, mainly the Old Firm, pick out seven or eight snaps, caption them and get them wired to Manchester. And, after that, I had to collate everything, quotes, breaking news, etc. that came in after the games and piece together a back page.

I would phone John Maddock and tell him we had one main story or something that could be broken into two or three separate pieces. For instance, if I thought we had three articles that deserved to stand alone with merited headlines, I would tell John to expect a main piece of fifteen pars, one of ten and another of six. He would relay the message to the lay-out artists and they would draw up the back page with the information received. Yes, it could get a bit hectic.

I wasn't too sure about accepting the job until John Maddock told me what I could pick up for one day's work. I would be on London rates, by far higher than those of Glasgow and he would throw in an extra half-shift per week if I could shave thirty minutes off the existing publishing schedule. And, of course, I would get expenses, no questions asked. And I would be finished by six o'clock. I was, believe it or not, something known as a 'permanent regular casual'. No, I still haven't got a clue what it means, either. What was a boy to do?

John Maddock told me to sleep on it and get my answer to him early the following week. We went down to The Montrose Bar on the Broomielaw for a couple of pints before he got his flight back to Manchester. As the first beer touched the bar, I gave him my answer in case he changed his mind. 'Yes,' I said, and I kept that shift going for eleven years until I quit to join the Sunday Mail in the summer of 1987.

I knocked the required half an hour off the People's publication times and picked up my weekly 'bonus' on top of the other cash. However, from day one, I was astonished at the hostile atmosphere in such a small office. The three sports reporters, John Blair, Bobby Bogan and Douglas Ritchie, clearly couldn't stand the sight of each other. We had a certain amount of friction among far superior numbers at the Record, but this was something else altogether. God knows how they got on the rest of the week, but I welcomed that certain time on a Saturday when they vacated the office and went to cover their respective games. That was when peace broke out.

As it happened, I got on very well with John and Bobby, but Dougie took a wee bit of watching. He had worked solo for so long on the old Sun newspaper before Rupert Murdoch came on the scene, transformed it into a tabloid, introduced bums and tits on page three and the rest, as they say, is history. Dougie wasn't used to someone else looking at his copy before it went south and, to be honest, he didn't welcome what he obviously perceived as an intrusion. He would actually get a copy boy to smuggle stories to the old Wire Room before they were filed to Manchester. I had to have them retrieved to have a clue what was going into the paper. It would never have been too clever to receive a tip-off from someone, write the story and then find Dougie had already filed the same tale earlier in the day. It happened once. And only once.

To me, John Blair was a jolly type of character, very old school and like something out of a Dickens play. Samuel Pickwick is usually portrayed as a round-faced, clean-shaven, portly gentleman wearing spectacles. Just add long, bushy grey sideburns and you've got John Blair. Unlike most of the sports reporters of my acquaintance, John was not a pub person. I invited him down every Saturday and I think he came twice, both just before he retired at the required age of sixty-five. John didn't bother with my excursions to the pub, but he positively frowned on either Bobby or Dougie going for a quick snifter. Bobby enjoyed a wee dram, but Dougie, as you might have guessed, was happy to do his own thing. I'm not sure he liked the company of people (no pun intended).

Bobby used to try all sorts of elaborate ploys to sneak down to The Copy Cat for a couple of swifties early on a Saturday. The Sunday People offices were situated at the back of the newspaper building at Anderston Quay, so there was no way Bobby could be detected once he got to the front door. In *The Great Escape*, the POWs named their three escape tunnels Tom, Dick and Harry. I'm sure if dear old Bobby could have persuaded another two colleagues, he would have quite merrily dug away knowing there was a large Grouse at the end of the dark shaft.

Even when it was raining, Bobby would leave his jacket draped over his chair. The umbrella would remain at the side of his desk; taking the brolly for a trip to the Wire Room on the fourth floor would have been a bit of a giveaway. 'Just popping upstairs, John, make sure everything is okay,' Bobby would say and he would be out the door only a matter of seconds when John would sidle up to me and say, 'That's him away for a drink; thinks my head buttons up the back.'

On one such occasion, Bobby made sure everything was in place; jacket over chair, umbrella left in plain view. 'Just popping upstairs.' He would run the one hundred yards or so to The Copy Cat, have a couple of drams, sprint back to the office and nip into one of the toilets at the Record and dry his hair and make sure there wasn't a splash of mud or rainwater on his shoes. He would compose himself and then walk along the corridor to the Sunday People offices. He was convinced his little act of deception had worked. John, straightening like a sergeant major, stood up at his desk, eyed him suspiciously and growled, 'Where have you been?'

'I've been up in the Wire Room, boss,' Bobby replied, the epitome of innocence.

'And is it raining in the Wire Room?'

Bobby, bless him, wore spectacles. Tiny particles of rain were quite visible on the lenses. He was caught bang to rights; the evidence as plain as the specs on his nose.

Chapter 57

The ecstasy and the agony

I scooped Fleet Street with my exclusive story of Stevie Archibald leaving Spurs for Barcelona in July 1984 - and got my backside well and truly booted for my efforts.

An oft-repeated observation from my old mate Hughie Taylor went along these lines, 'Journalism is the only industry where they hand you a medal, you stoop forward to receive it and then you get a kick up the arse.' Back then, I realised exactly what he meant by those prophetic words.

I was the Chief Sports Sub-Editor at the Daily Record, and my remit was purely that of production; edit the stories, get the right ones into the right places, check the facts, make it look bright and readable and get it out on time. It was a tough enough job editing a sports section in a national newspaper, but, through my freelance magazine work, I picked up the odd story or two and, at the same time, struck up friendships with certain players, Stevie Archibald among them.

You know, it's quite remarkable how things work out in life, isn't it? I probably wouldn't have had that tale of Stevie moving to one of the biggest clubs in the world if it hadn't been for a chance meeting with his dad, also called Alex. (Stevie has a brother named Alex, too, so it looks as though he's doing his best to surround himself with people called Alex.) I lived in Burnside at the time and Stevie's father worked as a taxi driver in the rank at Rutherglen main street. I was heading into work early one afternoon and I telephoned for a cab. One duly arrived and I was nattering away with the driver en route to the offices at Anderston Quay.

'What do you do in the Record?' I was asked. I told the driver. 'How about getting me some pictures of my son?' he asked. An unusual request even from a cabbie, I thought. 'Who's your son?' I asked, just a tad intrigued. 'Steve Archibald. Plays for Clyde. Have you heard of him?' I nodded my head, I knew the name; there weren't too many Archibalds in

Scottish football. 'Will you get me some snaps?' repeated the driver. 'I'll have a rummage around in the library and see what I can find,' I answered. 'Promise?' asked the cabbie as he dropped me off at the newspaper office. 'I promise,' I said.

I recall it was a Sunday afternoon and those days could be fairly hectic as you set about compiling all the weekend sports news while making certain the Daily Record did not repeat any of the stories that had already appeared in the Sunday papers. Freelancers had a habit of simply regurgitating what they had sent out twenty-four hours earlier. I got about twelve Sunday publications delivered at home and I had already scoured them before heading into work. I would usually give myself an early start on this particular day simply because it was so frantic. The sub-editors would begin rolling in at 5pm to start their shift and it was always a good idea to have a multitude of stories ready for them to get wired into. The early pages would be drawn up and the stories, with style sheets attached, would normally be waiting for them.

That day, as luck would have it, I was running even earlier than normal, something like an hour-and-a-half. I thought I would pop into the library department on the second floor and check out the picture file on Stevie Archibald, assuming there was one. There wasn't. I knew there was another file tucked away in the vaults stamped 'CURRENT FOOTBALL'. Basically, it was a huge pile of action photographs from all the games in Scotland that had been submitted by staff snappers as well as freelancers. These were the photographs that never saw the light of day in the paper, but were shovelled into this file. They would remain there for a couple of months before being trashed and replaced by another bundle. I sifted through the snaps in the hope of finding a couple of the Clyde player. It would have been extremely helpful if the pictures had been in some sort of alphabetical order; of course, they weren't. There were at least a couple of hundred. After about thirty minutes or so checking out scores of sundry images, I found four of Stevie Archibald. I returned the file, went upstairs to my desk and put the snaps in an envelope which I placed in my top right-hand drawer. Amazingly, I remembered to take it home with me that evening.

A couple of days later, I was waiting for a taxi to head into the office again. I heard the usual tooting of the horn outside my front door and was halfway down the garden path when I recognised the driver: Alex Archibald. I about-turned and went back inside to fetch the envelope with the photos of his son. I had left them on a table in the hallway because I just knew I would be meeting Mr Archibald some time soon. I handed over the envelope and, of course, the proud father couldn't wait to see his son in pictorial action for Clyde. It dawned on me those would be the first proper pictures Alex had ever seen of his boy playing football. Honestly, he was overjoyed. I was dropped off as usual and Alex asked me for my home telephone number. I gave it to him and thought nothing more about it. A couple of days later I got a call at home. It was Stevie Archibald. Very politely, he thanked me for the photographs and we had a wee chat.

That was in 1974 and he was earning £6.50 per week playing part-time for modest Clyde. Ten years later he was to join Barcelona for £1.25 million and be well on his way to becoming one of the highest-paid players in football.

We kept in touch all the way through his days at Clyde, but, rather astonishingly, never once met face to face. I knew nothing of his transfer from Clyde to Aberdeen in 1977. We had chatted a week or so earlier on the phone and if Stevie knew of any impending deal with the Pittodrie outfit, he did a good job of keeping it quiet. Three years later, I got a whiff of Stevie preparing to leave Aberdeen for Spurs. Once again, my mate was displaying talents that would have got him an executive position in the Secret Service. As I have said elsewhere in this book, I was aware Jim Rodger, the original 'Scoop' among sports reporters, had a tie-up with the London outfit after years of friendship with the club's former manager, Bill Nicholson.

When I was given the nod about the possibility of a transfer, I decided to phone Stevie and put him on the spot. 'How do you know that?' he asked. 'I've been told not to speak to anyone or the deal is off.' That sounded very much like a warning from Jim Rodger; it was a trademark order. Immediately, I believed the accuracy of the tip-off. Stevie asked me to sit on it. I followed his request, but I knew with 'The Jolly' around, it wouldn't remain hush-hush for much longer.

All was revealed in a press conference with Spurs paying £880,000 for the player who had been working as a car mechanic with Rolls-Royce (he would later buy one) while turning out for a pittance at ramshackle Shawfield only three years before. To be fair to Stevie, he gave me an exclusive interview. There was a great line about him swithering over the move and only making up his mind when he read the motto of the SAS; 'Who Dares Wins'. That swung it for him.

I have to say here and now that I have heard from many people over the years that Stevie and Scrooge are one and the same; you'll never see them in the same room at the same time. Okay, my wife Gerda and I might still be waiting for our wedding gift, he eats us out of house and home when he's in Scotland and pops in to catch a game on Sky and BT Sport and, yes, he forgot to fill up my car with petrol after using it for a month - free of charge - when he was over from Barcelona on business a few years ago, but, hey, let's cut the boy some slack. Actually, I know the Daily Mirror and The Sun in London would have happily written cheques for around £2,000 - a fair chunk of cash in those days - for a 'first person' piece with the new Spurs player. Stevie did his interview with me for the Daily Record for free.

Of course, he had a stupendous career in England, as I would have predicted. We still kept in touch, but we had still never met. Everything was done over the telephone and it looked as though fate had decreed our paths would never meet. I received a handwritten letter - remember them? - every now and again on official Tottenham Hotspur notepaper and I returned the compliment. For all our communications, I could have been standing beside Stevie in a telephone booth and he wouldn't have had a clue who I was or what I looked like. He told me his dad described me as resembling the 'bloke from *The Rockford Files*'. Presumably, he was talking about James Garner, the star of the American TV detective show from the seventies. He's a handsome lad, no doubt about it, but I don't look a bit like him. Not even with the lights out. Besides, he was almost half a century older than me!

I know you are desperate to know this, so I'll put you out of your misery. Stevie and I did meet when he joined Hibs in 1988. We had arranged to hook up in a pal's restaurant called La Vie En Rose which was just off Edinburgh's famous Rose Street. Stevie said, 'Don't tell me what you look like and don't acknowledge me when I arrive. Let me find you. Okay?' I was there that night, sitting at a table with a girlfriend, when in came the bold boy. Remember, we had been talking to each other for fourteen years and never been within touching distance of each other. Stevie looked around the restaurant and promptly walked over to a diner. The guy was taken slightly aback. He was also about eighty years old. Stevie smiled, shook hands with the bloke and came straight over to me. 'I knew it was you all the time.' The rest, as they say, is history.

Four years after Stevie's shift to Spurs the jungle drums were beating; my boy was getting restless again. He had told me of friction between himself and some of the White Hart Lane backroom team. There had been a public bust-up with manager Keith Burkenshaw. Despite winning a UEFA Cup medal - where Stevie struck a decisive penalty-kick in the nerve-shredding shoot-out with Belgian side Anderlecht - and two English FA Cup badges, I was aware he wasn't happy.

Back then, I was the Scottish correspondent for France Football and L'Equipe, two absolutely superb French productions which were both way ahead of their time. One of France Football's journalists was a Parisian gentleman by the name of Max Marquis (Marquee, as he pronounced it) and he worked out of their London office. I spoke to Max once or twice a month, but I never met him, either. I got the impression he might have been Agatha Christie's original prototype for Hercule Poirot; not the Peter Ustinov or Albert Finney versions, but, in fact, more like David Suchet, who later took on the role of the dapper Belgian detective for television. Max would chat about all sorts of things and he gave me the impression he was a bit of a wine connoisseur. I could only tell him I liked copious amounts of lager and made a mental note to never invite him to The Scotia Bar in Stockwell Street any time he was in Glasgow.

Anyway, I was talking to Max one day and he just happened to mention he had heard through the London grapevine that Spurs were about to sell a Scottish player, Stevie Archibald. Did I know him? 'Yes', I answered. 'Any idea where he might be going?' I asked. Max replied, 'I was enjoying a nice claret in a London drinking establishment the other day,' - in hindsight, I think it might have been the Scribes Pub owned by Terry Venables - 'when someone mentioned a Spanish club showing an interest. Apparently, they were willing to pay a substantial amount of cash.'

Sometimes the jigsaw comes together very easily. Venables, of course, had just taken over as manager of Barcelona and he was on the look-out for a replacement striker for Diego Maradona, who was heading for Napoli. I knew Venables wanted to sign Archibald for Crystal Palace in 1980 before he agreed to go to Spurs. Could it be that simple? I put a call into Stevie. He stonewalled me! He told me nothing; not a dicky bird. We can laugh at it now, but I wasn't too impressed in 1984. He had clammed up.

I was positive 'The Jolly', with his Spurs contacts, was on the scene and a long-term friendship was forced to take a back seat. There wasn't even an off the record hint from Stevie. Can you blame him? He wasn't about to put a life-changing move in jeopardy. I phoned him again a couple of evenings later. 'I'm running with the story, mate,' I told Stevie. He said nothing. I trusted him enough for him to tell me not to, because a tale like that would have back-fired fairly spectacularly in my kisser if I was off target.

'Good luck with the story,' was all he said.

'Good luck with the move,' I returned.

From Clyde to Catalonia … Stevie Archibald

I went with it. I wrote the story, drew up the back page and placed it there with a massive 'EXCLUSIVE' tag. I've always believed self-praise is no praise and there is little point of pinning medals on your own chest, but I have to admit I was happy enough with my tale. The following morning, before I started my afternoon shift, I switched on the radio and the news firmed up the transfer; it was definitely going to happen. I sighed with relief. Then I received a telephone call from my Editor, Bernie Vickers. 'Good story,' he said, adding, 'See you when you get in.'

Would it be Cristal or would we slum it with Dom Perignon? Would caviar be on the menu? (Actually, I'm not a big fan of champagne or fish eggs.) I couldn't help but wonder on my drive to the office, earlier than usual to give me plenty of time to soak up the applause. Bernie was sitting at his desk on the editorial floor and I walked straight towards him, requiring plastic surgery to remove the smile from my face. I realised my Editor looked far from satisfied with my efforts. Where did I go wrong? Bernie actually looked a trifle embarrassed. He said, 'Sorry, Alex, but I've just been kicked upside down and I've been told to pass it down the line. Consider your backside booted, as well.' I looked for the tell-tale hint of a smile. There was none.

It was my bad luck that Robert Maxwell had just taken over the Mirror Group that month. The megalomaniac known as 'The Bouncing Czech' was clearly enraged his newly-acquired Daily Mirror did not get a copy of my story. 'Why would I send it to them?' I asked logically. Although the Record and the Mirror came out of the same stable, we were still rivals on the newsstands. As far as I was concerned, I worked for the Record and they were my only concern. The Mirror meant as much to me in Glasgow as the Record meant to a hack in London; zilch. Dear old Hughie Taylor's words drifted back in that instant.

Pardon me, if I don't dwell on the horrendous Maxwell Years at the Daily Record and Sunday Mail; I've always been a sucker for a happy ending. I met the guy once and thought he was easily the most bizarre, undefined mass of protoplasm masquerading as a human being it had ever been my misfortune to come across. His face was chalk white and caked with make-up and his hair was jet black, dyed almost on a daily basis. With his extended belly, I doubt if he had seen his feet in years. Normally a bloke like that would be in a circus or certified.

He brought chaos to Anderston Quay through his sheer greed; there was no need for some of his despicable deeds, least of all, standing on the doorstep on the newspaper building on day one and promising there would be no need for anyone to fear for their jobs, then going straight upstairs and sacking chairman Derek Webster. With this bloke around, there was always the opportunity for a plague of dullards and 'yes men' to make progress if they danced to his tune. Some so-called 'executives' were as comfortable with the written word as Maxwell was at attempting to stay afloat. I saw some pathetic spectacles back then.

Glad I got that off my chest. Okay, time to get on with the story.

Hughie's words echoed around my head again on November 3 1992, more than eight years after the Archibald fiasco. By then, I was Sports Editor of the Sunday Mail. Lennox Lewis was being tipped as Britain's first world heavyweight boxing champion of the twentieth century and he was due to fight Canadian Donovan 'Razor' Ruddock in a WBC Eliminator at Earls Court in London on October 31. As usual, there was a lot of publicity surrounding the fight, but unlike Joe Bugner, Henry Cooper, Brian London and another colony of no-hope journeymen, it looked as though Lewis had a genuine chance of taking the title. He had won the 1988 Olympic gold medal at the weight, had fought twenty-one pro bouts, won the lot with an impressive tally of eighteen knock-outs. Ruddock was no slouch, either, with twenty-seven wins from thirty-one fights, twenty inside the distance.

The fight had been hyped up for weeks, but on the days leading down to the head-to-head encounter, the publicity machine went stratospheric. The fight was due for a Sunday morning start around two o'clock because Sky were beaming the action back live to the States.

I had a word with the production people to make sure we could get coverage of the fight in the Sunday Mail. There was little point of them putting it into the newspapers at the tail-end of a run. Obviously, if we could anticipate everything being done and dusted in a reasonable time, then we could get thousands more into Glasgow and surroundings areas. I thought we should go with the fight. They agreed. I volunteered to cover the event and write it from Sky TV's pictures. I began my shift at just before 10am that day and worked all the way through to the boxing action. In all, it was a seventeen-hour shift. (*What a man*, I hear you say.)

I mapped out a prominent space for it on the back page. I left room to accommodate sixteen paragraphs. I pre-set three headings to cover a win, a loss and a draw. Next up, I had to choose a couple of colour snaps and get them down to the process department early to give them a chance to prepare them for the paper. One had Lennox Lewis with his hands in the air (after a previous win) and the other was a simple action shot. I wrote three captions to cover the eventualities.

The eighties and nineties had seen a revolution in marketing of the sport. In Muhammad Ali's days he just about always wore pants endorsed by the 'Everlast' label across his waistband. Lewis, I noticed, was changing his sponsors and his shorts almost fight by fight. That presented a problem because I didn't have a clue what backer's name would be on his waistband the night he fought Ruddock. Get it wrong and you could be sure some eagle-eyed reader would spot it and tell the world. I cropped the photo of a triumphant Lewis to take out the sponsor's name.

So, come the morning everything was ready to go. A couple of fight fans remained in the editorial to watch Lewis v Ruddock on the telly. The Londoner must have been aware of the Sunday Mail's 'off stone' production times. He walloped his opponent all over the place and a thudding right sent the Canadian toppling towards the canvas at the end of the first. I was already writing the intro. 'Lennox Lewis's dream of becoming world champion is alive after his demolition job on Donovan 'Razor' Ruddock in the early hours of the morning.' Something along those lines. I would leave the second par blank to put in how he won, knock-out, which round, on points, opponent retiring etc. I could fill in the remaining pars with some of the early action.

Lewis continued the assault in the second round and decked Ruddock again with a ferocious right to the chin. The Canadian, who was actually favourite to win, got up at the count of nine, but his legs had turned to jelly. He was gone and it was only a matter of time. Lewis went in for the kill. Crash! Bang! Wallop! It was all over. TKO in the second round; thank you, Mr Lewis.

My copy was sent to the type-setter, it went through a very quick process and was then delivered in what was known as monotype. Or 'wallpaper' as some preferred to call it. Then it could be pasted onto the page by a caseroom operator, I cut it to actual size, one last look and then it was off to cook downstairs before being delivered oven-ready to the machine room. I'm pretty sure these are not the technical terms, by the way. I drove home and was fairly satisfied with the way things had gone. I came back to work on Tuesday morning and I was told the Production Manager had sent a memo to the bosses saying things couldn't have gone better and he actually praised me by name. That was a bit unusual and I thanked him for his gesture.

One of Maxwell's former mini-Rambo minions, now touching his forelock in the direction of major shareholder the Bank of England after Cap'n Bob's Canary Isles 'calamity', slithered in my direction at some point that morning, looked at the back page and I wondered if he was actually going to compliment me. 'That photograph's a bit dark,' he mumbled and shuffled off, presumably to shed some scales in an appropriate damp and dark corner.

It was an image of Lennox Lewis, born of Jamaican parents, in the shady confines of an indoor boxing arena. Maybe if Lennox Lewis had been thoughtful enough to reverse the Al Jolson trend and 'white up' for the night and someone had arranged to have the bout fought under glaring floodlights, then the Maxwell-trained little toady might have been satisfied.

Like the gent with the long black sideburns and the blue suede shoes, I left the building, never to return, sixteen months later.

What did dear, old Hughie Taylor say again?

Chapter 58

Damn that Rummenigge

It was the evening of November 7 1984 and I wondered if someone had switched April Fool's Day. I was having an après work drink (well earned) in Henry Afrikas, a nightclub on York Street in Glasgow. A gorgeous specimen of womanhood adorned a stool at the bar and appeared to be paying me no little attention.

Here was a vision to whom Botacelli would have struggled to do justice. The face of an angel and the body of a supermodel, she made Raquel Welch look like a brickie. I pondered if a prankster had pinned a large sign on my back proclaiming, 'Kiss This Man And Win Instant Cash!' I could only believe my change of aftershave was doing the trick; no-one seemed overly-excited in the past when my Brut was in evidence.

Buddy Rich was giving it pelters inside my rib cage as Miss Wonderful, shapely legs up to her ear lobes, sashayed in my direction, flashing a smile that came straight from a Farrah Fawcett poster. She swept her blonde tresses back from her flawlessly sculpted features, vibrant blue eyes dancing with mischief. She bedazzled me again with her gleaming, even teeth and, as my quivering knees almost buckled under the weight of anticipation, she asked me, in sexy, husky tones, the question I will never forget.

'Are you Karl-Heinz Rummenigge?'

'Eh? Whit?' was my worldly retort. (James Bond didn't have the copyright on all the smart one-liners.)

'Are you Karl-Heinz Rummenigge?' she repeated, looking less attractive by the millisecond.

Unfortunately, I was standing alongside the German football legend and Liam Brady in the night spot. Both had played for Inter Milan against Rangers at Ibrox that evening in a European tie (they won 4-3 on aggregate) and the players had been allowed some free time before flying back to Italy the following morning. I had introduced myself to Brady, whom I got to know a lot better when he became manager of Celtic in 1991, as we had a mutual friend, Tony Roche, a journalist who had just completed Liam's autobiography.

Tony asked me where Liam and a few of the Inter players could go after the game at Ibrox for a couple of drinks without being mobbed by fans, well-meaning or otherwise. I nominated Henry Afrikas and Tony told me I should make myself known to Liam if I spotted him. And so I did. It was then I realised I had, somehow wondrously, been transformed into a babe magnet. Until those fatal words.

'Are you Karl-Heinz Rummenigge?'

I'm 6ft 2in and, back then, fair-haired (now grey) and Karl-Heinz was 5ft 11in and blond. As soon as I pointed out her error and stepped aside to introduce her to the sporting icon, her interest in me dissolved at a rapid rate.

Yes, you're right. I could have lied. Mind you, given the fact that my German was pretty much non-existent and I didn't own half of Bavaria, I think I might have been rumbled in double-quick time.

Chapter 59

Press passes - part two

There had been a spate of thefts on the Daily Record editorial floor when security officers hatched a plan to catch the light-fingered culprit.

In the early hours of the morning, they removed the television set from the News Editor's desk and replaced it with a cardboard box which had a TV aerial balancing on top of it. They rubbed black boot polish on the box to make it look more authentic. The security officer then slid under the desk and waited to nab the thief.

At one stage, he needed to go to the loo. He was away a matter of two or three minutes.

When he returned, the cardboard box was gone.

*

The old press box at ancient Hampden was a bit of a phenomenon. It actually leaned out at a forward angle and you could clearly hear the players having a go at each other, even when there was a noisy six-figure crowd crammed into the ground.

You could pick up what some of the fans were shouting, too. During one Scotland v England international, one of the Tartan Army was far from pleased with the performance of the match official.

'You're shite, referee,' he hollered.

'He'll no' understand you,' yelled another fan. 'He's French.'

'You're merde, referee,' came the quick-as-a-flash reaction.

On another occasion, I picked up the words of a supporter making his way towards his mates during the interval with the snacks. 'Hurry up and eat these pies before they get warm,' was the exclamation.

*

You knew you were in for a bumpy ride when you were greeted by an anxious secretary as you took your first step through the lift doors on the editorial floor.

There was one particular mean-spirited executive who gave me the impression he had been thrown out of the Gestapo for being just a shade too nasty.

On occasion, the weary secretary would give you the nod that all was not well with this individual. In her most apologetic tone, she would whisper, 'Sorry, Alex, but Jim's himself today.'

*

Frank Gray was a brilliant Picture Editor of the Sunday Mail. He could be an excitable chap, too.

He was in the editorial TV room watching the 1980 Scottish Cup Final between Celtic and Rangers. It was a tense encounter that was settled in extra-time with a goal from Celtic's George McCluskey. All hell broke loose at the end with both sets of fans swarming onto the pitch to try to knock each other good looking.

Comedian Andy Cameron told me, 'Aye, I was on the pitch that day. This Celtic punter ran at me and I just belted them over the head with a bottle. I'm told she was off school for at least a week.'

Hampden Park resembled a war zone as mounted police, batons drawn, waded into the fighting throng. It was as disgraceful a scene witnessed inside a football ground in the country's history as Neanderthals waged war on each other on the sacred turf of our national stadium. It all got too much for Frank Gray. He raced out of the TV room and down the editorial floor towards the executives on the back bench.

He yelled, 'It's Armadillo at Hampden ... bloody Armadillo.'

It was just as well it wasn't part of Frank's remit to write the headlines.

*

John Begg was one of the most prolific sports freelance reporters of the sixties and seventies. Jock Stein often availed himself of the services of this thoroughly likeable character.

John's nickname was 'Take A Peg' which was the long-running slogan for the whisky by the name of John Begg, 'the whisky supplied to all the ROYAL PALACES for over 70 YEARS', so said an advert for the product in 1923.

Unfortunately, John, then at the veteran stage, was hospitalised and the surgeons had to amputate a leg.

'That's taking the nickname just too far,' said one unsympathetic hack.

*

'Not a lot of people know this, but I'm very famous.'

That's a fitting mantra for those unseen individuals known as sub-editors. One of these guys can make a bad writer good, a good writer great and a great writer exceptional. They possess the skills and have the power. They don't mind working in the darkness of anonymity and have little or no desire to see their name in print.

One such excellent professional is a bloke called Robert Melvin, who just happens to be a lifelong pal. Robert was one of the most diligent newspapermen with whom it has been my pleasure to share a Sports Desk. He was a sub you could depend upon and, for me, was an absolute treasure to the Daily Record.

I recall the fabulous job he did the night Jim Watt won the WBC world lightweight championship by beating tough Colombian Alfredo Pitalua in front of a frenzied sell-out crowd at Glasgow's Kelvin Hall on April 17

1979. It was a Tuesday evening, with a midnight start to suit American Cable TV. Watt won when New York referee Arthur Mercante stopped the fight in the twelfth round.

Hopefully I'm not being boastful, but the Record also wiped the floor with the opposition the following morning. Dick Currie's report caught the raw emotion and wild nationalistic pride of the evening as well as an unbeatable summary of the action. Robert's pinpoint editing couldn't have been bettered, and George Hunter was the photographer who must have doubled as high wire daredevil to take some outstanding snaps from scaffolding inside the arena.

We finished our shift around 4am and, as we were both off that day, I offered to buy Robert a very late champagne breakfast in The Montrose. Unsurprisingly, he accepted. So, about one o'clock, Robert, rightly proud of his sterling efforts in the early hours of the morning, made his entrance at the pub. A round of applause and a fanfare of trumpets wouldn't have been undeserved.

John McIntyre, the Daily Record's Circulation Manager, had been in for an early lunch with one of his colleagues. He looked over his shoulder, saw Robert and said, 'I'll be with you in a minute.'

Alas, Robert had been mistaken for a taxi driver.

*

Bill Corke was a good, old-fashioned news hack at the Daily Record. The only time he wasn't half-sozzled was when he was completely sozzled. News Editor Fergie Miller never realised his reporter took a drink until he caught him sober once.

Bill was a proud Welshman, massive rugby fan and always insisted on wearing something red. Certainly, he worked hard at his bright florid complexion. Bill would arrive at the Copy Cat and announce, 'Sorry, I'm in a terrible rush. I can only stay for about six or seven.' He wasn't being funny. I liked the guy.

There was one afternoon we were propping up the bar, probably discussing his heartfelt belief that a bottle of Jameson's was the birthplace of all dreams. I noticed he was wearing a scarlet V-neck sweater that had the letters WA embroidered on the chest. I could understand that the W could stand for William, but the letter A was a bit more baffling. I had to ask.

Bill explained, 'Well, you know it was the Welsh rugby team's centenary year in 1981, don't you? I decided to treat myself and buy this tribute sweater. Then I noticed there was a loose thread at the letter 'y' at the end of the 'centenary' stitching. I just pulled it, you see. It should read, "WALES RUGBY CENTENARY".

'Now I'm just left with WA.'

*

A photographer at one of the Daily Record district offices was known to enjoy a pint and a punt. Or, if you prefer, a bevvy and a gamble. Distinctly bad bedfellows, methinks.

Hands up, I have been known to knock back a beer or two in my time, but I've never been drawn towards cards, horses, football or any other source that will undoubtedly help denude the contents of my already-depleted wallet. At a push, I might play the card game 'Snap' with someone afflicted with a stutter. Otherwise, no thanks.

Anyway, this particular lensman got in a bit too deep one night when he was involved in a heavy card school. The steady flow of brandy didn't sharpen his concentration, either. By the end of a reckless evening, he had been cleaned out. After losing all his cash, he was told his credit was no good. He couldn't very well gamble the house; even in his inebriated state, he realised the wife and three kids might not fancy sleeping rough for the rest of their lives. They had got used to a roof over their heads, after all. In desperation, he made one last frantic play to turn around his fortunes.

I'm still not sure how he explained the loss of the company car to the Record bosses.

Some guys took strange routes to roles into journalism. A former Deputy Sports Editor of mine at the Sunday Mail was a bloke by the name of Alex McLeod who was a massive rugby fan. He went on so incessantly about the oval ball sport that the rest of the Sports Desk ended up nicknaming him 'Wee Pointy Heid'. He took it as a compliment.

But Alex didn't leave school eager for a career in newspapers. Instead, he joined the Navy. Somehow that didn't work out and, by some circuitous route, he arrived at journalism. I was never able to work that out. Having said that, though, he was an excellent newspaperman.

I heard the story of an electrician who was doing a job at the STV studios in Glasgow. He was quite well spoken, wasn't unattractive and had good manners, opening doors for females and the like. A producer liked the cut of his jib and, just like that, he was invited to host sports shows on the telly. Obviously, he was a bright spark (sorry, couldn't help it).

There was another chap I met on the Daily Record's Sports Desk. His name was Jim and I often wondered what on earth he was doing in newspapers. He wasn't God's gift to the written word, that's for sure. If I was cruel, I could say that if talent was a disease he would have been the healthiest man on the planet. But I'm not that cruel.

Anyway, one day I asked him what had propelled him towards a career in journalism. Apparently, he had started on the ground floor of the old Evening Times building in Buchanan Street. He was at the front counter where they dealt with 'Hatches, Matches and Dispatches.' Or, as they are properly known, 'Births, Marriages and Deaths'. The public would come in, fill out the relevant forms, count the words - I think it was something like one shilling (5p) per word back in the sixties - and he would check it for spellings and so on before passing it onto the proper department to be processed into the newspaper.

However, he was relieved of these duties one day for failing to control his laughter when a wee old lady filled in a Memorial form for her dearly departed husband who lost his life at sea during the Second World War.

Every year on the anniversary of his sad passing, she would make her way to the Evening Times offices in Glasgow to carefully fill in that form. She would pay her money, say, 'See you next year,' and then leave quietly through the side exit. Naturally, it was an emotional day in her calendar. So, the last thing she needed was Jim roaring with glee when he read her heartfelt message for her dead husband. So, what tickled Jim's fancy? The memorial announced,

'My Wee Tam was always nice and clean,

'He went to meet God in a submarine.'

*

The Sunday Mail Sports Desk's Christmas parties had the habit of becoming slightly boisterous affairs. Each year we would select a hostelry to stage our annual re-enactment of something akin to the Siege of Mafeking.

On this particular festive occasion, the patrons of the very fine Babbity Bowster establishment on Blackfriars Street in Glasgow city centre were treated to the impromptu antics of the journalists and guests who dovetailed throughout the year to help produce the biggest-selling newspaper in the country.

As you are probably able to anticipate by now, strong drink is a pre-requisite for this particular day out when war is declared on alcohol. I don't recall too many abstainers at these functions. The afternoon at Babbity Bowster had hurtled into evening and there were a few dead men walking. One of our number decided to serenade a young couple sitting in the corner of the restaurant, steadfastly minding their own business among the revellers.

Dropping to his knees in front of their table, he performed a hearty and extremely thunderous version of *Oklahoma!*, a rendition, it must be said, which bore no resemblance to the one made famous by veteran Hollywood crooner Howard Keel in the movie of the same name. Pub dwellers that evening probably decided in unison that Archie Macpherson was much better suited to commentating on football.

However, Billy McNeill wasn't bad on the harmonies…

*

The tell-tale sign of the hopeless gambler is often his mode of transport. When they are on a winning streak, they are often seen zooming around in a gleaming Porsche. If things ain't so good, it's often the rust-bucket Volkswagen. 'My car's in the garage. I'm just using the wife's this week.' Aye, right.

There was one Celtic player in the early seventies who was never going to be seen driving around in anything too sleek. I'm not a gambler, but I've got a fair idea 'mug punter' is not a term of high praise for those who like a wee flutter.

Davie Hay assures me this is a true story. 'Everyone was well aware Lou Macari was a guy who liked a bet. Lou had a great knowledge of horses and I think he won more than he lost. He had an exceptionally quick brain when it came to sizing up situations - and I'm not just talking about when he was in the opponents' penalty area.

'I recall a day when we were whiling away the hours watching TV in the players' room at Celtic Park waiting for kick-off. To be honest, it can get a bit boring on these occasions because you are primed and ready to go; this is what you have trained all week for and the adrenalin is always pumping away. On this occasion, there were cartoons on the telly and no-one was paying any particular attention. Lou noticed that something called *Wacky Races* was coming on. For a bit of fun, he opened a book and started to give odds. Unbelievably, he hooked in one of our players. No-one could believe this bloke took odds of 2/1 on one of the characters.

'Maybe he had never seen the show before or he just felt extremely lucky when he stuck on his fiver. No-one had the heart to tell him Dick Dastardly and Muttley never ever got to come first.'

*

Bernie Vickers, the Daily Record's Editor, was in the mood for change and wanted to jazz up the Saturday sports section.

Back at the start of the eighties, he conjured up the idea of a 12-page pull-out and asked for any thoughts on his plan for a revamp. I liked the innovation and told him so. Actually, it didn't really matter what my view was on the project because Bernie would have gone ahead and pushed it through, anyway. He also fancied further giving the pull-out its own identity with a change in colour from the rest of the newspaper. He thought pink would be ideal.

I could recall the Saturday afternoons when the pink Evening Times and the green Evening Citizen were produced mainly for football fans in the West of Scotland. Again, I agreed with the Editor. He also came up with a slogan which he would run along the top of the newspaper every Saturday. I'm afraid we weren't reading from the same sheet on this one and I just couldn't subscribe to his chosen formation of words. He pointed to his imaginary stripes.

So, every Saturday morning for about two years, hot-blooded sports fans throughout the country were encouraged to ...

'PULL OUT THE PINK UN'.

Chapter 60

The mistress and the ringing endorsement

A well-known Scottish international star with one of the Old Firm clubs had been playing away from home for a considerable time. He had even set up his mistress in a flat on the south side of Glasgow.

Most of the guys, including me, on the Daily Record's Sports Desk knew of the situation. The guy in question was extremely popular with the press, so everything was hush-hush. It was the early seventies and no-one blew the whistle. The long-suffering wife hadn't an inkling.

The player covered his tracks fairly expertly. He had told his missus he wanted to go into management when he quit playing. 'That means I've got to go to a lot of away games to keep my eye on up-and-coming players. I've got to be ready when I get the call. So, I might have to take in a few evening games in Aberdeen, Dundee and wherever. Unfortunately, there will be overnight stays. You understand, dear?'

You could picture the scenario. The trusting spouse had learned to live with the constant demands of football. Her husband had also to travel with the reserve team when they had midweek games just to try his hand at coaching. 'Got to be prepared, dear.' And off he would go for an evening with his girlfriend, who was completely at ease with her position in the long-term deception.

All went well until the wife received an unexpected phone call. She was informed by the anonymous female caller that her husband had been spotted out on the town with a young lady on his arm. She thought he had been away with the reserve team in Berwick that evening. She decided to confront her husband the following day. 'Innocent,' was the plea. 'Must be someone who looks like me.'

A couple of weeks later, the wife received another phone call from the same unknown source. Once again, her hubby had been spotted with a rather attractive companion. They looked like they were having fun. She was sure her husband had told her he was with the reserves for a fundraiser for a team in the Highlands. Once again, she took it up with her man when he returned after training the following afternoon.

'Innocent,' was the cry again. This happened a couple of times over the next month or so. An unknown well-meaning (vindictive?) female appeared to be keeping tabs on the errant player and maintaining a steady line of information to his wife.

The footballer knew it was time to do something about these nuisance calls. He hatched a plan with his mistress. He made sure he was in one evening and a telephone call was expected around 9pm. Sure enough, the instrument shrilled. The wife answered. 'Oh, my man, is out on the town again with his girlfriend, is he? Are you sure it's my husband? Funny that, because he's sitting on the sofa beside me and we're just about to watch the Max Bygraves Show. I would suggest you never phone me again. If you do, I'll just hang up. Okay?' With that she slammed down the receiver.

'So sorry, darling,' she said. 'You know I never doubted you for a moment, don't you?'

The player smiled and accepted the apologies of his wife. The mistress had played a blinder. He related the story to me one day over lunch.

Just a week or so after his divorce.

Chapter 61

Ali and the ringside seat ... in Glasgow

Muhammad Ali ... and the late-night thrillers

I was among five million UK television viewers who stayed awake to witness challenger Cassuis Clay's world heavyweight championship fight against Sonny Liston at 4am at the Convention Hall, in Miami Beach, Florida, on February 25 1964. The historic event was beamed by the BBC, the first boxing match to be shown live across the Atlantic. Britain was one of fifteen European countries receiving the action via relay satellite.

I had just turned twelve and little did I realise I would be 'covering' Muhammad Ali title fights fourteen years later for the Daily Record. Unfortunately, though, never from the ringside in exotic locations such as New York, Las Vegas, Kinshasa or Manila. Nope, my beat was Anderston Quay, tuned to the American Armed Forces radio station.

The byline in the newspaper was either 'Peter Wilson or Frank McGhee at the ringside', but it was really Alex Gordon at the Daily Record Sports Desk in Glasgow. Wilson was succeeded by McGhee as the Chief sportswriter of the Daily Mirror and the superior budget of our London cousins allowed them to send their sports reporters worldwide. We would often 'lift' their copy and present it as our own in the Record. All perfectly above board.

However, there was always a problem with boxing matches starting at times such as 2am or 3am on the other side of the world. Normally, Wilson or McGhee would have their copy wired to the London offices of the Mirror. Alas, back then, it could only be sent to one site. Then a wire room operator would have to type it all out again and forward it on to Glasgow. Of course, there were no such things as faxes in those days. It was an exceptionally slow process and the words from Wilson or McGhee could be running more than an hour late. Believe me, that is a massive sixty minutes in production times early in the morning when the presses have stopped and are awaiting the news. The fight could go the distance and the Record would just be receiving coverage of round one.

Given those circumstances and with critical time restrictions, it would have been virtually impossible to get the fight verdict into the newspaper the following morning and it would mean our readers missing out. The Record prided itself by going that extra yard to beat our rivals in an effort to continue topping up circulation. Very early in my career, I was impressed by a scenario that had been painted by a veteran newspaperman. 'Imagine you're working on a building site and everyone stops for a break,' he said. 'There are three guys having a mug of tea. One's got the Record, another's got the Express and the other's got the Mail. The Record reader has the absolute latest news the other newspapers have missed. It won't be too long before the other two blokes ditch their papers and start getting the Record.' Simple enough little tale, but one that stuck with me.

Back in the early hours of February 25 1964, I was excited as I waited for the Clay v. Liston fight to begin. Of course, what I knew about the craft of the Noble Art back then you could have written in large letters on a postage stamp and still have had plenty of room left over. But Cassius Clay, who, of course, reverted to his Muslim name of Muhammad Ali the day after he beat Liston, had really captured my imagination like no other boxer. Football and boxing were my main sporting interests and I had been brought up on fighters such as Henry Cooper, Brian London and Jack Bodell who had two things in common; they would never win a world title and they liked to lead with their chin.

In an era when most heavyweight boxers possessed cauliflower faces, Cassius Clay was charismatic, colourful, a genuine showman. I was hooked. That particular morning, my mum made up a bed settee for me in the living room. She left a flask of tea and told me to remember to switch the telly off after the fight. She worked in a bakery at McNeill Street, in the Gorbals, at that time and she would be leaving for her shift about 10pm. My dad was also working a nightshift at Polmadie Railway station. My sister Betty, six years older than me, was staying overnight with a friend. I had the house to myself as I made myself comfortable before the TV treat.

That was the start of a love affair with Muhammad Ali. I've got every single fight of his on video or DVD. I own about fifty books on his life and times. My wife Gerda bought me a model of Ali, standing twenty inches tall, that's got pride of place in my study at home. Press a button and you'll hear his unmistakeable voice, asking, 'Who's The Greatest?'

I couldn't even hazard a guess at how many times I've watched that bout against Sonny Liston in Miami Beach. I don't think a solitary boxing 'expert' tipped the upstart who had been labelled 'The Louisville Lip'. Many believed the brash contender was too lightweight compared to the brute force of Liston, who didn't believe in boxing. He was a fighter; pure and simple. He went into the middle of the ring, stood toe to toe with his challenger, and normally battered them into submission. On September 25 1962, Liston won the world championship when he knocked out Floyd Paterson in the first round. He took all of two minutes and five seconds before clubbing his opponent to the canvas. A rematch was called for on July 22 1963 and Paterson did marginally better; he lasted two minutes and NINE seconds before his bloody capitulation. Liston brought controlled mayhem to the boxing ring.

Next up was Cassius Clay, the first poet of fisticuffs. 'When the crowd laid down their money, they didn't dream they would see a total eclipse of the Sonny.' Okay, it owed more to McGonagall than Burns, but it was all captivating stuff. Liston didn't bother with banter. He growled menacingly, 'I'm gonna pull that big tongue out of your mouth and stick it up your ass.' That was the best he came up with. I couldn't wait to view that fight. I danced around our tiny living room when Liston failed to come out for the seventh round; Clay winning on a technical knock-out. He screamed into the microphone, 'I shook up the world! I shook up the world! I'm a bad man. I just upset Sonny Liston and I don't have a mark on my face. I must be the greatest.' And, of course, he was just that. To me, anyway, and billions of others.

I actually volunteered to cover his early morning fights. (I hope older readers will forgive the deception.) I'm no technical wizard - just ask my wife! After twenty years I have now mastered the microwave - so I would get someone to set the dial on the Sports Desk radio for the American Armed Forces network and heaven help anyone who went anywhere near that fount of all knowledge. I wanted to be one of the first to know how my hero had fared. It's amazing how much you can do with one little gem of information. The ringside reporter could say something innocuous like, 'Ali is keeping his left in the face of the challenger' and you could spin about fifty words out of that grain of knowledge.

The BBC, after their original telecast, dropped out because it became too expensive with Ali's handlers all too aware they had something special to barter with. BBC Radio eventually cottoned on, but, back then, it was the AAF you had to rely on. Pay-Per-View and cinema screenings came into play later on, but, although the Odeon in Glasgow beamed back several Ali contests, they were useless for big fight coverage because of the lack of telephone facilities in the cinema. So, it was just me, as Peter Wilson or Frank McGhee, sitting beside the radio with a typewriter at the ready in the early hours of a morning.

I recall one incident, beyond the witching hour, when Editor Bernie Vickers came wandering along the editorial floor. (I talk about this excellent and eccentric executive elsewhere.) It was fairly obvious he had had a few drinks. Bernie thought nothing of spending a few hours in The Rogano of an afternoon and just continue the topping-up process as the evening wore on. The Sports Desk, at that time in the morning, looked as though the Calgary Stampede had taken place. There were empty cans of lager lying around, plastic cups upside down, paper strewn all over the place, stubbed-out cigarettes, the usual mess that greeted the poor cleaners when they started their shifts at 6am. Bernie was not impressed by the cluttered and shambolic state of the place. He looked at me.

'Clean up this fookin' mess right now,' he ordered in his Mancunian tones.

'Sorry, Bernie, I'm just waiting for the Ali fight to begin,' I replied reasonably.

'Clean up this fookin mess right now or you're fired,' said the weary boss.

'I'm not cleaning up anything.' I was indignant.

'Then you're fired.' Bernie had spoken.

'Who's going to cover the Ali fight?' I asked.

'Okay, you're fired in the morning,' said the Editor, who about-turned and sauntered back in the general direction of his office.

I can't recall that actual fight, although I have an inkling it might have been against Joe Frazier on March 8 1971. Ali, after refusing to be inducted into the US Army, had been out of action for three years and had only two fights in 1970 - TKO wins over Jerry Quarry and Oscar Bonavena - before coming up against Smokin' Joe at Madison Square Garden in New York. (Ali lost on points after fifteen pulverising rounds.) I've got a framed photograph on my study wall taken years later at the famous Big Apple venue, with a massive billboard behind me hailing it as 'The Fight of the Century'. What I would have given to be there that night. Instead, I was in Glasgow getting fired for my trouble.

I loved the quote I dug up among the mountain of words that was written about the fight the next day. Smokin Joe said, 'I hit him with punches that would bring cities down.'

Incidentally, I saw Bernie Vickers the following day. I asked him if I was still fired. He waved me away. 'Good work,' was all he said. I assumed I still had a job.

Damn! Missed the fight ... me at Madison Square Garden in 2005

One of the last fights I covered from the radio was Ali's remarkable loss on points to the unfancied Leon Spinks on February 15 1978 in Las Vegas, almost fourteen years to the day I had seen him beat Sonny Liston. He won the world title back from Spinks, of course, in August later that year in New Orleans. On June 27 1979 he announced his retirement and, privately, I thanked him for the awesome journey. Alas, he was tempted to make two comeback fights in 1980 and 1981; two losses against Larry Holmes, his former sparring partner, and Trevor Berbick, a boxer I reckoned my missus, in a good mood, could beat. On December 12, a day after the loss against Berbick, Ali, just a month before his thirty-ninth birthday, decided enough was enough. Thankfully, he didn't have a change of mind,

The last word has to go to The Greatest. He was asked, 'How would you like to be remembered?'

In an instant, he replied, 'As a man who never sold out his people. But, if that's too much, then just a good boxer and I won't even mind if you don't mention how pretty I was.'

Chapter 62

Tommy Gemmell's booze brothers

Jinky and Gordy may sound like a comedy double-act. But when those two got together it was no laughing matter. Certainly, Tommy Gemmell, then the Dundee manager, didn't see the funny side after a booze-fuelled incident back in 1977.

The Lisbon Lion, another quality human being it has been my utmost pleasure to spend time with, related the extraordinarily funny yarn when I co-authored this genuine legend's autobiography, *All the Best*, which was published by CQN Books in 2014.

Here is the story as Tommy told it …

I thought I had pulled off the signing coup of the century when I tempted my old Lisbon Lion team-mate Jimmy Johnstone to Dundee during my first few weeks as boss of the Dens Park club. He had left Celtic two years earlier in 1975 on a free transfer, first to San Jose Earthquakes and then onto Sheffield United. After his stint in England, Jinky was up for grabs again. He was only thirty-two years old at the time and I had every faith there was still mileage in those little legs of his. I believed he could do a real turn for Dundee and help me settle into management at the same time.

I contacted my wee pal and the whole town was buzzing when the news leaked that there was the possibility of the great Jimmy Johnstone signing for Dundee. Ten years earlier he had been my Celtic colleague when we beat Inter Milan to win the European Cup on a glorious day in Lisbon. I had brought in Willie Wallace as my assistant and now there was the chance of three of that historic outfit teaming up on Tayside. Could the magic rub off once more? It seemed beyond the most outrageous hopes and dreams of the Dundee support. One telephone call put the wheels in motion.

Jinky agreed to have a chat and I promised him I would put together a contract that would suit him and the club. I can tell you that if Jinky had stuck to the deal and all had gone well, he would have earned more than me at Dundee. I was on £10,000 per year and, to help with the comparisons of the time, Ally MacLeod was the Scotland manager on £15,000 per year. If Jinky kept himself fit and played in all our games he would have walked away with fifty per cent more in his pay poke than yours truly and the same as the country's international team boss. I was perfectly happy with that situation. But, of course, I knew Jinky better than most, possibly better than the Wee Man himself. Basically, he had to be making appearances and performing for the two-year deal to be worth everyone's while.

I had arranged a reasonable basic wage with an excellent signing-on fee spread over the length of the contract. There would be bonuses for points and our position in the league. There were all sorts of other add-ons that would have made Jinky one of the best-paid players in Scotland although we were a First Division side at the time. In all honesty, if I had still been playing, I would have snapped up a deal like that and made sure I spent the next twenty-four months earning every penny. Jinky, though, saw the world from a different angle from most people.

I was delighted when he said he would sign for us. I then laid it on the line that he would have to work hard to get his financial rewards. He assured me he would and I believed him. He may have been a bit wayward, a happy-go-lucky character, if you like, but there was another side to Jinky that a lot of people never saw. He was a very sincere, well-meaning person. The reason he couldn't retire at thirty when he left Celtic was because he hadn't put together a pot of gold. He wasn't financially secure.

Jinky earned good money at the club, but he wasn't the type of individual to save for a rainy day. Believe me, that is the case with most footballers. I realise it is totally illogical, even to the ones who don't have all their brains in their feet, that a day will dawn when the ability you possessed for such an important part of your life has ebbed away. The power in your body has simply dissipated. And one former Scotland international of my acquaintance, who was a genuine tough guy, told me he knew it was time to retire from the playing side when his heart went. He no longer relished thundering tackles and realised he was being bowled over by fitter and younger opponents. It's something you have to accept.

However, I looked at Jinky on his first day of training with us and I was impressed. He had been on a family holiday and looked tanned, fit and ready to go. There was a problem, though, and I hope my wee pal will forgive me for this observation, because there normally was with him. He fretted over all the travelling entailed as he wanted to continue living in Uddingston, in Lanarkshire, with his wife Agnes and the family. I had the solution to that particular obstacle. I had bought the Commercial Hotel in Errol for £34,000 as my financial safety net. It was a six-bedroomed nineteenth century building and I knew it was a good going business concern. I told Jinky he could come and live there free. He could stay during the week and, after the game on Saturday, take off immediately for home to spend the remainder of the weekend. That seemed to do the trick, the final piece in the jigsaw.

The Dundee directors were ecstatic. Jimmy Johnstone joining Dundee was making news on the front and back pages of the press. Our First Division outfit was suddenly vying with Celtic and Rangers for coverage in the national newspapers. The signing caught everyone's imagination. Mine, too. I still had visions of the Wee Man dismantling defences with those mazy runs, cutting a swathe on his way to goal, leaving defenders spinning in his wake. Don't get me wrong, I am not a dreamer. I knew Jinky could never replicate that sort of heyday stuff with Dundee. What I did believe, though, was that he still had the ability with one electric burst every now and again to unlock the back door of our opponents and give the rest of his team-mates the opportunity to capitalise on a moment of sheer brilliance.

One back door he wouldn't be unlocking, though, was the one to the Commercial Hotel in Errol. Or the front door, either. I had deliberately not given him a set of keys to the hotel. I wanted to know what time he was getting home and he would have to knock on the door or ring the bell to get access. If he mingled in the bar with some of the punters he was bright enough not to do anything silly right under the nose of his boss. It was impossible to keep a twenty-four hour watch on the Wee Man and that became a problem.

When he arrived for pre-season training, he looked in good shape, as I have said, but his fitness wasn't at a level that satisfied me. The Dundee support, quite rightly, were excited at seeing one of the most exciting footballers ever produced by this country playing for their club. However, there was little point in him going out, showing a sporadic flash of splendour, and then spending the next hour or so absolutely knackered. Being fit and being matchfit are two entirely different things. So, I got Willie Wallace on the case. I told him to work Jinky hard in training. And I also knew the Wee Man would respond. Despite his excesses away from football, Jinky was a great trainer. Jock Stein would never have let him near his first team if he wasn't convinced he could give everything for the entire game. I had the same attitude. Skill is nothing without fitness.

Jinky and Gemmell - no laughing matter

Jinky, I'm glad to say, buckled down. It was great to see he was taking everything so seriously. Listen, we all knew Jinky was devastated when Big Jock told him he had no future at Celtic. Parkhead was his spiritual home, Celtic was his team, and the club had become his life. He loved it there. He thrived on those supporters singing 'Jimmy Johnstone on the wing' on matchdays. But, fair play to him, he picked up the pieces when he went to the States and then Sheffield United. To me, that showed a gritty determination to carry on playing. I must say I wasn't surprised.

Apart from the financial situation, I realised only too well there was an inner core of steel within that small and sturdy frame. But, alas, he possessed the concentration span of a gnat. The Wee Man could get bored too easily. He could put in a fabulous morning at training, impress everyone, and leave with a big smile on his face. 'See you later, boss,' he would laugh. Normally, I was at the office until around five o'clock, so Jinky was out of my vision for four hours or so. I couldn't exactly put an electronic tag on him, but it would have come in handy to monitor what he was getting up to.

I was heartened when he took to going on long walks in the countryside, or doing a bit of fishing on the Tay. I had introduced him to the use of the rod while we were at Celtic. We would take off for some quiet location in Perthshire, or some such place just to sit by the banks and idle away a couple of hours or so. It was great for relaxation and, if you were extremely lucky, you might even catch a fish. Had Jinky turned over a new leaf? I hoped so, but I was still wary. The Wee Man was full of great intentions, but he had to be watched. He was a massive celebrity on Tayside and everyone wanted to mingle with him and to spend some time in his company to be regaled by some of his marvellous exploits on and off the field. He was a magnetic personality and that's what brought about his downfall in Dundee.

Jinky always found it difficult to say no. I realised that was a problem with George Best, too. Bestie would agree to give so much of his free time to spend on engagements or just meeting people and, like Jinky, rarely got a moment's peace. Could you have ever imagined either Jinky or Bestie sitting peacefully in an armchair, no distractions, feet up and absorbed in a good book? Me, neither.

It didn't take long for Jinky to start heading for the pub with some team-mates and some newly-acquired hangers-on after training. He would never have believed he was actually being a bad influence, but a lot of the younger players were in awe of him and were hanging on his every word. It wasn't the Wee Man's fault, but it was becoming the worst case scenario. I noticed he was settling into a routine and he was coming back to the hotel later and later.

I took him aside on a daily basis. 'Look, Jinky, screw the heid, will you?' I implored. 'We've got loads of dosh I want to give you, but you've got to earn it. Forget the bevvy and get on with taking care of business. Go crazy at the weekend with your pals in Uddingston, but watch what you're doing up here.' Rearrange the following into a well-known phrase or saying: Ears Words On Falling Deaf.

I thought it would be a good idea to pair Jinky with Gordon Strachan in training. Wee Gordy was another who appeared to be in awe of Jinky and I thought his natural enthusiasm would spark my pal. It appeared to be doing the trick for a few days, too, until Gordy injured a toe which became infected. A few days rest was required. I think Jinky picked up a strain of some kind around the same time. Boredom kicked in big-style, unfortunately, with the Wee Man. He couldn't even get to training in the morning and there were many other distractions. Jinky had taken a liking to his new team-mate and it was reciprocated by a fresh-faced teenager.

I never had any doubts about Gordon's dedication and application. I also knew he was a youngster who kept his word. I was told Manchester United had offered him a trial before he actually signed any contract at Dundee. However, because he wouldn't go back on a promise, he rejected United and put pen to paper on schoolboy forms at Dundee, left school at fifteen and became an apprentice on the ground staff in 1972. Ironically, he was signed by John Prentice, the manager who gave me my international debut in 1966 against England at Hampden. That man could spot a player.

From a raw kid to a veteran at Coventry City via Aberdeen, Manchester United and Leeds United, playing into his forties, he never lacked enthusiasm. Ron Atkinson, the manager who took him from Pittodrie to Old Trafford in 1984, once said, 'There's no-one fitter at his age - except, maybe, Raquel Welch.' Now that's a compliment.

So, I had nothing to worry about with Gordon as far as his professionalism was concerned. And when I paired him with Jinky, I genuinely believed they would feed off each other. I also told Gordon to push the Wee Man and I thought Jinky would respond. Well, it looked sound enough in theory. Things can often go slightly awry in practice, as we all know. Anyway, one day Jinky, with nothing to do, invited the injured and sidelined Gordon out for lunch at the Queen's Hotel in the city. Innocent enough and there was no way my young player would knock back such an invite from a true football legend. Jinky was always good company and had a steady line of anecdotes. Wee Gordy was hooked.

The drink was flowing by the time lunch was over and done with. Now, Gordy was no drinker. He was a lightweight and I was aware of that, but it's easy sometimes to lose inhibitions once radical thought is dismissed as the alcohol goes to work. Gordy would have been trying to keep pace with Jinky without even realising how much he was consuming. He always admitted he wasn't in the same league as Jinky as a footballer. He discovered that day he wasn't in the same league as Jinky as a drinker, either. Not too many were, in fact.

A barman at the Queen's later told me my two players had consumed four bottles of wine with their meal. The bright thing after that would have been to go home and have a bit of a kip. Indeed, I later found out that they went to Strachan's home, had a few more drinks and then fished out a ball and had an impromptu kickabout with some local kids in the street. That sight must have bewildered passers-by.

After that, it was off to the pub. And then another pub. They must have been fairly puggled by this stage because someone thought it would be a great idea to get a taxi to Errol and have a few more in the Central Hotel. Not a particularly good idea considering the hotel was only fifty yards across the road from the Commercial Hotel, where the proprietor, of course, was a certain Mr T. Gemmell Esq. I noted Jinky hadn't returned, but wasn't overly concerned. He could have been fishing by the Tay for all I knew. That notion was knocked on the head when one of my regulars came in. 'Hey, Tommy, did you know two of your players are over at the Central trying to drink the place dry?' he asked. Not for the first time my heart sank. 'Jinky and who else?' I responded. 'Wee Gordon Strachan's with him. He's totally blootered. Wee Jinky's no' much better.'

I was fuming. How stupid could they be? It was bad enough going on a pub crawl, but to do it just across the road from their manager was unbelievable. I marched across the road, just in time to see a sloshed Strachan staggering through the door. He weaved unsteadily towards me without lifting his head.

'Where the fuck are you going?' I bellowed.

'Where the fuck am I going? I don't even know where the fuck I am,' slurred Strachan.

'Do you know who you're talking to?'

'I don't even know who I am.'

I wasn't sure if he was trying to be funny. Then he focused, blinked one eye, and managed to make out my image and burst into tears.

'Sorry, boss,' he uttered. 'Sorry, sorry, boss. I don't suppose you could get me a taxi?'

'Get over the road,' I ordered. 'I'll deal with you in a moment.' I then went into the bar to give Jinky a piece of my mind. The wee bugger had scarpered. The sixth sense that came to his aid so often on the football pitch worked just as well when he was blotto off it. 'You've just missed him, Tommy,' the barman informed me. 'He left a couple of minutes ago.' I caught up with Strachan and all the time he was crying, 'Sorry, boss, really, really sorry. Can you get me a taxi?'

There was little point in giving Strachan a dressing down. He was obviously out the game. I made sure he got home in one piece - he would now be his wife Lesley's problem - and I awaited with the greatest of interest when Jinky might grace my establishment with his presence. Eventually, there was a racket at the front door. It was about two o'clock in the morning. I opened the door and there was the Wee Man. Putting it mildly, he was the worse for wear. Before I could say a word, he looked up, bleary-eyed and muttered, 'Ach, we were only having a wee bit fun.' I got a hold of him and huckled him to his room and chucked him into his bed. As I closed the door behind me I heard a muffled, 'Ach, it was only a couple of fuckin' drinks.'

The following day, once they had properly sobered up, I had a good old-fashioned heart-to-heart with both. Gordon Strachan swore it would never happen again. As far as I am aware, that remained the case throughout his career. At least, Jinky did him a huge favour that day. My old team-mate was contrite, too. 'It just got a wee bit out of hand,' he said. 'I didn't see it coming. Sorry, Big Man.'

I have to be completely honest here and say I was heartbroken that things did not work out for Jimmy Johnstone at Dundee. It could have turned out to be a grande finale to a wonderful career. That would have been fitting after all Jinky had contributed to the game. He deserved sustained applause at the final curtain on what really wasn't a job of work but his vocation. Alas, it wasn't to be. He started only two games for us and made a substitute appearance in another. We knew it was all over after about three months.

I had the secretary draw up a waiver stating that Jinky's contract with Dundee Football Club was being terminated with immediate effect. I promised to pay him the second part of his signing-on fee. I don't think he was even thinking about the money when he signed the form. We had been through so much together, going way back to the days when I trained to be an electrician at Burnbank Technical College and Jinky took a course in welding. That was in 1960. This was 1977. There had been a lifetime in between.

He signed the waiver, handed it back, looked at me, smiled and said, 'Thanks, anyway, Big Man.'

My heart plummeted like a stone. We had a wee cuddle and he was on his way. His taxi arrived at the front door of Dens Park and, with that trademark cheeky grin, he glanced back at me, smiled again and waved. I felt my eyes welling up. There was a strange feeling in the pit of my stomach. If an individual can't get emotional at a time like that, then they should check and make sure they still have a pulse. As the vehicle took off, I couldn't help but wonder about the Wee Man's destination.

Football chairmen and directors often have the backbone of a banana. So, it is to the credit of the Dundee board that they afforded Jinky the opportunity to relive the glory days. A lot of boards, realising the Wee Man's wayward, carefree reputation, wouldn't have even considered it. If that jigsaw had come together - and Jinky had behaved himself - it could have been a marriage made in heaven.

Football is loaded with fairy tales. Sadly, this wasn't one of them.

Chapter 63

Sign of the times

Daily Record's Sports Editor Jack Adams asked me if I had an ego. I was only fifteen years old at the time and had just joined the Sports Desk. I told Jack I was born in the Gorbals and brought up in Castlemilk. 'We don't do egos in those places,' I told him.

The incomparable Jack Adams

'Good,' he returned, 'keep it that way. Egos are dangerous things that constantly need fed. You're better off without them.' Wise words from a wise man. Words, in fact, that have followed me around all my life.

My mother would often say, 'Remember, son, the truth hurts, but the lies will kill you.' That advice stuck, too.

However, I have met a few members of the media over the years who have quite a high conceit of themselves for reasons that will forever remain a mystery to yours truly. There's one guy who features regularly on the radio and, apparently, his ego, like the Great Wall of China, is visible from Outer Space. Maybe if I'm spared an extra lifetime I'll find the years to work out why his self-esteem is so prominent. You get the drift that he believes sincerely that when he dies God will be sitting by HIS right hand.

This bloke is fairly embarrassing, truth be told. I've been in airports when the football teams have been coming back from foreign trips; the Scottish international squad and the top club sides. If this character is through customs before the professionals, he deliberately hangs around until the players come out and then he mingles with them. Of course, there is normally a cluster of autograph hunters looking for a signature from the stars. And there's our guy in the middle of the throng, grabbing autograph books from the kids and scribbling his name. Pathetic or what?

If I was ever heading in that direction - and, believe me, I never will be - it would have been knocked out of me in an instant one afternoon when I was coming out of Shawfield after a league match between Clyde and Hibs. I was last out of the chicken run that doubled as a press box at the ground after filing my match report to the Sunday Mail.

As luck would have it, the Hibs players were just coming out of the away dressing room at the same time. They had Peter Marinello in their team back then and he was a trendy young guy who later signed for Arsenal and was labelled the 'new' George Best. He was nineteen - two years older than me - when he went to the London club in 1970. The Edinburgh side also had a collection of long-haired 'groovy' guys such as Peter Cormack, John Blackley and Alex Cropley.

Anyway, I was coming through the exit with the Hibs lads when a friendly little cherub with the face of an angel pushed his autograph book at me. 'Will you sign, please?' he asked in a voice that could have been set to music.

'Sorry, son, I'm not a footballer,' I said.

'Well, fuck off and don't waste my fuckin' time,' he spat back.

Chapter 64

Spanish cries

I called it 'The Ole Grail' when Stevie Archibald attempted to give an ambitious Spanish kiss of life to Airdrie Football Club in the summer of 2000. The former Barcelona star was poised to revolutionise the Scottish game thanks to his extensive network in his adopted country.

I had known for about four years of my mate's desire to own and run a football club. He talked to me at length about the 'Airdrie Project' months beforehand. If the enthusiasm of exciting, if unlikely, imports such as David Fernandez, Javier Sanchez Broto, Antonio Calderon, Fabrice Moreau and Jesus Sanjuan matched that of the club's new owner (liquidators, shareholders, creditors permitting), then there was every chance of a glorious new era for the team and its supporters.

Archibald believed he had unearthed football's most passionate and animated set of players when he observed the keenness of the squad on the coach heading for Inverness for their opening fixture against Caley Thistle. There was an eagerness about his players that was almost tangible. The former Scotland international striker admitted, 'I was massively impressed by the attitude of everyone. It looked like a genuine 'one-for-all-and-all-for-one' spirit among the squad. I was sitting at the front of the coach and I could detect the excited babble from the players behind me. This makes it all worthwhile, I thought. All I needed to do was give them a quick pep talk before kick-off and then let them loose on Caley Thistle. In that mood, I fancied our chances.'

As the coach neared its destination, Archibald realised his players were getting even more frenzied as they eagerly chatted away. He stood up, looked around and was amazed to see his latest acquisitions, eight Spaniards, a Frenchman and an Argentine, sitting with their video cameras poised and ready to go. 'Maybe they've fallen in love with the beautiful Scottish Highlands and want it all on film,' he thought. Then he realised no-one was actually shooting anything. The players and the gear were primed, but the equipment wasn't in use. 'What are they up to?' wondered Archibald.

He asked Donald Mackay, the former Fulham and Blackburn Rovers manager he had brought on board, to find out what was going on. Mackay had a word with one of the players and reported back, barely concealing a large smile on his face.

'You'll never believe this, Stevie,' he said. 'They're all waiting to film the Loch Ness Monster. They've all been told the monster lives up here and they want to capture it on film. I didn't want to let them down. I've told them it might be taking a day off.'

Archibald went out of his way to make sure his foreign legion settled in well to their new surroundings. He did all sorts of deals to get them reasonable accommodation. He handed out his special mobile number to the players to phone him, night and day, if they had a problem. 'Don't hesitate,' he told them. 'Get on the phone and I'll be there.'

Everything was going okay until one morning Archibald received a call from one of his players who was in a state of obvious confusion. Stevie told me, 'He was frightened out of his wits. I told him to calm down. I wondered what on earth could have got him into such a state. I asked him to tell me why he was so scared.'

'It's a bomb,' he said. 'Someone wants to blow me up.'

Stevie said, 'He hadn't played particularly well in the previous game, but I didn't think anyone might want to blast him to bits. I told him to stay indoors and I would jump into the car and get over to his apartment. As I drove there, I thought about phoning the police, but I didn't want to waste anyone's time. I was fairly sure whatever it was that alarmed the player, it was not an explosive device.'

Archibald approached the player's front door. There was, indeed, a suspicious-looking box on his mat.

Upon closer scrutiny, though, it was discovered to be a plastic container for any unwanted glass objects, courtesy of North Lanarkshire Council.

Chapter 65

Dead wrong

It was drummed into me at an early age to always check my facts. Not every journalist abided by that golden rule, though. Certainly not one reporter on the Daily Mirror back at the start of the nineties.

Rangers legend Willie Waddell, outstanding winger and obstreperous manager, died in October 1992 of a heart attack and, as per norm in these circumstances, there is always a ring-round to get tributes from relatives, friends, former colleagues and opponents.

A lot of the homages are fairly repetitive and normally go along the lines of 'he was a great man and will be sorely missed' etc. There is always the temptation to add a few quotes from people who would have known the recently deceased. If the eulogy goes along the usual route, there isn't likely to be any comeback.

The Mirror hack decided to quote Willie Thornton, who had been a Rangers team-mate of Waddell back in the mid-thirties stretching into the fifties and had also been his assistant manager.

Thornton, it was reported, 'would miss his wonderful pal' and would 'always treasure their memories.'

One snag; Willie Thornton passed away in August 1991, more than a year BEFORE Waddell.

Chapter 66

Gaga Gazza

Gazza ... ready for a night out

Paul Gascoigne was so blotto he couldn't remain upright to accept his Player of the Year award from the Scottish Football Writers' Association in 1996. This is one of those so-called glitzy occasions where anything can - and often does - happen. But, trust Gazza, this was a first.

I made my debut at the end-of-season bash, always termed in the press as 'a glamorous evening at a plush hotel', back in 1974 when I was twenty-two years old. The entire Scotland World Cup squad that was heading for West Germany later that summer took the accolades; a nice touch from someone at the SFWA. I've been at every one of these functions since and, quite remarkably, I can remember most of them. It's an evening when the notebooks and recorders are put away. Big Brother has switched off for the night and everyone can have a kick of the ball (or each other as has happened on occasion).

I can recall a Premier League manager and a very distinguished Fleet Street sportswriter grappling on the floor of the upstairs lounge bar of the Albany Hotel and people stepping over them, not one of them giving a hoot. Well, it was about three in the morning. I was there when two Celtic players, big, brawny guys, decided to indulge in some impromptu Sumo wrestling in the same bar in another early morning melee. Unfortunately, both decided the best way to re-enact the sport was to strip off and cover their modesty with little white towels appropriated from the loo. It wasn't long before they were repeating the scene from *Women In Love* where our old chum Oliver Reed and Alan Bates go au naturale for a bit of Greco-Roman wrestling.

Just as well those pesky mobile phones with the cameras weren't around at the time or two established first team players, one a defender, the other a forward, would have had some explaining to do to Big Jock.

There was one hilarious moment back in 1979 - Morton's Andy Ritchie was the deserved winner that year - when my old Daily Record colleague Hughie Taylor, a former president of the SFWA and a top table guest, had made an early start to the evening.

Someone said, 'Hughie, slow down, for fuck's sake. Keep drinking at that rate and you'll be pissed at the dinner.'

Hughie looked him straight in the eye and mumbled solemnly, 'Too late.'

Anyway, Ernie Walker, the Scottish Football Association secretary, was in the middle of addressing the five hundred 'distinguished' guests when suddenly there was this almighty clatter followed by a loud expletive. Hughie had fallen off his seat and, holding onto the table cloth for dear life, had dragged plates, glasses, bottles, cutlery and candelabras with him as he crashed to the floor. Ernie didn't break stride. He merely glanced to his right where Hughie was lying in a heap and said, 'Thank you, Hughie. I must remember to do the same for you some day.'

But no-one came close to matching Gazza's performance in 1996. This guy obviously didn't do dull. The dinner was normally billed as 7pm for 7.30, but I could never recall it kicking off on time. This one at the Glasgow Hilton was different. As we turned up and headed for a snifter at the bar, we were told to get upstairs immediately; for the first time in history the annual event was actually going to start ahead of schedule. It was soon fairly evident to everyone why there was a bit of a rush to get the function underway.

And that reason was the guy in the bright pink suit slumped in the middle of the top table. Gazza, the Guest of Honour, was sloshed.

The running order of the evening had to be hastily redrawn. In normal circumstances, the guests get through the lumpy stuff (food to the uninitiated) and settle back with a few drinks as the speeches are made. There is the usual preamble and then there is a ten or fifteen minute segment of footage of the star performer and his daring deeds throughout the season. As I said, that would have been in normal circumstances. Is there such a thing with Gazza in the building?

This is the same Gazza who once turned up hours late for training and had Walter Smith fuming. The Rangers manager didn't have to ask his AWOL footballer for a reason; Gazza was still wearing his thigh-length green waders. 'I lost track of time, boss,' he explained. 'And the fish were biting.'

On this particular evening, though, Gazza couldn't bite his teeth. The organisers had to reverse the running order. It was usual for the Player of the Year to receive his award at the end of the night, make a 'witty' speech, thank his manager, his team-mates, his mum, his dad, his goldfish etc. That would usually take place around 11pm. However, this was four hours earlier and there was no way Gazza was going to perform a Lazarus job. He was presented with his award, remained seated, uttered something incomprehensible - strong ale and a strong Geordie accent don't do each other any favours - and then we raced through the film of his wonderful campaign.

That wasn't quite it for Gazza for the night, though. I was sitting with my back to the top table and chatting to my good friend David Leggat when I was suddenly, and without warning, walloped across the back of the head. Someone being playful had got their timing out somewhat, I thought. Swiftly, I looked round and there was the bold Gazza, swaying, smiling and slurring. 'Awright, canny lad?' He slumped into a vacant seat to my right. I didn't require the skill of Hercule Poirot to deduce he was wired to the moon.

As I said earlier, this was an evening when indiscretions are normally overlooked. This was one night when the notebook went out the window. Unfortunately, one guy at our table couldn't look the other way. He made his excuses, disappeared to the Gents with his mobile phone, filed a story and the Daily Record had a wing column on their front page the following day about a boozed-up Gazza struggling to make an acceptance speech. That reporter was immediately banned and has never been seen at the soiree since. Pity, that; I invited him as my guest.

The last I saw of Gazza at that 'five-star gala occasion' was in a hallway being propped up by his Ibrox team-mate Richard Gough and sportswriter Ken Gallacher. He resembled a giant flamingo that had just been hit by a train. 'Anything I can do to help?' I enquired. 'Just waiting for a taxi,' said Ken. And I wondered who would actually pick up a guy that wasted.

But, hey, this was Gazza. This was his night. And it was memorable. Well, to most of us, but, alas, certainly not to the Guest of Honour.

Chapter 67

Dial M for Mayhem

I don't think it's an exaggeration to say that new technology has had a tsunami-like impact on some of the veteran hacks of my acquaintance. Some have embraced the runaway revolution, while others, alas, have been swept into oblivion.

One Sunday newspaper sports reporting icon had reason to curse the space-age upheaval one afternoon while he was covering a Hibs v Rangers game at Easter Road. The match had just ended and he was desperately trying to dial the copy-takers in the Glasgow office (the advent of the laptop was just around the corner). Feverishly, he pushed the buttons and held the receiver to his ear. Nothing. He repeated his actions. Not a thing. He looked at the instrument and tried one more time. 'Hope it's not the batteries,' he said. 'That's just what I need.' He pressed the numbers again. Once more without success.

He turned to the left where my Sunday Mail colleague Don Morrison was sitting beside him in the press box. 'Here, Don, you're better with this stuff than me; will you have a go?'

Don took the 'mobile phone', looked at it for a second and handed it back. He said to his stressed-out pal, 'I don't think it's a problem with the reception or the batteries.'

'How do you know?'

'That's the remote control for your television.'

Chapter 68

At Death's door

Most journalists are prone to the odd over-exaggeration. 'Never let the facts get in the way of a good story,' is how it is often put. I suppose it comes with the job. Only the most basic of reporters will write 'cat sat on the mat'. Using a little bit of flair, a writer will conjure up something along the lines of 'The luxuriant Persian flourished radiantly upon the rich, lush pile of the extravagantly-woven floor-covering fabric.' Or some such nonsense.

Personally, I don't think there is anything wrong with adding a little colour to liven up a grey tale, but there are some journalists who can go just a little overboard. My good friend Fraser Elder could spice up a story with the best of them - as he proved one Saturday evening amid the chaos and clamour between editions of the Sunday Mail.

I liked Fraz's style of creative writing and I thought he was wasted simply doing 'the cat-sat-on-the-mat' routine match reporting. The Premier League games were covered by staff reporters, while Fraz operated as a freelance. I decided to get him to choose his First Division *Match of the Day* every week and I could give it and him a better show within the pages of the newspaper. Fraz was well up for the idea and I believe it proved to be a winner with the readers which, at the end of the day, was what it was all about.

Fraz was at an Airdrie game one Saturday when their goalkeeper, John Martin, took a kick on the head and had to be carried off. Fraz duly reported the incident, the photographer got a couple of snaps and everything fitted snugly. And then Fraz caught up with the other match reporters in the Copy Cat which was the norm on a Saturday evening. They would discuss the merits - or demerits - of their particular game as the booze flowed behind their neckties. Most clubs were quite generous with their aftermatch hospitality to reporters in those halcyon days. Celtic had a chap by the name of George who looked after the press in a wee room under the stand as they awaited the verdict of Jock Stein, Billy McNeill, Davie Hay or whoever was in the hot-seat that particular season. I can only believe George had shares in The Famous Grouse judging by the manner he tried to get rid of copious amounts of the stuff. I've seen reporters go into that room stone cold sober and come out legless an hour or so later.

I have to think that someone in the Broomfield hospitality room was too vigorous on the generosity front while dispensing the largesse the day the home side's goalkeeper, John Martin, got a boot on the napper. On a normal Saturday, if there was such a thing at the Sunday Mail, it was always a pleasure to hear the hum and thunder of the presses running down in the bowels of the building and be safe in the knowledge the streets edition was running on time. I would take the opportunity to nick down to the Copy Cat for half an hour or so, catch up with the match reporters, have a quick chat over a beer and get back upstairs for the evening conference with the Editor and the heads of the respective departments around eight o'clock. Then it was back to hammering out the editions and, more frequently than not, another break about ten o'clock. My Saturday shift would start just before ten in the morning and would run to the back of midnight. All knackering stuff, but worthwhile when we saw the circulation figures at our first conference of the week on a Tuesday morning.

Fraz appeared a little more animated than usual this evening. He grabbed me as I came into the Copy Cat. 'Alex, we've got a biggie,' he said. 'Front page stuff. John Martin's on a drip at Monklands General Hospital. The kick on the head is much worse than we thought. He's at death's door!'

I about-turned and raced back up the stairs to the editorial on the third floor. I had to notify the News Desk and the photographers and get someone over to Monklands immediately. I wondered if there was anyone at the Martin home to answer the phone. I asked one our sports reporters to put in a quick call. He duly did and I saw him discussing something with the person on the other end of the line. Our reporter placed the receiver back on the cradle and smiled, 'There goes the splash. That was John Martin.

He's got a bit of a sore head, but, other than that, he's got his feet up and waiting for *Match of the Day* to come on the telly.'

Goodness knows what Fraz was drinking that evening, but, in an instant, I wondered if Monklands General Hospital had a spare bed for a freelance sports reporter who had come in contact with a wrecking ball.

Chapter 69

Flaming Hell!

We are all aware of the image of your typical Scotsman being, at worst, a skinflint or, at best, careful with his pennies. I've always thought it was silly propaganda from our cousins across the border to keep the focus off them. (Please don't accuse me of being anti-English because my wife was born in Birmingham. Then, again ...)

However, every now and again a tale comes to the fore that makes you cringe. How about the former Scotland international footballer who used to earn a fortune in media work? A TV company by the name of Zig-Zag wanted to do an 'at home' piece with the well-known pundit at his Southport mansion.

It was reported he was paid for the interview and, apparently, he was a more than welcoming host as he showed the producer around his palatial pad. They chose a suitable area to film him in front of his living room fire with the ex-player leaning against the ornate mantelpiece. To add a little ambiance to the interview, he suggested putting the fire on. The producer agreed it was a good idea. Everything went well until the tight-fisted former Talking Head asked the TV company to pay a share of the gas bill.

Alan Hansen's spokesman refused to comment.

Chapter 70

The hard man and burying the hatchet

I was interviewing a well-known footballer who had a reputation as a bit of hard man, on and off the field. I intended on doing the player a wee favour and conducting one of those exposes that show the public the other side of the character; how he helped old grannies across the road, dragged babies out of burning buildings, rescued kittens from tree tops, that sort of thing.

The player agreed to it, but pinning him down was a bit of a problem. This bloke could have ducked and dived with Arfur Daley. We met one day at a pub in the Gallowgate, but that turned out to be a disaster. Everybody, and I mean EVERYBODY, knew this guy and didn't think twice about interrupting an interview. I didn't exist. They would drag up a chair, turn their back on me and start chatting away to their mate. Even the wonderful Michael Parkinson would have found it difficult to conduct an interview in such circumstances.

He was most apologetic, but what could he do? He couldn't ignore his pals. I thought I would get him away from the Calton and attempt to get this one-on-one dialogue elsewhere. Unfortunately, he didn't 'do' lunch, so that was out of the question. It would have to be a couple of beers elsewhere. We arranged to meet one afternoon in a wee howf in the city centre.

Thankfully, it was quiet and we were able to assemble a reasonable question and answer piece. Now, please remember, the main aim of the entire feature was to turn around everyone's perceived notion that this guy was merely a thug in football boots. I got some great stuff and realised the bloke wasn't anywhere near as bad as he had been painted. I think you could say he was an 'excitable' character on a football pitch. Anyway, after a couple of hours, I was fairly satisfied that I had enough to be able to go away and cobble together something reasonable in an attempt to try to remove some unfair stains from his character.

As we were leaving the pub, there was this huge gorilla of a bloke leaning on the bar chatting to a wee chap. The big guy had an angry scar that ran from his forehead and down his cheek ending somewhere under his chin. By the looks of it, he had never had it stitched properly. It was a combination of purple, crimson, yellow and blue as it dominated this individual's rugged features. As I did my best to hurry past this hulk, he growled, 'Hi, pal.' Unfortunately, he knew the footballer and stopped him in his tracks. 'How ye doin'?' I made my excuses and told the player I would see him at the exit.

A couple of minutes later, the player caught up with me. 'Who, or WHAT, was that?' I asked.

'Oh, he's an old mate I grew up with. Mean-looking big bastard, eh?'

I wondered how the footballer might attempt to describe an extremely ugly version of Frankenstein's monster. I nodded. 'What happened to his face?'

'Oh, there's a good story there. He was blotto one night when the son of one of his pals came into the pub. Apparently, the boy was a bit cheeky, so the big guy made a mess of him before bouncing him out into the street.'

'And?'

'Well, the boy ran home and told his dad. He came down with an axe and stuck it in the big bloke's face.'

'Really?'

'Aye. See that wee chap he's talking to? That was the guy with the axe.'

I suppose that's one way of burying the hatchet.

Chapter 71

Last orders with Yogi

One of the most rewarding aspects of writing an autobiography with a big-name celebrity is discovering facts that have never hitherto seen the light of day. I suppose many of the book-buying public with no interest in sport simply believe football tomes are all about kicking balls around, winning/losing Cup Finals, arguing with the refs/managers/opponents, dating super models, talking nonsense on the telly and earning far too much money. Well, yes, those aspects could figure prominently in some publications.

Sometimes, though, you can hit a rich seam that makes everything worthwhile. Some information will come to the surface you realise will hold a reader's interest. And, basically, it's got nothing to do with football.

I got lucky when I was co-authoring *Yogi Bare*, the warts-and-all life story of Celtic great John 'Yogi' Hughes, the seventh-highest goalscorer in the club's history. He made his debut for Celtic as a very raw seventeen-year-old centre-forward in August 1960 and went on to hammer in some truly memorable strikes as he blitzed his way to a stunning one hundred and eighty-nine goals total for the team.

As you would expect, the actual football-playing side of Yogi's extraordinary career had been well covered over the years. But what wasn't so well known was what happened after the football boots had been cleaned and put away to merely gather dust. Yogi – nicknamed after the popular TV cartoon character 'Yogi Bear' – and I would meet at least once a week at the Burnside Hotel to put his thoughts down in print. It was always an enjoyable experience - and the fish suppers weren't bad, either. Here is an extract from one chapter in his autobiography that I found particularly interesting. It is reproduced with the kind permission of the man himself.

The guy wearing the multi-coloured balaclava looked quite menacing. The shotgun he was pointing at my head was fairly intimidating, too. Immediately, I sensed he hadn't lost his way to the après ski jamboree. This was Balornock, Glasgow, and I was standing at the bar of my pub, The Brig, confronted by the threatening sight of someone who gave the impression he had just wandered into my boozer after participating in the Gunfight at the OK Corral. I had a fair idea what his mission in life was this particular morning.

'Gie's yer fuckin' money,' he rasped.

I stood motionless, absolutely rooted to the spot. This wasn't exactly how I had hoped the day would pan out.

'Gie's yer fuckin' money,' he repeated, waving the weapon at my napper. His mean, dark eyes were fixed on mine, his finger curled round the trigger of the gun.

'Listen, mate, you could have picked a better time,' I said reasonably, trying to sound calm in slightly trying circumstances.

'Oh, and why is that, ya bastard?' asked the menacing masked man.

'Well, it's 11am and I've just opened,' I replied. 'The till's empty.' I felt like asking him to come back in twelve hours when he might have better luck.

285

He said nothing, but kept the shotgun trained at my forehead. At that precise moment, my barman Michael appeared from the stock room. The would-be robber pointed the gun in his direction. 'Don't fuckin' move,' he growled.

Michael froze for a moment. The next thing he did was quite remarkable. He smiled. Then he laughed. 'Oh, for fuck's sake, Jimmy, put the armoury away before ye dae yersel' a mischief. And take that fuckin' stupid thing aff yer heid.'

The gunman was speechless. Michael picked up an empty glass and began pouring a pint of lager. 'Put the fuckin' gun away, get rid of the daft balaclava, I'll gie ye a free pint and we'll say nae merr aboot this fuckin' nonsense.'

'Nae filth?' asked the slightly deflated failed mugger, looking less scary by the minute.

'Nae cops,' said Michael. 'Ah'm sure this is just a wee bit o' fun. Right, Jimmy? A wee lark to get the day aff to a good start?'

'Aye, that's right, Michael,' said the incompetent thief with the bad sense of timing. 'Just a wee laugh.' He took off the balaclava and rested the shotgun on the bar. 'Ah could ferr murder a pint,' he said.

I was beginning to understand this was not an abnormal incident in a particularly interesting locale of Glasgow. I hadn't spent too much time scouting the area before I bought The Brig boozer. It was up for grabs, my accountants and I had a look at the books, the figures stacked up and I thought it would be a sound investment. I had been warned about some 'tasty' individuals who roamed the streets of Balornock, but I figured I wasn't exactly taking over a pub in the Bronx. I didn't feel the urgent requirement to invest in a bulletproof vest while swapping my Audi for a Churchill tank. Anyway, I was over 6ft tall and it took a lot to scare me. Mind you, I hadn't figured on looking down the barrel of a shotgun which was levelled at my head.

I feared the worst as soon as I drove into the housing scheme on my first day. I hadn't even seen The Brig Bar and I was following instructions on how to get to my destination. I made my way to the Red Road Court where, sure enough, there was a row of shops. However, alarmingly, no sign of my newly-acquired pub. I looked again at the map. It should have been opposite the shops. I searched around and, completely baffled, I asked a little lad, 'Hey, son, can you tell me where The Brig Bar is, please?' The wee boy didn't hesitate. Helpfully, he informed me, 'It's doon that ramp, ya stupid big bastard.'

'Welcome to Balornock, Yogi,' I thought to myself.

Yes, an interesting place. Don't get me wrong, though. There were many fine people in the area and I enjoyed spending time in their company. But there were also more than a few renegades who took a wee bit of watching. These were blokes who, sadly, basked in their own notoriety and were quite fond of a little mindless violence to while away the hours. Actually, they were cretins who went out of their way to make life hell for everyone around them. Unfortunately, that included me. I think they must have been watching far too many gangster movies. I was often 'invited' to take out insurance for the pub. They were running their own protection rackets and it was a case of agreeing to give them a couple of hundred quid at the end of each week or the place would be wrecked, razed to the ground or become a suitable target for the pyromaniacs of the district. Real charmers. I told them to get lost. Or words to that effect.

There was one evening when I had been warned three or four neds were coming to pay what was euphemistically termed 'a wee visit'. Unfortunately, I had an unbreakable prior arrangement. Honestly! I couldn't be there to meet and greet these basket cases, but I knew the pub was in good hands. The bar staff could more than look after themselves which, rather sadly, was a pre-requisite of trying to earn a decent, honest living in less-than-salubrious surroundings. 'We'll be fine, Yogi,' I was told. 'We'll take care of business. Don't worry.' I half-expected a phone call that evening to inform me the pub was up in flames, but, thankfully, that wasn't the case. The following morning, I opened up and one of the bar staff arrived to start his shift. 'All quiet last night, then?' I asked. 'Oh, there was a wee incident, but we took care of it,' he replied.

I was curious. I wondered what came under the heading 'wee incident' in this part of the world. I asked him to elaborate. 'Aye, they came in, right enough,' he said. 'Four of them. Just as we were closing. They made the usual threats and I tried to reason with them. "Listen, lads, it's been a long day," I said. "I just want to get up the road and put the weans to bed. Okay? Maybe we can talk another time?" They didn't seem too interested in having a wee chat. So, I had to use the equaliser.'

'The equaliser?' I asked, somewhat puzzled. 'What the hell is the equaliser?'

'Oh, didn't you know, Yogi?' he said matter-of-factly. 'I keep a crossbow behind the bar.'

'A what?' I practically screamed. 'A crossbow?'

'Aye, I don't like guns,' he answered. 'I prefer the crossbow. Great weapon. Gets the job done close-up with the minimum of fuss. Whoosh! And there's an arrow in the bastard.'

'Have you ever used it?' I was genuinely fascinated by now.

'Well, I did last night.' Once again he could have been discussing the downturn in the climate or the price of milk. 'This halfwit, I think he must have been the leader, came up to the bar and demanded the contents of the till. I told him to fuck off, but he didn't back away. He fumbled for something and I thought he was going to pull a knife. I went for the crossbow. I pointed it at him and do you know what this daft bastard said, Yogi?'

'Go on,' I urged, anxiously awaiting the next thrilling installment of the gripping saga that had been played out in my pub the previous evening.

'He looked at the crossbow and said, "It's okay, lads, it's a fake!" I looked at the guy. "What the fuck are you talking about?" I said. "How can this be a fake? You can get a fake gun, but this is a fuckin' crossbow with a real arrow. It's not fuckin rubber, you moron." And then, Yogi, do you know what the arsehole said next?'

'Go on,' I repeated. This was better than any radio adaptation of a thriller.

'He said, "Go ahead and prove it!" That's what he said. Could you believe that? Prove it was a real arrow!'

288

'And?'

'Well, I fired the fuckin' arrow into his chest, didn't I? You should have seen his face, Yogi. It was priceless. His mates bounced off each other as they crashed through the door and left him standing there with an arrow sticking out of his chest. Honest, it was so funny. The halfwit looked at the arrow and then me and said, "Ya bastard. Ye've tried tae kill me." I could hardly stop laughing.'

'Aye, I could see how that might tickle your funny bone,' I said. 'What happened next?'

'Well, he stood there for a minute or so, just gawping at the arrow. There was a bit of blood and I thought he was going to faint. Eventually, he turned around and headed for the door. He kept saying, "Ye've tried tae kill me," all the way out. Actually, if I had pulled the twine to maximum strength, I might have wiped him oot. But I had left it fairly loose. Anyway, he managed to get through the door before he collapsed in the street.'

'Christ,' I exclaimed. 'You didn't kill him, did you?' I wondered for a moment what he had done with the body.

'Naw, nothing like that, Yogi,' said my barman with the William Tell instincts. 'Luckily for him, he fell on his back. If he had pitched forward, the arrow would have gone right through his chest and oot the back. That would have been tricky. Naw, he was just lying there muttering to himself when I came out and stood over him. I said, "So, ya daft bastard, do you still think it's fake?" I pulled the arrow out of his chest and said, "You'll no' be needing this. I might get some more use out of it if you ever turn up again. Okay? I take it you won't be visiting our establishment ever again, will you?" The poor bastard just lay there looking up at me. He shook his head. I grabbed him by the shoulders, pulled him to his feet and booted him up the arse. "Fuck off and don't come back," I said. He stumbled off, clutching his chest and mumbling that I had tried to kill him. I don't think we'll see him or his mates again.'

'No, I don't suppose so,' I nodded. It would be fair to say my barman had engaged my attention with his little ditty. I came to realise this was merely part of Balornock's rich tapestry of life.

Chapter 72

Big Leo's off-day

Big Leo enjoyed what he often referred to as 'a wee goldie' before starting his shift in the Caseroom department of the Daily Record. The only problem was that Big Leo's idea of 'a wee goldie' might be the combined alcohol intake of a particularly thirsty rugby team on a wild weekend.

I first encountered Big Leo when I was sixteen years old, in 1968. The newspaper back then was produced by 19th century technology known as hot metal and Leo was a linotype setter. A very fine linotype operator, too, I hasten to add. Even after 'a wee goldie'.

Basically, the paper copy from the Editorial on the second floor of the Hope Street building would land at the main desk in the Caseroom, a floor above, via a tube. The bosses would then hand the copy to a linotype operator and he would retype it to enable it to be inked over to produce the words in hot metal form. The page number would be printed on the top left hand corner of the paper copy with the catchline on the right. The story, once it had gone through the linotype process, would then be put in a galley tray and delivered to the relevant page where a page plan, drawn up by the Editorial, would be followed, fitting the words into the allotted space.

That is a basic and simplistic form of describing the function of the Caseroom department, a workplace packed with as many colourful and zany characters as the lot who occupied the floor beneath them.

Big Leo always volunteered to do the back shift which started at 3pm. In those days, pubs used to close their doors at 2.30pm with the usual fifteen minutes drinking-up time. They opened again at 5pm and usually closed five hours later. The opening time was normally 11am. Perfect for Big Leo. He had chosen the Garrick Bar (it's had about a hundred different name changes since then) on Waterloo Street which was a five-minute stagger from the back door of the Daily Record at Cadogan Street.

Commissionaires at the front door in Hope Street frowned upon anyone turning up for their work the worse for wear. I doubt if Big Leo ever used the front door in his many years at the Record.

Late January 1968 had been the winter from Minsk and Big Leo must have decided to get into the pub early for some warmth and to manoeuvre himself on the outside of vast quantities of Johnnie Walker Black Label; something at which he had become quite expert. The Garrick operated a 'knock-three-times-and-ask-for-Lizzie' system if you didn't possess the patience to wait for legal opening times. Big Leo must have arrived that morning about seven o'clock. Maybe he hadn't gone home the previous evening.

Around about 2.45pm, Big Leo was slumped over the bar, completely comatose. Guttered. Zonked. No-one had a clue what he had shifted that day, but there must have been a hasty re-ordering of stocks of Johnnie Walker Black Label by the pub owner that same afternoon.

A couple of Big Leo's workmates saw their colleague in obvious distress. Big Leo had earned his nickname. No-one was being ironic. There was a 6ft 4in, eighteen-stone football referee at the time by the name of Tom Wharton and he was nicknamed 'Tiny'. How droll. Unfortunately, for Big Leo's colleagues, he was called Big Leo because he topped 6ft and what he weighed in at was anyone's guess.

So, Big Leo, with a large smile on his face, was happily dozing at the bar.

'He starts work at 3pm,' said Jim, one his co-workers.

'How can he work in that fuckin' state?' asked Tom, another colleague.

There was a rather stern Caseroom gaffer by the name of Matt who was known as 'Mahogany Heid'. He was totally bald and bore an uncanny resemblance to Telly Savalas. 'Mahogany Heid' would later become known as *Kojak* after the popular TV programme made its debut. However, at that stage, Matt was simply known as 'Mahogany Heid'. He told people it was because he always made sure his bald pate was well looked after and shiny. I was told by Caseroom workers it was because he was as thick as a tree stump. I wasn't surprised, either, to learn he had been in the Military Police during the war. He never quite shook the Army attitude in civvy life.

Jim thought fast. 'We'll get Leo up the backstairs, smuggle him along the back of the Caseroom away from the bosses, find the furthest away linotype machine and plonk him there. He'll be out of sight and he'll be okay once he sobers up.'

'IF he sobers up. Next question: How the hell do we get him from here to there?'

'You take one arm and I'll take the other. Let's see how far we can go. Okay?'

'We don't have much choice, do we? Leo's on a couple of warnings, isn't he? Another one and he'll be in P45 territory. Let's go.'

Jim and Tom manfully hauled Big Leo to his feet. Before they got a chance to get their plan into action there was a huge crash as Big Leo lurched forward headlong into the wall before flopping backwards onto a table that practically disintegrated into a pile of sawdust under his considerable weight.

'This isn't going to be easy,' noted Jim, never prone to exaggeration.

'We'll have to call round for some reinforcements.' Tom raced to the phone in the public bar to seek help from colleagues in the Record. A few minutes later a couple of hardy volunteers arrived. The four of them began pulling Big Leo this way and that as they carted him off in the direction of the pub exit. I was passing on my way to the nearby Rapallo Cafe to get a packet of 10 Woodbine for a colleague. 'Hey, kid, give us a hand, will you?' shouted a guy I recognised from the Caseroom.

'Have you checked he's not dead?' I asked. Certainly, there was little sign of life.

'He was farting a minute ago,' answered Jim, who, clearly, had missed out on his vocation in medical science.

I grabbed a leg and, miraculously, we carried Big Leo to the back door of the Record at Cadogan Street. We only dropped him about three times.

'Now all we have to do is get him up the stairs, get him along the back alley, prop him up at a machine and it's job done,' said Tom.

I looked down at this fallen hulk, still smiling and snoring. And farting. I imagined it would have been an easier task to fend off a charging angry buffalo with a feather than cart Big Leo up three flights of stairs. 'Oh, shit,' I said.

'Right, let's go, kid,' said Jim. 'Grab a leg. It's all for a good cause.'

All five of us grabbed a piece of Big Leo's anatomy and pulled and hauled him up all three flights, his head banging off walls and stairs. We propped him up against the wall in the landing outside the main door of the Caseroom. The five of us were shattered. We fought for breath, my lungs were burning, my legs were jelly. Of the six of us, Big Leo, still smiling, looked in the best shape.

I was well aware 'Mahogany Heid' was despised and dreaded by his fellow-workers on the third floor. So, the last guy they wanted to see that fateful afternoon was their ruthless boss. Sure enough, though, it was the much-feared 'Mahogany Heid' who came through the Caseroom door at that precise moment and immediately espied Big Leo, totally out the game, sliding down the wall.

'Mahogany Heid', summing up the situation, narrowed his eyes and growled, 'What the fuck's happened to Big Leo?'

There was a collective intake of breath.

And then 'Mahogany Heid' grinned his wolfish grin and uttered the words that are still embedded in my memory bank.

'It's his day off.'

Chapter 73

The Milky Way

He was by far the best footballer of the time and one of the most recognisable faces in the country. You could go as far as saying he was the David Beckham of his generation.

All that meant precisely zilch early one morning when the maverick sportsman couldn't find a taxi in Glasgow for love nor money. The player was known to indulge big-time in the *joie de vivre*. Wine, women and song, as they say. With a little roulette and black jack thrown in for good measure.

He had stumbled out of a casino and found it pretty much impossible to maintain an upright stance in the taxi queue at Gordon Street beside Central Railway Station. An idea penetrated the fog; he would walk in the general direction of East Dunbartonshire and was certain to intercept a cab on his way home. This was Glasgow in the early sixties. Anyone out late, or if you prefer, early, in that era had more likelihood of spotting a Martian than finding a cab. I think there were about ten cabs on the road back then. Or maybe it just seemed like it.

Anyway, this bold character, who displayed nifty footwork on a football field, teetered, staggered and pirouetted his way towards the sanctuary of his neat three-bedroomed bungalow in the leafy suburbs of Bearsden after another frantic night of merrymaking. As he trudged towards home, his hopes were beginning to sink. Where were all the taxis? As he weaved his way along the deserted streets, he was vaguely aware of night turning into day. A glance at his genuine Rolex told him it was almost 6am. And it was then he espied a mode of transport that would take the load off his weary pins. After a bit of negotiating and a quick autograph, he was made welcome by the driver.

Anyone catching sight of that milk float would have no doubt have been more than a little surprised to see the footballer, almost nodding off, entrenched between crates of milk, with his legs dangling over the edge of the vehicle, his toes practically dragging along the road.

Taxi for Baxter

Upon closer inspection, they would surely have made out the unmistakeable features of the Rangers and Scotland superstar Jim Baxter.

(Copyright: Alex Cameron)

Chapter 74

Jousting with Jolly

Jim Rodger was a journalist who broke some of the biggest and most sensational sports stories for almost four decades. His headline-grabbing scoops spanned from the late fifties to the mid-nineties. It may surprise you, then, to discover he could barely write his name.

There is absolutely no malice intended in that observation. I thought the world of the man who was known to everyone as 'The Jolly'. However, I have seen what is known as the 'virgin' copy from this unique character and it could have been written by a three year old. What he lacked in the written word, though, he more than made up with his list of 'insiders'. He possessed a contacts book that was a veritable 'Who's Who' of just about everyone who was important on the planet.

Jolly Roger, a better friend than an enemy

I'm not over-exaggerating when I say that. 'The Jolly' was a staunch Labour supporter and mixed with politicians from all parties. On one occasion a female politician was visiting Glasgow for a charity function and didn't know her way around the city. 'Follow me, hen, and you'll be fine,' said our man. He was talking to Margaret Thatcher, who just happened to be Prime Minister at the time.

My good friend Alex Cameron told me of the day in 1989 when 'The Jolly' revealed he had just been awarded the OBE. Chiefy thought his old chum was at the wind-up. 'Genuinely, I thought he was kidding,' Chiefy told me. 'We were in Glasgow city centre and Jim insisted in dragging me off to one of the public telephones in Central Station. He jotted down a number and told me to call it. I inserted my coins and wondered who would come on the other end. Imagine my surprise when I got straight through to Harold Wilson at No10!'

'The Jolly' was heavily involved with the West of Scotland Press Fund - I'm talking from experience here - and would make sure he had personal telephone numbers for dignitaries he believed should be Guests of Honour at the annual fund-raiser. As well as Maggie Thatcher and Harold Wilson, he had numbers for former Prime Ministers Jim Callaghan, John Major and Tony Blair in his bulging black book he never let out of his sight for about half a century. Believe it or not, he even had a number for Heaven under 'H' in his contacts book. I didn't check under 'G' for God.

On another occasion, he was looking for a suitable main speaker at the annual charity bash. He was going through his book. 'No, they were here a couple of years ago. No, they'll be doing it next year.' And so on until he reached a name and number. 'This could be a possibility,' he said. He then telephoned the number and eventually got through to Bill Clinton at the White House. Now that is impressive.

When Rangers were drawn to play Spurs in the European Cup-Winners' Cup in season 1962/63, it was labelled 'The Battle of Britain' and tickets were like gold dust for the games in Glasgow and London. Ticket distribution was a problem back then and Spurs knew their ground at White Hart Lane would be heaving under the demand for briefs. They steadied themselves for an invasion from the north. Bill Nicholson, the Spurs manager, was a good friend of You-Know-Who and asked for some help with the Rangers allocation. 'No problem,' said 'The Jolly'. 'Just send them to me at Shotts and I'll take care of them.' Thousands of tickets were driven and dropped off at his home and 'The Jolly' slept with them under his bed for an entire weekend before having them deposited at Ibrox.

British Rail soon discovered the full extent of the reporter's involvement among the movers and the shakers of the political world. Unwisely, someone in BR had taken the decision to close the Shotts line. The Railway people incurred the considerable wrath of 'The Jolly', who had never driven in his life and went everywhere by public transport or taxi. He launched a blistering campaign on BR and, very swiftly, they shelved the proposal. Only 'The Jolly' could derail British Railways.

Football, of course, was his first love, although it's doubtful if he ever kicked a ball in anger. The sight of 'The Jolly' in a football strip is well outwith the scope of my imagination. He was a pit boy after leaving school and worked down the same Lanarkshire mine as Jock Stein. They became great friends. Likewise Sir Matt Busby and Bill Shankly, who had also been miners. They had an affinity that was never broken.

God only knows how many transfer deals he was involved in. He was the original Mr. Fix-it and I can tell you he never took a penny for his efforts. The exclusive story was enough for him. To scoop every rival newspaper was always his main aim. He was behind the great Dave Mackay's move from Hearts to Spurs in 1958. He triggered Jim Baxter's deal from Rangers to Sunderland in 1965 and 'The Jolly' would never have taken the credit, but you better believe he pulled a lot of strings in getting Denis Law from Italian side Torino to Manchester United in 1962. Alan Gilzean leaving Dundee for Spurs in 1964 was another massive transfer story of its time. Guess who was behind that?

Thankfully, although we worked for rival publications at the time, he took to me early on. Heaven help the poor soul who got on the wrong side of this guy. 'The Jolly' could make life utterly miserable for those who crossed his path. He was a peculiar wee rotund chap who favoured a big heavy gabardine overcoat, even in the days when we used to enjoy that phenomenon known as summer in this country. Sometimes he would carry a miner's lamp around with him, hidden within the network of his clothing. He would produce the metal contraption, slam it down in front of someone and say in his strange, Peter Lorre-sounding voice, 'Ah, son, I remember the days I used to go down the pit to make a living.' (If you

298

are fortunate enough to be too young to have heard of Peter Lorre, may I recommend the DVD of the fabulous film noir *The Maltese Falcon*, starring Humphrey Bogart? Lorre goes around that film continually muttering 'Who's got the falcon?' You'll see what I mean.)

I believe 'The Jolly' went out of his way to appear to be a figure of ridicule just to see which poor unfortunate took the bait. He would waddle around like a sluggish penguin, sometimes with a trilby perched on his head, and he practically dared people to snigger at his appearance. I never did.

I first met the man back in 1970 when I began covering games for the Daily Record while 'The Jolly' was at the Daily Express. There was an age difference of twenty-nine years between us; I was eighteen and he was forty-seven. It would be fair to say we didn't share the same hairdresser, tailor or musical tastes. The common ground was football. I was well aware of the reputation of Jim Rodger; I had heard a lot of the stories and I reckoned if even half of them were true, then this guy deserved the utmost respect. He could dress up as Batman for all I cared; it was what was working under the trilby that intrigued me.

In Sir Alex Ferguson's superb autobiography, *Managing my Life*, he talks of his fears about his move from Dunfermline to Rangers falling through in 1967 'until Jim Rodger came on the scene'. Ferguson had just returned from a Scotland International Select's tour of Australia and Canada and tells it like this.

'The throng of reporters asking questions about Rangers was almost unnerving until I noticed, off to the side with my wife Cathy and my brother Martin, the reassuring figure of Jim Rodger. Jim was a legendary sports journalist and an invaluable friend to me. Once I knew he was on the case I was sure that, from my point of view, he would have everything under control. Cathy confirmed as much as we escaped in Martin's car. As usual with Jim, there was to be more than a hint of the MI5s about our dealings, with him contacting me by making calls under a false name to a neighbour in Simshill. There was still no development by the time I had to report back for training at East End Park, but I had the Rodger guarantee that Rangers were negotiating.'

And, as per normal, 'The Jolly' was as good as his word. Sir Alex also revealed in his book that Jim Rodger, by then working for the Daily Mirror, was one of the first people he contacted when Manchester United chairman Martin Edwards made his move to take him from Aberdeen in 1986. So, the pedigree of the man was never open to debate, as far as I was concerned. But I believe he would have been exasperating to work with. I can give you two instances. One was before my time, but I was told it was a true story. 'The Jolly' was at the Daily Record when Dundee centre-half Ian Ure was one of the hottest properties in British football back in 1963. There was a lot of speculation about him leaving Dens Park for pastures new and he seemed to be linked with every top club in England. 'Leave it to me, son,' was the call from Wee Jim. 'I'll get it sorted.'

Dundee, back then, came off the first edition of the Daily Record, combining the North and North East. So, if there was anything happening on the Ian Ure front, it stood to reason the newspaper would want the story in the relevant edition for maximum coverage and impact. Around 9pm was the cut-off for first edition material. About an hour before the edition was due to go to press, 'The Jolly' made a phone call to the Sports Desk. 'Ian Ure's signing for Sunderland tomorrow, son,' was the message. 'Transfer fee will be £60,000. Okay? Bye.' That was all the information a good newspaperman required. The story was rattled out, twelve paragraphs in all with a lot of background material, a headline fitted in, an 'EXCLUSIVE' banner across the top of the page and everything was okay with the world. Well, you would have thought so, wouldn't you?

The presses were about to roll when 'The Jolly' phoned the desk again. A sub-editor picked up the receiver.

'That'll show them, son,' came the unmistakeable drone from the sports journalist.

'What do you mean, Jolly?' asked the sub who, by now, must have been used to the reporter talking in riddles.

'Ian Ure's not going to Sunderland, son. No, he's signing for Arsenal for £62,500.'

'What are you talking about? What do you mean Arsenal? You said Sunderland.'

'Aye, son, I know. But they're bugging my phone. I'm phoning from a call box now ...'

'What? For Christ's sake, Jolly, are you sure?'

'Aye, son. Arsenal tomorrow for £62,500. I'll let you go now because I know you're busy.'

What the sub said after that is probably unprintable, but I was assured by my new colleagues when I joined the Sports Desk four years later that is exactly how it happened. They had to stop the presses, rewrite the story, replate and start again. If you say it quickly, it doesn't sound too frantic, does it? Trust me, to alter a story at the last minute is heart-attack material for everyone, from the editorial to the machine room and all the way to the van drivers sitting in Cadogan Street round the back of the Hope Street office waiting to whisk that night's offering away to the furthermost northern reaches of the country. Chaos doesn't begin to cover it. 'The Jolly' would have gone home to his house in Shotts no doubt delighted after a good night's work. Where on earth he got the idea that other newspapers were bugging his phone is anyone's guess.

I was on the receiving end one afternoon in the summer of 1977. I was in charge of the Daily Record Sports Desk when 'The Jolly', then with the Daily Mirror, rolled up. Given the veteran reporter's near-spherical shape that could almost be taken literally. I dined with 'The Jolly' on several occasions and you never got between this man and the gateaux trolley. That was tantamount to taking your life in your own hands. Anyway, Celtic were due to play a handful of games in Australia during the last week of July as they prepared for the new season. They had already flown out that morning when 'The Jolly' heaved into view.

'Everything okay, son?' It was his usual greeting.

'Aye, fine, 'Jolly'. Thanks for asking, How are you?'

'Okay, son.' Then he fixed me with his usual stare when he was about to impart a gem of knowledge. As ever, though, 'The Jolly' wouldn't get to the point. He loved playing this game.

'Pictures, son,' he said.

'Pardon, 'Jolly'? What about pictures?' I was bewildered as was usual chatting with this guy. He never touched alcohol. I often wondered if I could persuade him some day.

'Pictures at the airport, son. Have you looked at them?' He was smiling.

'I've got a selection. I'll pick a couple for the paper later.' I said. Sports photographer Eric Craig, a magnificent lensman, had taken the usual selection of snaps of players lounging around the airport, looking at books, having a coffee, queuing on the steps up to the aircraft, all that sort of thing. 'Do you want a look?' I asked.

'No, son, I don't want a look. I think YOU should have a look.' Again, that annoying grin.

'Jolly, have you anything to tell me? I'm quite busy.'

'Pictures, son. You'll need to see ALL the pictures. Bye now.' And with that he trundled off through the corridor to the Daily Mirror office.

So, there I am, drawing up the pages for the following day's sports section, rifling through the stories that are coming in from our reporters, plus wire copy via the Press Association, Reuters, UPI and AP from all over the world. Freelancers' tales would also be arriving via the copy-takers. There were also check calls to the district offices at Aberdeen, Dundee, Ayr, Falkirk and Edinburgh to find out what was happening in those areas. In truth, I didn't have time to sift through a mountain of negatives.

Eric Craig was a dedicated, top-class professional and always made certain you received snaps that offered a wide selection and covered all bases; square, deep and shallow. It helped the design of a page if the picture made you look twice. So, if Eric could manage to get you something thin that would virtually run from the top of the page to the bottom, then it had an impact in a tabloid newspaper. Unfortunately, Eric was so damn good he took, what seemed that afternoon, hundreds of pictures. The silly thing to have done was ignore 'The Jolly'. I knew, in his inimitable fashion, he was trying to tell me something, but I would have to follow the rainbow before I found the pot of gold.

I asked the Dark Room to print up contacts from the negatives and I would have a squint at them. I sifted through them once. And again. And

302

once more. Bang! The light went on. There was a rather famous face missing from the travelling squad. Kenny Dalglish was nowhere to be seen. At that time there was speculation about Celtic's best player quitting the club. He was linked with the usual suspects; Manchester United, Arsenal, Liverpool, etc.

Why was he not on the flight to Australia? Clearly, Jock Stein hadn't mentioned the situation of the AWOL superstar to the travelling press corps and, in any case, they were hardly likely to do a head count of the Celtic players at the airport. I'm in Glasgow, Alex Cameron is thousands of feet up in the air heading for Melbourne and we've got a bit of a puzzle. You wouldn't need to be a devotee of Agatha Christie or Sir Arthur Conan Doyle to put two and two together on this occasion. I believed Kenny Dalglish had played his last game for Celtic. He would be transferred within the next few weeks, but it was also obvious no business would be done while Jock Stein was elsewhere. He would certainly be around to oversee the transfer.

I went through to the Daily Mirror offices where 'The Jolly' was sitting at his desk, grinning at me as soon as I walked in with a pile of contact photos.

'Pictures, son,' he said. 'Did you look at the pictures? ALL of the pictures?'

'Aye, Jolly, no sign of Kenny Dalglish. You wouldn't happen to know where he is, would you?'

'Well, son, that would be telling, wouldn't it?' That infuriating smirk again.

'Look, Jolly, I'm running the story along the lines of 'DALGLISH MYSTERY' and I'm going to have to speculate. If you've got him joining Manchester United tomorrow in the Mirror you're going to make me look a wee bit foolish.' I had often hit blind alleyways dealing with 'The Jolly', but, deep down, I knew he liked me. And that was a major plus in my favour.

He looked at me shrewdly over the rim of his spectacles. 'You run that story, son, and you'll be okay,' he said.

I trusted him and, again, it worked for me that 'The Jolly' realised that very important aspect of our friendship. I think that particular quality was important to this wee chap from Shotts. I left the Mirror office and returned to the Record's Sports Desk to pull apart the back page and start again with the Dalglish story. I knew Chiefy would telephone whenever he was on terra firma, but I wasn't too sure of his travelling schedule and when that would be, so I just steamed ahead with what I had. A couple of reporters tried to track down Dalglish, but, no surprise, he had come off the radar. I knew there was every likelihood 'The Jolly' had him stuck in a hotel somewhere away from our clutches. He could have been on Saturn for all I knew. I also realised 'The Jolly' would not have told anyone else about Dalglish. I stuck the tag 'EXCLUSIVE' on the story. I think 'The Jolly' would have approved.

Kenny Dalglish did, in fact, play one more game for Celtic; a friendly against Dunfermline at East End Park on August 10 1977. The guessing game of 'will-he-or-won't-he?' was now into overdrive. Of course, I have heard all sorts of fanciful notions put forward about the player's move to Liverpool. They are rare and varied and, mainly, ludicrously inaccurate. Transfers and all the subterfuge, innuendo and nonsense that go with them can often take on an absurd life of their own. Some of the 'informed sources' who know all about such-and-such, the inside story are wearisome characters who would be better off dwelling on a desert island where they could bore the hell out of a coconut.

Here is the REAL story about the night Kenny Dalglish left Celtic for Anfield for £440,000, at that stage the highest transfer fee in Scottish football history. I was working that evening and was hoping to get away at the back of 10.30pm. I had been in since 2pm and had worked through my break. I was beginning to wilt a little. However, it was obvious something was going on as far as Dalglish was concerned. For a start, although he had played against Dunfermline, the player had been stripped of the captaincy; Danny McGrain was the new Celtic skipper and it was easy to comprehend it was not a one-off appointment. As the clock ticked and tocked its way towards 10.30pm, I was told to be prepared for a 'stunning exclusive'. Apparently, we were sharing the story with the Daily Mirror and that meant only one thing to me; 'The Jolly' was on the case.

We would need to make quick changes in the editions. Via 'The Jolly', I was given a clue - Dalglish was signing for Liverpool. The fee had yet to be confirmed. The back page and the main sports spread were redrawn and a slot was allocated on the front page for a huge cross reference. Eric Craig had taken a superb snap of Dalglish following McGrain onto the pitch at East End Park. It was a clever photograph: the deposed skipper behind the new leader. 'The Jolly' and the Daily Record's Ken Gallacher were the only two reporters who were aware that Liverpool manager Bob Paisley and his chairman John Smith were tucked away in the crowd; two anonymous faces under bunnets who were about to capture Celtic's prize asset.

Dalglish returned on the team bus to Parkhead and then went to his father-in-law's pub, The New Orleans, in Rutherglen for a drink with goalkeeper Peter Latchford. A telephone call told him to return to Celtic Park. Shortly afterwards, the record deal was completed and Dalglish was warned not to breathe a word to anyone. It would have been a bit of a surprise, then, when the newly-transferred player arrived at his home at Newton Mearns on the south side of Glasgow after midnight to be confronted by Eric Craig, camera at the ready. Eric possessed a velvet tongue and persuaded Dalglish to pose for some pictures. That was the final piece in the jigsaw. We had our exclusive, Eric had his pictures, Kenny had his transfer and Liverpool had their man. Everyone was happy. Except, of course, the Celtic fans who would learn the following morning they had lost their best player.

'The Jolly' loved the cut and thrust and the mystery of transfer wheeling and dealing. Here's another little tale where I was convinced he had stitched me up good and proper. It was 1973 and 'The Jolly' was with the Daily Express. We had been sharing press boxes for about three years and I had grown to like this quirky little guy. The Record and the Express were by far the two biggest-selling daily newspapers in the country at that point. So, of course, there was a fair bit of rivalry. After one game at Broomfield, 'The Jolly' grabbed me by the arm. 'File your report, son, but don't leave early. Okay?' I nodded. 'Fine,' I said and, by that time, I had long since ceased to try to unravel the workings of this guy. What did Winston Churchill say about Russia? 'It is a riddle, wrapped in a mystery, inside an enigma.' He could have been referring to a wee man from Shotts.

Airdrie's best player and top scorer was Drew Busby and he was being linked with clubs all over the place, including Rangers. He had scored 43 league goals in 93 games for the club, which wasn't a bad ratio for a frontman performing in a team that was on the back-foot most of the time. I duly filed my report to the Sunday Mail and collected some quotes from both managers and a couple of players for my follow-up piece for the Daily Record on Monday. Broomfield was just about deserted, the rest of the press boys had long since departed and the players were drifting out. 'The Jolly' summoned for me to follow him and suddenly we were in the tight confines of the home dressing room. Drew Busby was still towel-drying his hair when 'The Jolly' pinned him in a corner. It was fascinating watching this bloke at work close up.

'You're signing for Hearts on Wednesday, son,' he informed the Airdrie player.

'What?' he asked, clearly totally unaware of any forthcoming transfer.

'Aye, son, it's Hearts,' repeated the Express man. 'Leave it to me. Okay? Not a word to anyone.' Then he asked Busby his age.

'I'm twenty-six,' answered the player.

'The Jolly' obviously decided this was a shade too old. 'No, son, you're twenty-four. Remember that, you're twenty-four.'

'Right, Mr Rodger, I'm twenty-four,' agreed Busby. At a stroke, he had lost two years from his age. Couldn't get away with that today, of course, but, back then, it appeared no-one paid too much attention to birth certificates.

'I've got your phone number, son. I'll be in touch. Now, remember, not a word to anyone, okay?' I left with 'The Jolly' and we travelled through to Glasgow on the train. 'You happy with your story, son? A wee exclusive for you, eh?' I couldn't thank him enough, but why would he want to give a journalist from his newspaper's biggest rival that story? I couldn't hazard a guess. He also told me the transfer fee would be around £35,000. 'Write that and you'll not be far wrong.'

We parted at the train station and the following day I wrote my 'exclusive' story for the Daily Record. On the Monday, I had Drew Busby joining Hearts and 'The Jolly' had him signing for Sunderland in the Express. I was completely baffled. Had he staged all that stuff with Busby in the Broomfield dressing room as a red herring? Surely not. I felt a little disappointed and I believed I had been done over like so many others before me. On Wednesday, I received an early morning phone call. It was 'The Jolly' and I didn't even ask where he had found my home number. 'Drew Busby's signing for Hearts today, son. Tell your Sports Desk.' And, with that, he hung up.

Sure enough, Busby signed for Hearts at a fee of £35,000. I was congratulated by Jack Adams, my Sports Editor, for out-scooping 'The Jolly'. I told him the truth, but I'm not sure if Jack thought I was havering. A week later, I was covering a Morton game at Cappielow and, once again, 'The Jolly' was a press box companion.

'I've got to speak to you,' I said.

'Oh, what would that be about, son?' 'The Jolly' had perfected the art of playing the daft lad. Pity anyone who was taken in by his act.

We had a discussion over our pie and Bovril at half-time. 'The Jolly' chuckled. Apparently, he had had some sort of fall-out with an executive of the Express. He preferred me to him and, thus, he did me a favour to 'help your career along the way, son'. I told him I would never forget his act of kindness. And I never did.

I was among the many hundreds of mourners at Daldowie West Chapel crematorium on a glacial January 8 afternoon in 1997, when Jim Rodger bade his final farewell. The great and the good, Sir Alex Ferguson among them, were there to pay their last respects to this truly remarkable and wonderfully unique newspaper man.

I could afford to smile wryly in the certain knowledge 'The Jolly' had already negotiated a safe passage through the Pearly Gates.

Part Four

Hail to the Chiefy

Chapter 75

The legend known as Chiefy

Alex 'Chiefy' Cameron in the old Hampden press box

Alex Cameron was known by a variety of nicknames, including 'Candid' after his avidly-read column *Candid Cameron* which was lifted from the title of a TV programme at the time called *Candid Camera*. He was also known as 'Ace' and 'Commander'. Hardly anyone, in fact, ever called him by his Christian name. I only knew him as 'Chiefy'.

As I have already stated elsewhere, the tales of the Daily Record's fearless, intrepid sports reporter are legendary. I've dipped into the memory bank to select another few at random. Please enjoy.

One of Chiefy's requests when he was going on his many foreign trips with Scottish sporting squads, was for a hotel room with a sea view. He loved to greet the morning with a cup of tea, standing on a balcony and taking in lungfuls of fresh sea air. Redoubtable Sports Desk secretary Marge Davidson made certain Chiefy's orders were followed.

One morning, however, she received a frantic phone call from Chiefy. 'Marge, there must be some mistake with the room. I don't have a sea view.'

'You're in Switzerland, Chiefy,' Marge sighed.

'Ah, that would explain it,' said the Record's top man.

*

On another occasion, Chiefy left a press box just before the kick-off to a game in Germany to search out a loo. When he returned, he discovered, to his chagrin, that he had been locked out of the reporters' area. He thumped on the door. No reply. He kicked the door. Nothing doing. Chiefy was working himself up to an eruption when he saw what looked like a German stadium official. He grabbed the guy by the shoulders, spun him around and had him by the throat. 'Get me in now,' he barked. The bloke stared wide-eyed at his assailant and said, 'Alex, it's me, George - your butcher in Balfron.'

*

Chiefy also possessed a butterfly mind. He seemed to want to do about twenty things at the same time and was known to get his wires crossed on occasion. I was sitting about twelve feet from him one day in the editorial when Chiefy was dialling a number, his contacts book in front of him. Obviously, he was a little distracted that particular afternoon.

'Alex,' he shouted, 'who am I phoning?'

'Do you want to give me a clue, Chiefy?'

'My book's open at the letter M.'

Thankfully, he recognised Billy McNeill's voice the instant he answered the call.

Chiefy was seldom rendered speechless, but I was with him one evening in the Copy Cat when such a rarity occurred. We were in the company of a rather voluptuous female Features writer. For a little bit of devilment, Chiefy asked her. 'Would you ever sleep with someone to get a story?'

The attractive Record scribe didn't bat an eyelash as she replied, 'Is there an alternative?'

*

Chiefy was always immaculately attired and denims would have been well off limits. No doubt he believed those were the work clothes of a hillbilly baling hay on a farm. However, there was one evening in the Copy Cat when a female News sub-editor, standing at the bar with a pair of sprayed-on jeans, caught his attention.

'How on earth does someone get into those?' he asked the female.

'A couple of large gin and tonics would help for starters,' came the response.

*

On another evening, a punter, slightly the worse for wear, was in the pub and having great difficulty in mastering the art of making a telephone call. His fingers apparently had become sausages trying to fit into thimbles. He wasn't having much luck. Impatiently, he began hitting the receiver against the wall-mounted phone.

'Hey, you,' shouted the barmaid, Anne. 'Stop banging the phone.'

'Well, it's better than banging the staff,' said Chiefy, ducking for cover.

*

Of course, my good friend was as adept with a microphone as he was with a typewriter or keyboard. He was unusual in that respect because not too many journalists possessed the ability to switch from the written word to the spoken word in a seamless fashion. Many tried and many failed. Archie Macpherson was another rarity who could also excel at both.

Such were the vagaries of television back then, the English Cup Final was beamed live in Scotland while the Scottish Cup Final was only broadcast as a highlights package later on that evening on STV's *Scotsport*, or the BBC's *Sportsreel*. Anyway, Chiefy was at Wembley to bring commentary from the 1966 English showpiece between Everton and Sheffield Wednesday. He only covered one club game a year from across the border, so he did his homework. As ever, he was impeccable in his research before the kick-off. He would memorise how the teams got to this stage, the main players, the goalscorers, the managers. Nothing would be left to chance. He was well prepared to offer his expert view. Unfortunately, the best-laid plans of men and mice.

Sheffield Wednesday were leading 2-0 at one stage when the Merseyside men staged a spirited comeback. One Everton forward scored twice before Derek Temple netted the winner for the Goodison Park club. The player who kicked off the fightback was a guy called Mike Trebilcock.

How was Chiefy to know his unusual surname was pronounced 'Trebilco', rhyming with Bilko?

*

For a guy with a fly trap mind, Chiefy's absent-mindedness was legendary, too. Reporters lost count of the amount of times they saw their colleague sprinting along railway platforms in hot pursuit of a departing train hollering, 'My typewriter ... my typewriter.'

Remarkably, though, he never mislaid his trusty camel-haired coat. Well, that's not strictly true. Yes, he did leave it all over the place, but, somehow, it always made its way home, like the best homing pigeon. Chiefy's lovely wife Jan has had a look at a few of the things I have written about the icon that was her husband and she reminded me of that coat. I hope I'm not letting a secret out of the bag here, but Jan still has that trusty well-travelled garment in her possession. She confessed, 'I can't bear to part with it.'

I've got a photograph on my wall in my study at home where I am sitting writing these words. About twelve inches from my screen to the right is a framed photograph of Chiefy, myself and three of our best friends taken outside The Montrose pub on the Broomielaw where we spent some fabulous afternoons. It's a sad image, really. It was our last 'Wednesday Club' at the bar that had been home to our meetings every week for years. Jim Cullen, owner of this fine establishment, had reluctantly sold the hostelry to developers and that was the last lunch we had in the Montrose before the wrecking ball was swung in its direction.

Unfortunately, it is the last photograph I had taken with the bloke who meant so much to me. I'm not the maudlin sort, so I can say I smile every time I look at that image. And, yes, he's wearing that camel-haired coat.

Chiefy, in his treasured camel-haired coat, with three of the Wednesday Club, Don Morrison, me and (far right) David Leggat. Getting up close and personal with Chiefy and me is Jim Cullen, owner of our dining establishment, The Montrose on Glasgow's Broomielaw.

*

Chiefy would often fall into bad company on a Thursday. That was the designated day he would go for lunch with John Burrowes, the superb Daily Record Features Editor, Stan Shivas, the outstanding Chief Features Writer, and Martin Gilfeather, the gifted Picture Editor. The Four Men of the Apocalypse? Not quite. Chiefy did his *Candid Cameron* column every Monday and Thursday to appear in the following day's newspapers. On every occasion, bar one, I would arrive to start my shift around 2pm and that day's offering would be in the tray waiting to be read and placed on a nominated page.

One afternoon, though, the column was missing. I searched around the desk, but there was no sign of it. Possibly, Chiefy hadn't time to pen his words of wisdom and he could shed some light on the mystery when he returned from lunch. I have to say here that these Thursday outings with those four award-winning newspapermen could often become good old-fashioned boozy affairs. I hoped this Thursday wasn't one of them. My hopes were in vain. Messrs Cameron, Burrowes, Shivas and Gilfeather had gone at it with a furious gusto. Chiefy weaved his way towards me.

'Please tell me you've done your column, Chiefy,' I asked, knowing the worst.

'Nothing to worry about, my old commander,' he said. My heart sank. He only ever called anyone 'old commander' when he had had a few. 'Leave it to me. One column coming right up.'

And with that he wandered in the general direction of his desk. 'This will be interesting,' I thought.

Chiefy hammered away at the metal keys. These were the days of paper and that wonderful invention Tippex. Our dashing wordsmith always prided himself on his finishing work being immaculate. Most reporters would misspell a word and then just rattle a few xxxxxxxs through it. That's known as sloppy copy. Chiefy, on the other hand, would roll the paper out of his machine, tidy it up with Tippex, allow it to dry and then place it back in the typewriter and type over it. I couldn't help notice that on this particular day the Tippex was in full flow. Chiefy sat there in silence, typing away to produce what was normally the most controversial, provocative and thunderously-opinionated column in sports journalism. Many tried to copy his style; many failed. There was only one Candid Cameron.

After a couple of hours, and several black coffees later, Chiefy carefully shuffled his column together, normally about five or six pages of foolscap, and placed it in one of the trays in front of me. 'There you are, my old commander, nothing to worry about.' I lifted the copy and was dismayed to note it weighed about two stone. Slight exaggeration, but gallons of Tippex don't make for feather-light copy.

Before I had the opportunity to read the column, I noticed Chiefy was disappearing into his camel-haired coat. 'Shivas!' he shouted across the editorial floor. 'MD.' That stood for 'More Drink'. And off went the acclaimed Chief Sports Editor and the accomplished Chief Features Writer of the nation's popular top-selling daily newspaper to continue getting on the outside of an ocean of alcohol; one known to quaff a vodka, tonic, no ice; the other, gin, tonic, plenty of ice.

I read Chiefy's copy. To be honest, I just couldn't understand any of it. If there was a point in the main piece, it was lost on me. Maybe I was too sober. I offered the copy to a first-rate sub called Alan McMillan. 'Alan, have a look at this, please. I'm struggling to make head or tail of it.'

Alan carefully read the copy. Read it again. And then re-read it. 'Sorry, Alex, I don't know what Chiefy's trying to tell us, either.'

Another trusted sub was Robert Melvin. I wondered if he could bail us out. Robert, a very studious type of chap, took the sheets of paper, cleared his desk, sat down, put on his reading specs, perused what was in front of him for a moment, stood up, handed back the copy and said, 'I haven't a bloody clue.'

Now, please let me stress here that this was a one-off occasion. In the newspaper world, we probably went about our daily business in a fashion that most places of employment would find totally unacceptable. Back then, most journalists were known to have a few beers or whatever their favourite tipple was every working day. I've often been asked why newspapermen drink so much. I often answer, 'I can't remember.'

I can recall, though, the day a fresh-faced youngster by the name of John Docherty arrived from, I think, the Stirling Observer, and was naturally eager to make an impact on the world of national newspapers. Around 1pm on his first day in the Record, 'Doc' was ordered by a couple of his new colleagues, 'Right, come on, young lad, let's go for a drink.' The recent recruit flummoxed his hard-drinking mates by responding, 'I'm not thirsty.' No-one had ever heard those words on the editorial floor.

By the way, that's the same 'Doc' with whom I helped down pints of black Sambuca before and after his superb reporting at Wimbledon over the years. We never again heard those words 'I'm not thirsty'.

So, that merely serves to illustrate that no-one was in a state of panic when Chiefy had enjoyed a vodka, tonic, no ice or several with his lunch that particular Thursday. Don't stagger away with the idea, either, we spent all day bouncing off each other. Makes for good movies or TV sitcoms, but misses the bullseye every time. Anyway, I drew up the main sports spread and, as usual, left about three columns - most tabloid newspapers have seven columns on each page - on the right hander for 'Candid'.

I had another attempt at trying to decipher what Chiefy was informing the nation. Honestly, I just could not get a handle on it. At that stage I could have done one of two things. I could ask Chiefy to rewrite the column. Or I could drop it and face the consequences. However, I also realised *Candid Cameron* was such a thought-provoking, topical and anticipated column among our readers on a Friday that a no-show would bring about a lot of disappointment.

I telephoned Chiefy in the Copy Cat. 'Yes, my old commander,' he answered.

'Any chance you could have a look at your column, Chiefy? Couple of wee points that may need to be explained. Okay?' I said, hopefully.

A small percentage of journalists I worked alongside could be precious. Querying their copy was a bit like asking God to rewrite the Ten Commandments. Chiefy could have ordered me to publish his column - he was my boss, after all - and that would have been the end of the matter. My fingerprints would be removed from the feature and the responsibility lay with the author. Many of these scribes appear to write for themselves and not the reader. Their stuff can be so convoluted it can only make sense to one person - the originator of the prose.

Thankfully, my friend did not fall into that category. Chiefy, I was well aware, cared passionately about the readership of the newspaper and, of course, he had the utmost pride in his work.

'I'll be up in a minute,' he said, just finishing off a vodka tonic, no ice.'

He was as good as his word. The camel-haired coat was back on the peg, the jacket was thrown behind the chair, the sleeves were rolled up, paper was put in the typewriter and our man, without a murmur, began hammering out the words. Inside an hour, the column had been completely rewritten. Once more, Chiefy handed me the copy and I wondered what lay in store. It was well-nigh perfect. I realised in that moment I had just seen a consummate professional at work. No tiaras and no tantrums, just a first-class operator going about his job.

'Okay?' asked Chiefy, slipping into the camel-haired coat. 'May I go back to my vodka, tonic, no ice now?' And off he went. From somewhere, Chiefy had found the resources to produce yet another excellent column.

The following morning, my telephone rang at home. Chiefy was on the line.

'Alex,' he said, 'I was just wondering why we needed a new column. Can you tell me where the original is?'

'Chiefy, are you in the office?' I asked.

'Yes,' he said. 'Just arrived to pick up my car. Why?'

'Where are you sitting?'

'At your desk. Why?'

'Do me a favour, please, and open the top drawer to the right. Your original column is in there.'

There was silence for a moment followed by, 'Right, I've got it.'

'Can you do me another favour, please? Will you read it?'

More silence. 'Yes, I see,' came the considered opinion after scouring his work, followed by, 'Clear as fog, isn't it? Yes, might have baffled a reader or two.' Then he laughed. 'May I buy you lunch today?'

Some megalomaniac scribes would have spat their dummies into orbit: their copy was sacrosanct and had to go in the paper without anyone touching it. Didn't seem to matter that it made absolutely no sense to anyone else on the planet. Thankfully, Chiefy didn't dwell on Cloud Cuckoo Land. If he thought someone could enhance his copy with a word or two here or there he was always grateful.

So, instead of my head on a plate, I was served a rather succulent well-done T Bone steak at the Buttery that afternoon. That little tale speaks volumes for a man who could have had an Everest-scraping conceit of his undeniable ability if he so desired. In fact, many so-called essayists, with only a scintilla of Chiefy's talent, had such an inflated opinion of themselves, I'm certain they possessed egos that actually had their own post codes.

*

There was also the time, back in 1969, the Daily Record had arranged a gala evening to honour a top sportsman at the Central Hotel in Glasgow. Chiefy, of course, had been instrumental in pulling the glittering event together. On the day of the function, Chiefy was, as usual, going through the routine of keeping all the plates spinning on their sticks. It was a black-tie soiree and Chiefy was leaving it late in getting home to change into his penguin suit.

The Daily Planet's Clark Kent could get away with changing into his Superman outfit in a telephone booth in Metropolis, but that wasn't quite the done thing in Glasgow. (Not in the sixties, anyway.) Eventually, Chiefy managed to transform into his finery and was driving back towards the city centre, realising time was against him. The last thing he wanted to do was take his place at the top table ten or fifteen minutes late.

As he gunned his car in the general direction of the Central Hotel, he thought he was being carved up by a driver in another vehicle in front of him. Chiefy tried to go on the inside and was blocked off. He attempted to go on the outside and found the other car obstructing his progress. Both cars were sitting at a set of red lights, when a frustrated Chiefy wound down his window and fired some choice words in the direction of his 'opponent'. I don't know what was said in the heat of the moment, but I trust the recipient was more than a little surprised.

Jackie Stewart was also in a bit of a rush to get to the city centre hotel. It wouldn't have done for the newly-crowned world champion racing driver to be late for the function that was being held in his honour.

*

Another thing that's worth stating about Chiefy was his generosity. If you let him out of your sight for a moment, you would discover he had hoovered up the lunch bill for about six or seven of us at the 'Wednesday Club' and would exit the pub with that mischievous and endearing grin on his face. He was never slow to the bar, either. Quickly, he became one of my favourite drinking partners.

When he returned from foreign trips, he would always have a gift of some sort for secretary Marge. He would often drop off a bottle of perfume or two for the girls in the copy-takers who had typed out his reports. And there would be a bottle or two of something slightly stronger for the blokes. After the 1980 Moscow Olympics, Chiefy brought me back a key ring with a specially-designed silver track shoe. Allan Wells won the gold medal in the 100 metres, of course, and triumphant competitors had exclusive trinkets made in their honour. Allan passed one on to Chiefy and he, very courteously, presented it to me. It was a lovely gesture and I treasured the memento. I put it on my car keyring and it followed me around for years. Then I put my car in for a service and got it back. Minus Allan Wells' shoe. Some light-fingered bugger had nicked it off the chain. I never went back to that garage. (They didn't do a particularly good job on the car, either!)

*

Chiefy was at the World Cup Final in Buenos Aires in 1978 when the host

319

nation Argentina beat Holland 3-1 in extra-time. The telecommunications from South America to the UK back then were utterly abysmal. Chiefy would phone and there was never any time for niceties. Being the good-mannered chap he was, he would often ask, 'Everything okay? Are you well?' You had to make the most of him when he was on the line because, inevitably, he would be cut off. So, you just had to get straight to the point. 'What's Ally MacLeod saying today? Any team? Any injuries?' Everything would be jotted down before switching the call to the copy-takers. At least, those rapid-fire conversations meant you had a safety net in the realisation Chiefy, without warning, would be left hanging on the end of a barren line. What we would have given for Sky Sports back then.

We were chasing to get the report of Argentina's victory over the Dutch into the paper and Chiefy had come on bang on the final whistle. They had yet to make the presentation to Mario Kempes and Co. Chiefy was dictating his story and it was being faithfully typed out when he paused and said to the copy-taker, 'By the way, you might hear some rounds of applause while I'm dictating this.'

The copy-taker answered, 'It's good, Alex, but not THAT good.'

Four years later, Chiefy was at the World Cup Finals in Spain and was preparing to phone his report on Italy's 3-1 triumph over West Germany. His intro was, 'Magnifico! Magnifico! Magnifico!'

The copy-taker responded, 'Okay, Alex, I heard you the first time.'

*

Everything Chiefy did was larger than life. He was a stand-out character among outstanding characters. We had a ball working together in the days when your occupation was also your vocation. Truly, it was a labour of love. Sure, we propped up the bars at the Copy Cat, the Montrose and Off The Record of an afternoon and evening. But the Daily Record always came first. We were both gratified to be associated to play our parts in the success story of the newspaper. I was proud to call him a colleague.

And prouder, still, to call him a friend.

Epilogue

I hope you've enjoyed our excursion through the world of newspapers, an arena where March hares are made to feel right at home.

Life in this particular planet is many things, but dull it ain't. I've been involved in so many crazy, colourful capers in the pursuit of stories and interviews that it becomes second nature. It's only when you reflect on these madcap years that you think, 'My God, did I REALLY do that?'

That exclamation is normally swiftly followed with the time-honoured question, 'How come I'm still alive?'

It's been a wonderful odyssey. When I look back, I realise this is just a sample of my experiences in a career spanning almost half a century. There might just be some more off-the-wall revelations to come from inside the eccentric world of publications.

JINX

DOGS

BURNS

NOW

FLU

TWO?

Stranger things have happened, dear reader ...

Some other books from Ringwood Publishing

All titles are available from the Ringwood website (including first edition signed copies) and from usual outlets.
Also available in Kindle, Kobo and Nook.
www.ringwoodpublishing.com

Ringwood Publishing, 7 Kirklee Quadrant, Glasgow, G12 0TS

mail@ringwoodpublishing.com
0141 357-6872

A Man's Game
Alan Ness

On a Saturday afternoon in central Scotland, both Davie Thomson and Stuart Robertson have scored goals for their respective football clubs: Cowden United FC and Glasgow Athletic. Once team-mates in the Athletic title-winning side of 1997, their subsequent fortunes could not have been more different. Whilst Robertson had gone from strength to strength, winning titles and the love of the Scottish public, Thomson had slipped out of the team and down the leagues with alcohol and a weight problem contributing to his fall.

Whilst scanning the results, James Donnelly, reporter for the Daily Standard connected the two and remembered the tragic events which would forever link them and their team-mates from that ill-fated side.

ISBN: 978-1-901514-27-8   £9.99

Scotball
Stephen O'Donnell

Peter Fitzpatrick returns home to Kirkintilloch with his Czech wife after five years in Prague. Resuming his previous career in banking and financial service, he feels unfulfilled. His application to host a television programme discussing the hot topics relating to Scottish football eventually finds favour. 'The Scottish Football Debate', or 'Scotball' is born.

Scotball is a searing examination of the current state of Scottish football and the various social, political and economic forces that combine to strangle its integrity and potential.

ISBN: 978-1-901514-13-1   £9.99

Paradise Road
Stephen O'Donnell

Paradise Road is the story of Kevin McGarry, who through a combination of injury and disillusionment is forced to abandon any thoughts of playing football professionally. Instead he settles for following his favourite team, Glasgow Celtic, whilst trying to eke out a living as a joiner. It considers the role of young working-class men in our post-industrial society.

ISBN: 978-1-901514-07-0   £9.99

A Subtle Sadness

Sandy Jamieson

A Subtle Sadness follows the life of Frank Hunter and is an exploration of Scottish Identity and the impact on it of politics, football, religion, sex and alcohol.

It covers a century of Scottish social, cultural and political highlights culminating in Glasgow's emergence in 1990 as European City of Culture.

It is not a political polemic but it puts the current social, cultural and political debates in a recent historical context.

ISBN: 978-1-901514-04-9   £9.99

Silent Thunder

Archie MacPherson

Silent Thunder is set in Glasgow and Fife and follows the progress of two young Glaswegians as they stand up for what they believe in.

They find themselves thrust headlong into a fast moving and highly dangerous adventure involving a Scots radio broadcaster, Latvian gangsters, a computer genius and secret service agencies.

Archie MacPherson is well known and loved throughout Scotland as a premier sports commentator.

"An excellent tale told with pace and wit"

Hugh Macdonald -The Herald

ISBN: 978-1-901514-11-7   £9.99

Yellow Submarine

Sandy Jamieson

Yellow Submarine explains how a small football club from a town of just 50,000 inhabitants became a major force not just in Spain but in Europe.

The success of Villarreal offers supporters a model of how they too might live the dream, without having to rely on billionaire benefactors.

ISBN: 978-1-901514-02-5   £11.99

Celtic Submari

Sandy Jamieson

An invasion of Villareal by 10,000 Celtic supporters in 2004 created a set of circumstances that has led to a lasting friendship between supporters of Villarreal and Celtic. This friendship is unique in football and offers the wider football world a model of camaraderie and togetherness that shows how football can be a force for good.

ISBN: 978-1-901514-03-2   £9.99